Operations Management

The Art & Science of Making Things Happen

What the business schools don't teach you to survive and flourish

James T H Cooke

Operations Management

First published in 2012 by

Ecademy Press

48 St Vincent Drive, St Albans, Herts, AL1 5SJ, UK
info@ecademy-press.com
www.ecademy-press.com

Book layout by Neil Coe.

Printed and bound in Great Britain by TJ International Ltd

Printed on acid-free paper from managed forests. This book is printed on demand to fulfill orders, so no copies will be remaindered or pulped.

ISBN 978-1-908746-63-4

Dedicated to my friends and former colleagues of the Metropolitan
Police, London, including many tragically killed in service
1976 - 2009

REVIEWS

If you're having to manage and lead in the tough conditions that dominate everywhere today, you need James Cooke's guidance. He's crammed more than three decades of coal-face experience into a book that is destined to become a touchstone for anyone who wants to succeed in business, public service or life in general.

Patrick Mercer OBE
Member of Parliament for Newark

Clear, concise and informative, each chapter comes alive with examples, stories and case studies. You can read it from cover to cover or jump in at any point for pearls of wisdom that will help you take your life and business to the next level of success.

Bev James
Best Selling Author of Do it or Ditch it!
CEO of The Coaching Academy

Essential reading if your personal and professional goal is long term effectiveness and high performance as an Operations Manager.

Andrew Priestley
Business Coach & Ecademy advisor

REVIEWS

Leadership and management starts with the 'self' and Cooke has rightly brought this in to context within the needs of the individual, the team and the task. He is more than an ex-police officer. He is a leader, a manager, a coach and businessman. He uses his experiences from his public and private life providing a well-balanced, informative and insightful book that captures the essence of operations management. This is a must have book for any aspiring or current leader.

Lieutenant Colonel Stewart Hill
Professional Leadership Speaker and
former Army Officer (severely injured in Afghanistan)

This is a book full of wit, wisdom and professional clout. It's written by a former high ranking police officer who has been in the thick of it and knows what he is talking about. This is not another run of the mill management tome but a sharp and intensely, practical book. It is sprinkled with small learned gems that send out the right message to various audiences such as wearing a uniform cap when exiting a police vehicle at an incident. Some will miss the value of such tiny details of wisdom but they are the nuggets that mark James out as a consummate professional. He also throws in vivid funny scenes such as a drunk woman resisting arrest and leaving James having his keys caught up in her stockings. Every manager who reads this book will be a better manager for it. Switch off the television and get stuck into Operations Management. It's worth it. Highly recommended.

Paul Marsden
Former Shadow Transport Minister and
Member of Parliament for Shrewsbury

CONTENTS

Section 1

You as an Individual Manager

CONTENTS

Section 2
Making Things Happen and Work Successfully

CONTENTS

Section 3
Developing Your Team

Conclusion
All Pull Together

CONTENTS

References

Foreword

What you *do* in life has always seemed to me to be far more important in moving things forward than what you say. All too often, words, no matter how eloquently delivered by politicians, leaders and managers can become just empty rhetoric.

Consequently, bringing ideas and concepts to life, shaping them into something real and tangible to benefit others has been the driving force behind much of my life's work.

Making things happen and work successfully propels a civilisation forward with purpose and ambition. This is at the heart of operations management, translating ideas and strategies into delivery and action.

There is something deeply admirable about those who do this, and if you are interested in joining their ranks as a highly effective operations manager, then this book is for you.

The demands on a modern operations manager, whether in either the service or manufacturing sector, are intense. If you are to succeed there is no room for compromise in the standards you set and you must have an acute sense of awareness of both yourself and the environment around you.

Without this you will not survive, let alone thrive.

Having followed several post-graduate management courses, I can vouch for their value in providing many of the tools to get the job done. However, practical experience has also highlighted how much remains untaught in the classroom about the prime importance of how to manage others and how to deal with the many hidden agendas that require navigation in the work place. These include knowing how to handle your line manager, dealing with difficult personnel, building self-confidence, working your way around organisational politics and understanding the intricate dynamics of team leadership. Your growing competence in these areas will eventually lead you to become an outstanding manager.

However, the raw brutal realities of some of these factors must be fully appreciated before you can move into the realm of high performance delivery.

In a police career with Scotland Yard that spanned thirty-three years between 1976 and 2009 I faced many challenges as a manager and was involved in some of Britain's biggest social history events of contemporary times, such as the Regent's Park IRA bombing, the Brixton riots, the miners' dispute and the growing trends in gang, gun and drug culture.

Such events have frequently tested my resolve and resilience at times of great stress. In the imperative moment of getting a job done under extreme circumstances, niceties get thrown out of the window. However, these challenges have all given me a unique perspective on the business of operations management.

The learning that comes from such experience is profound and extensive and I hope is conveyed through this book in a way that will help you enter the upper echelons of operations management, whether you are currently new to the role, or already 'blooded'.

If I can spare you some of the pain that I have suffered, then this book will have succeeded. Consequently, this is written not as an academic management text, of which there are already many, but as a very practical guide that offers what I believe is a unique take on the dynamics of fast-moving situations, like those I have witnessed. This combined with the information and insight it offers on the science and art of making things happen, creates what I hope will be an inspirational manual for your success.

Introduction

What is Operations Management and Why is it Important?

The Pivot Point

In any act of human enterprise, several things happen. There is a need to look forward and plan what needs doing to accomplish the designed aims successfully. This plan has to be effectively communicated to all those directly involved. Finally there is the actual delivery of what you have planned in a way that meets an expected standard.

The operations manager sits firmly in the last of these areas at what is a unique point in the enterprise – the translation of blueprint to reality.

Even more, this manager has to both meet and reflect changing customer needs while proactively charting a course that actually delivers the strategic vision of the organisation through its products or services.

Translating that vision into practical action is pivotal in many types of public and private sector activity, ranging from the military, the police, local and central government, through to industrial companies, small businesses and entrepreneurs.

It is in the quality of the outcome achieved – a battle won, crime levels down, roads becoming safer to use, well designed products that get a job done, or expertise that is there at the time and place of need – that people judge the success of any enterprise.

So, the operations manager sits at the crossroads between the end-user and the senior management team, not just initiating the planned strategy but just as importantly influencing its development through feedback and real-time experience. This dynamic is unlike any other part of the enterprise, as it is the operations manager who has to be both proactive and reactive, quickly improving and adjusting output to meet any change in circumstances.

Not surprisingly, this is an extremely demanding role, requiring a particular combination of skills and aptitudes. Consequently, operations managers must be exemplary leaders, creators, problem solvers, organisers and communicators if they are to be effective.

The Duke of Wellington, for example, although renowned for his success at the Battle of Waterloo, won his reputation not just by bold leadership and decision-making but also by giving painstaking attention to detail in the supply of stores and logistics. This ensured that those under his command in the Indian and Peninsular campaigns did not have to plunder the surrounding lands for food causing additional resentment and rebellion among the locals. Just as it was for Wellington, getting materials, equipment and expertise into position at the right time and place is an ongoing requirement of a good operations manager.

The Translation of Strategy into Action

Delivering real action sets operations managers apart from all others, as they are the link that matches aspiration with the hard realities faced by any enterprise. This means that they need to be very practical and tenacious, but with an intuitive sense of judgment that enables them to visualise the ideal service or product and reverse engineer the actions necessary to bring it to fruition. Many elements go into this role, from being able to first thoroughly understand a situation, to co-ordinating available resources and then having the flair to create a solution that not only meets user needs but is also cost-effective.

Operations and Project Management

The classic definition of operations management dwells on its 'ongoing' nature, the need to maintain a consistent standard and quality of output day after day. In contrast, project management is normally considered to be a set piece of work with a beginning and an end with appropriate milestones between the two. The construction of a new building, process or product would be examples of this. In my experience, the modern operations manager must be comfortable with both and be able to move from one to the other seamlessly, improving overall outputs through daily operational consistency, but also initiating projects to solve particular problems and issues.

Outcome vs Process

There is a real tension between these two aspects of management. However, quality of outcome must always take precedence over process, as it is this that ultimately defines the success of an operation and allows you to answer the question: 'Have I achieved what I set out to achieve in the most efficient and effective way possible?' For example, in my final role in the police this meant asking: 'Have the most dangerous offenders been identified and controlled so as to prevent them from murdering or grievously wounding others around them?'

In the police, while there were countless processes in many different police departments dealing with different crimes, there was no overarching mechanism in place to properly identify those who were offending across different crime types. Consequently, numerous opportunities were missed to give many offenders the risk rating they deserved and therefore manage them properly through earlier intervention. In other words, the desired outcome had been lost in the complexity of the process.

That said, once the most appropriate outcome is defined based on a thorough analysis and understanding of the situation, consistent processes are essential for managing its delivery and to maintain an enterprise's day-to-day effectiveness.

Who This Book is For

This book is based on my own development as a manager over many years. Consequently, it covers the broad sweep of my police career, from the initial difficulties I faced when first promoted to a junior management position, through to the challenge of creating high performance teams and the development of multiple 'fire-fighting' abilities as my rank and responsibilities increased.

As such, it will help equip the inexperienced manager with the survival instinct, the techniques and the attitudes they need to 'cement themselves into position'. It will also be of value to the much more experienced senior director who wants to gain new insights for the development of a high performance team and department.

Some observers will question whether my experience in policing is relevant to the rest of the private and public operations management sector. To this I would utter a most emphatic, 'Yes'.

While the objectives may have been different from those demanded of operations managers in the private sector, the business control methods that I employed were not. Nor were the business environments, which encompassed hierarchical rapid response teams through to the 'flatter' specialist teams consisting of highly experienced experts.

Though my work primarily embraced the public service sector, much of my later partnership work continually exposed me to manufacturing and service sector companies facing major crime threats. This, together with numerous joint ventures involving voluntary sector and government organisations ensured that my experience was well and truly tested under 'real world' conditions.

So whatever the nature of the particular operation or project, it has invariably entailed the application of problem solving, quality control and risk-management techniques to often fast-moving and non-replicable events of significance.

During my studies for a diploma and MSc in Operations Management at university, while working alongside executives from BT, British Airways, DHL, the NHS and many other corporate companies, it became clear to me how much of a shared challenge we all faced. In what were such diverse industries, getting the right service or product into position to meet a specific need and to do this within an available budget, were universals.

I hope the examples, stories and case studies I have used here will also be of interest to social history readers, as many touch upon notable national events of the last thirty-five years. The perspective from which I saw these important incidents might therefore give an additional understanding of their impact on all of us, police included. All this has allowed me to develop unique insights and knowledge, which I now want to share.

Summary of Main Themes

Through raw brutal experience, certain factors have become abundantly clear to me as to the essential qualities and skills needed to navigate your way through modern operations management and to come out at the other end with your sanity, health and reputation still intact. In this book I cover these under three main themes:

1. You as an individual manager.
2. Making things happen and work successfully.
3. Developing your team.

You as an Individual Manager

YOU are the main pivot point in the operational delivery within any organisation, but your performance can only ever be as strong as your own personal characteristics.

However, whether you are a new manager or more experienced, there is a tendency to ignore this and succumb to the overwhelming pressures placed on you to deliver, and so end up just 'getting on with things'.

That is a mistake. If you are to achieve long-term success, you must have three higher priorities. The first (*Know Yourself Utterly and Completely*) is fundamental to your longevity as a manager, while the other two (*Arm Yourself for Success* and *Position Yourself for Success*) require ongoing attention if you are to establish yourself in the top operations management echelon.

Know Yourself Utterly and Completely

Many of our personality traits remain largely unaltered throughout life and these have a direct bearing on our management behaviour. Though there is no one way of doing things, there is always a dynamic of cause and effect in the workplace that requires you to understand the impact your behaviour will have upon others and the situation.

Whatever your particular style of doing or saying things, you will inevitably, from time to time, be misunderstood, causing resentment among your staff. You may also have to compensate for not being a natural team player or communicator, particularly if you have had to work alone for extended periods previously, something that can show in your dealings with others.

Similarly, your own levels of motivation and determination will define you as an individual, so knowing just how far you can be stretched and challenged before losing self-control is an area of vital personal understanding that you must have before you enter the managerial arena.

Developing this awareness through personal honesty will help you to be much more proactive in your work and avoid the major pitfalls that might bring down the less mindful manager. You will need to be both scientific and intuitive in gaining such an insight but the rewards are significant, as you can then adapt to any given situation and play to your strengths and minimise your weaknesses.

This book recommends a number of techniques you can use so that you will know yourself better and be able to answer confidently questions such as:

- Who are you and what motivates you each day?
- What are your strengths and weaknesses?
- What is your leadership and management style?
- How can you best apply your particular style of leadership effectively?

Arm Yourself for Success

If you are to become an outstanding manager there are many things to consider.

1. **Looking after your health and wellbeing at all times is an essential.** Neglecting this is a fast route to disaster, but there will be a multitude of pressures on you both at work and home to do so. Ignore them. Your first responsibility must be to yourself before you can look after others and deliver results, and that means achieving a consistent state of physical and mental fitness. However, as it is highly likely that you will go through periods of stress, depression and possibly even injury if you are in a high risk role, this book also gives you the tools and a framework to manage such moments of crisis.

2. **Your mindset** is the core attitude you have to the people around you and the work that you do. It consists of:
    - Your drive and determination.
    - Being able to maintain and accelerate your momentum during crucial periods.
    - Being firm, assertive but also diplomatic and tactful to those you have dealings with.

- Giving others a clear sense of direction and purpose so as to truly motivate them.

- Being well organised, proactively planning ahead to put in place the resources needed to complete the necessary actions.

- Always seeking solutions. This means seeing problems as obstacles to be overcome, not as events sent by fate to trip you up.

- Building your resilience to setbacks that test your resolve and spirit.

3. **Developing your skills and awareness**. This is your personal quality control mechanism for constant improvement. It should be based on:

- Professional training to improve your knowledge and skills.

- Professional qualifications that show you are able to perform at a higher level of responsibility and accountability.

- A suitable coach or mentor (everyone aspiring to success should have one), who can encourage, draw you out and focus on your personal and work based objectives.

- Being aware of current events that could affect you in the future.

4. **Setting appropriate standards for yourself and others** is an essential element of effective management. You must think carefully what these will be, *before* hitting the 'factory floor'. This is likely to mean that you must have:

- High quality verbal and written communication to enable you to become very efficient at directing others to do what you need them to do.

- High standards of personal behaviour in terms of appropriate dress, language and demeanour that will set an example for others.

- A strong personal commitment to your work that is balanced with your other life objectives.

- A clear definition of the standard of work that you expect from others.

5. **Resisting compromise.** Line managers, customers and end-users will put you under constant pressure to compromise on quality, costs and schedule. Resist this vigorously. In the latter part of my career, my famous refrain to my line managers was: 'I don't do Skodas sir, only Rolls Royces'. This referred to Skoda's early reputational image for poor quality, and was a reminder to them of the strong emphasis I put on attention to detail, something on which I have built my reputation. You will have to decide how much compromise you are prepared to accept before your own reputation is threatened, then draw a line in the sand and don't cross it.

6. **Promotion and selection processes.** Failed attempts at promotion and selection littered my early years until I realised they were partly due to the scale of my own ill-preparedness. It was only then, when I began to apply the same levels of planning and organisation to my progression as I did to my work projects, that success flowed. This is a very important lesson for the selfless manager to learn. Don't short change yourself by trying to sketch out your future on the 'back of a fag packet'.

Position Yourself for Success

If you are to maximise your effectiveness and ensure career success you must make these areas your priority:

1. **Create for yourself a position of influence within your organisation or department**. Remember, you are not a minion doing the executive board's bidding but a central pivot point through which ideas, concepts and strategy are translated into action. As such you must ensure that:

- You attend key decision making meetings about current and future strategy and operations. Here, your input, knowledge and intuition will eventually become indispensable.

- You become 'a key person of influence' in your department so you can persuade and inform others.

- You are fully recognised as someone with the role and ability necessary to deliver a service or product to the end-user.

2. **Establish clear roles and responsibilities for yourself.** These should be clearly defined BEFORE you take up a new position. Therefore, you must know and understand:

- Where your responsibilities begin and end.

- How much room there is for individual decision-making.

- When decisions should be referred upwards.

- The mechanisms for staff appraisal, feedback and assessment.

- How to deal with disagreements between yourself and your line manager.

- The quality of outcomes and outputs that are expected from you

Making Things Happen and Work Successfully

The production of a tangible and real product or service of quality is what drives an operations manager onward as there is nothing that comes remotely close to the pride and satisfaction of seeing something conceived on paper and then brought to life.

This book discusses and explains the two core principles behind making this happen: awareness and response

Awareness

If your levels of awareness and understanding are to be outstanding then you must:

- Totally immerse yourself in the issues, needs and requirements of the end-user so you are fully aware of any changing circumstances or new dynamics.

- Fully understand the objectives and operating constraints of other organisational departments and, just as importantly, your external partners. Finding common ground and interest with others will propel your standing and reputation as a person who 'they can do business with'.

- Understand the hidden agendas and politics of your organisation and department. These are likely to revolve around asset control power politics, personal rivalries, private relationships and 'dominions of hidden power' where charismatic characters exert unaccountable power above and beyond their actual level.

To navigate around, over and through such obstacles requires a carefully thought through tactical response and the ability to identify alternative routes forward using champions, allies and 'lever points' of persuasion. Often this will entail stepping back from the fray so as to take a 'helicopter view' and identifying gaps and opportunities by using tools such as appraisals and audits, SWOT and GAP analysis, environmental scanning, PESTLE techniques and 360 degree staff feedback.

Problem Solving and Process Mapping

Sometimes from the methods above the source of problems will be obvious, but frequently the root cause or dynamic at work isn't clear. Then the situation requires more careful analysis, and hopefully then the methods recommended here for unpicking the difficulties and complications will give you greater understanding. Often, this requires deep lateral thinking or looking at the situation in fresh ways by seeking out the perspectives of others on the periphery. The diversity of their insights, unencumbered by any cultural or professional narrow-mindedness, will give the process both a logical and creative momentum.

So, for instance, the Scotland Yard problem-solving process that I explain in depth, uses incremental steps to analyse a situation or issue, identify the causes of it and then build a response through option appraisal and selection.

Process mapping techniques are also part of the analysis methodology and which, in suitable cases, can plot the entire continuum of sourcing, supply and distribution, so as to highlight points of weakness, vulnerability or inefficiency.

Managing Sudden Events and Crises

With the best will in the world 'stuff just happens'. Factors completely out of your control, like natural disasters, terrorism or illness of key members of staff, will impinge on your operations.

However, even though these events by their very nature are unpredictable, there is much that can be done in the way of contingency planning to ensure a high state of preparedness and flexibility of response. After all, business continuity is a major challenge facing ALL service and manufacturing operations. This book explains some of the techniques for doing this, such as scenario contingency planning, resource re-routing, sustaining core function and staff adaptability.

Response

What Needs Doing and How?

Once you have a clear understanding of your end-users' situation, the environmental context and the organisational factors you're faced with, you are ready to begin organising an operational response to meet those needs and to navigate the obstacles that might otherwise hamper effective delivery. This book details the four key components for doing this:

1. **Setting a clear outcome description.** This visualises how success will feel, taste, look and sound to the end-user. 'Start with the end in mind', as Steven Covey eloquently explains in his bestseller 'The 7 Habits of Highly Effective People'.

2. **Plan and organise.** Activities and responsibilities should be planned carefully with realistic milestones. A high degree of reverse engineering is needed here to draw together the resources necessary to create the best solution.

3. **Monitoring and adjustment.** Even the best of plans will be severely tested on 'first contact with the enemy' as unforeseen events impact capacity and capability. So the implementation process needs regular review with any constraints quickly being addressed.

4. **Evaluation and constant Improvement.** If an outcome is to be properly evaluated 'start point' data is needed to assess the subsequent progress and to authenticate an operation after its completion. Having such baseline data is also invaluable in helping you in the quest for constant improvement as it will enable you to see how outcomes improve when you keep 'tightening the bolts'.

Developing Your Team

The third part of my approach concerns those you gather around to assist in any enterprise. At first, these are likely to be just a group of disparate individuals with a variety of skills, attitudes and personalities. Your role will be to shape and galvanise them until they become a highly effective team working towards common goals. To do this requires from you abilities that are both artistic and scientific, and which you must bring together in an almost mystical mix. However, in essence there are only three main ingredients that go into creating a successful team:

1. **Choosing the right type of team for the function required.** Any operation needs different types of teamwork doing. For example, these can include research and development, analysis, process control and problem solving. All involve particular skill sets.

2. **Mixing and matching individuals to these teams.** The aptitude, ability and personality mix of a team is crucial to its success. Of course, you may not have the luxury of appointing a completely new team and so might have to just work with what you've got. In this case, profiling individuals using psychometric testing and observation can be extremely useful in determining the relative strengths and limitations of a broad range of people. By doing this, you will be well on your way to developing the right balance of leadership, creativity, critical thinking and productivity. This book will show you how you to achieve this.

3. **Team engagement and performance.** The individuals within your team need clearly defined roles and responsibilities. These then have to be reinforced using effective appraisal and coaching techniques so a sense of selfless contribution is developed in your staff towards the work effort. During this process, you will encounter an array of challenging people who must be handled firmly but fairly using appropriate techniques.

Conclusion - All Pull Together

The holy grail of all managers is to create *the* high performance team. If you are to achieve this then you must build your team through motivation and effective management so that their actions take on a momentum that is 'more than the sum of its parts'. When this is achieved, your team will be working seamlessly together, predicting each other's actions and performing with energy and drive towards a desired outcome. What makes for such a team is not easy to define, but there would seem to be a special mixture of qualities involving skill, understanding, loyalty to each other, humour and common purpose, that lie at its core. In this section of the book, I pull together key points to help you better understand how you can go on to create your own unstoppable team.

How to Use This Book

You do not need to read this book from cover to cover or its sections in any particular order, though the first section, which is about looking after yourself as an individual manager is a natural starting point, whatever stage you are at in your career. After all, the strength of what you build and deliver can only be as strong as the central pivot point and that pivot point is YOU.

Of course, you may prefer to dive into the 'guts of the book' – Section 2 – which after all is about making things happen based on the depth of your situational awareness and the quality of your response.

Or, if you are already an experienced operations manager, then Section 3 will give the insights and ideas you need to create a higher performing team that reflects your core standards and operates seamlessly and with synergy.

Each chapter is structured so that key points and messages are illustrated through examples, stories and case studies from my own career and reflections from other practitioners. I hope you will find these interesting as I have sought to reveal some of the factors that are crucial in not just surviving but flourishing in the world of operations management, but which are not obvious or taught in classrooms.

I also make reference to historical and contemporary leaders as their behaviour is often timeless in ANY situation, venture or enterprise.

Much of this content revolves around people, something for which I make no apology, as it is generally through the 'human factor' that your objectives will be reached. People are also frequently the greatest challenge to achievement and success.

I have also included internet links to exercises and profiling tests that can be used to assess your own personal and work circumstances and these can be found in the reference sections at the end.

As a learning aid for others, this book reflects my own management experience but it can only be an introduction to the key themes it raises. So if you would like further advice, training support, or to benefit from a range of self-help products, then contact me directly through my website at www.standingstartsolutions.com, or by emailing james@standingstartsolutions.com

Section 1

You as an Individual Manager

Introduction

The strength and effectiveness of a department depends on the skills, aptitude and drive of its leader. He or she sets the tone of the entire show and that someone is you.

Appreciate this and your mind will stay focused on developing and maintaining yourself as an individual who is the best they can be

But to do this, you need to first know yourself completely and utterly. All your foibles, idiosyncrasies and underlying characteristics must be laid bare to yourself and often to others – a humbling and awkward experience but vital and necessary.

This requires you to use analytical methods to completely dissect yourself and then to formulate a plan of self development that will amplify your strengths and control your weaknesses.

This plan must cover every area of your life from health and wellbeing through to your own standards of personal and professional conduct.

Conversely, if your self-awareness is only vague you will undermine your own authority and influence, quickly becoming a 'hostage to fortune' losing any sense of control as you blow in the wind.

Knowing Yourself Inside Out

If you are to become the best operations manager you can be, you need to know what makes you tick and to do that you must begin a process of self-understanding that comes from listening to your inner voice and knowing your values and beliefs.

Your Inner Voice

Talking to yourself is said to be the first sign of madness. I say 'Nonsense!' If used positively, it's both a natural and reassuring thing... and something I do all the time.

We all have an inner voice, one that whispers to us as we bump along the journey of life. It's our conscience – it is what holds us back from danger and pushes us forward in times of need – as such it represents both the light and dark of our nature.

Remember Gollum in the film Lord of the Rings?

He gazed into the water pool and saw the two sides of his character reflected back, vying with each other for control over his actions. One side was selfish, malicious and violent, the other side protective, selfless and kind. This was one of the most brilliant representations of the inner voice's struggle in human psychology I have ever seen and for which Andy Serkis, the actor who played him, quite rightly won several awards.

This inner voice talks inside your head discussing the rights and wrongs of a situation. I use this 'debate with myself' to assess the relative merits of a course of action or, just as importantly, to encourage myself with words of praise and support – a type of mantra that's fully recognised by psychologists.

Unfortunately, self talk can also have a very negative side too, with words of praise just as easily turning to self derision, over-caution and despondency.

For some reason, my inner voice has always spoken in a way that has given me a sense of exceptional self-belief even in the most difficult circumstances when all the evidence was telling me to give in. Yet this belief in myself did not prevent me from falling into periods of serious depression when I could literally not move my mind and body; almost a state of paralysis. But even in these darkest moments I knew my strength and ability was still there to achieve, contribute and to help others.

Where does such self-belief come from?

The answer lies I believe partly in how we are brought up; partly in how we are then tested by experience; and partly, as you might expect, in our DNA.

However, even if you don't have such self-belief and are the world's biggest pessimist, you will be heartened to hear that there are many ways to improve your inner voice so that it becomes a positive power for growth. For instance, trained counsellors, coaches and mentors use Cognitive Behavioural Therapy (CBT) and Neurological Linguistic Programming (NLP) to help train your mind so that it acquires a habit of positive, solution seeking, self-confident thinking.

Your Values and Beliefs

How we behave and interact with the world is guided by two sets of criteria.

The first focuses on what is truly important to us – our core values. For me these are integrity, a high work ethic, loyalty and a love of adventure. Once instilled during childhood and through contact with relatives and friends, these core values remain largely unchanged throughout life.

The second is our belief system. This determines how we interact with others and, in turn, they with us. Our beliefs are often very inconsistent and can lead us to into contradictory behaviours.

My beliefs about the world around me have changed a lot as I have gone through life. Assumptions that I once had have now been tested and found wanting. For instance, the sanctity of marriage which I thought was something that should never be broken was, when after 25 years of marriage, it became clear to both my ex-wife and I that we were staggering on as two completely incompatible personalities. Experience changes belief, particularly in what I call 'Crucible Test Moments'.

Crucible Test Life Moments

In everyone's life there come moments that truly challenge our very nature and inner strengths and weaknesses. These defining moments – 'crucible tests' – are often only recognised as such much later.

What's important though is that you reflect carefully back on these moments, drawing out from them learning and insight, a lesson I was taught by my former Police Cadet School Commandant.

Such moments, and for me there have been a number, test the strength of our values and beliefs both in ourselves and towards others.

The Police Cadet Corps

In 1976, aged 16, I left home in Hereford and joined the Metropolitan Police Cadet Corps. I was drawn there by a mixture of adventure and excellent mentoring from my future brother-in-law (a serving officer at Paddington Green) and in the knowledge that a relative had been in charge of the Grantham police area of Lincolnshire.

As well as providing an opportunity to continue my A level, the Cadets instilled in me relentless self-discipline towards my own physical and mental upkeep as well as self-reliance, since I was now responsible for all my own laundry, sewing, uniform pressing and time keeping.

The endless routines of fitness training, team activity and inter-house competition, forced me into constantly having to think ahead with a thoroughness and selflessness I had not been accustomed to.

I always remember the absolute frustration of having to build a daily bed pack out of my sheets and blankets, all to a particular order and shape. A task that took weeks of learning, practice and attention to detail to master, but what was the point? On reflection, it was probably learning the importance of good order, detail and organisation – standards that were expected of everyone without exception.

The Cadets also ingrained in me endurance and resilience. Long cross-country runs, night marches and punishment details got me into the habit of keeping going at all costs for fear of letting down anyone in the team. Learning how to show a good example is something the military do extremely well and was all part of preparing me for the challenges ahead.

Camaraderie and Esprit de Corps

There come rare moments in everyone's career when you join or develop a team of outstanding quality and performance.

Why one team works better than another is not always immediately obvious, but the hallmarks of the special camaraderie and performance that bind it together are always present. It's enriching going into work each day with such characters, a strange but perfect mix of personalities, skills and attitudes.

For me this happened twice: once at Paddington Green (1978-80) and then Notting Hill (1990-94) and I will forever have good and fond memories of the people and the escapades in which we were all involved

Humour, character, courage, friendship and trust all bound us in the same way as the company of men in the World War II TV drama 'Band of Brothers'. We worked extremely hard for each other with dedication, but the laughter and fun we had at the same time was extraordinary. It made going into work a joy, not a job.

Brixton Riots 1981

In July 1981 I was working on a series of contingency plans for important diplomatic and economic key points within the Paddington Green area. It was an eerie humid summer with swathes of low cloud. In Brixton, South London, there had been an extensive operation to tackle the massive problem of street robberies involving knives and guns. Unfortunately the stop and search tactics used, which was based on limited intelligence, had really infuriated the young black community in the area and major disturbances had broken out several weeks earlier. This had led to copycat rioting elsewhere, particularly in the Toxteth area of Merseyside. In July another spate of rioting started in Brixton and all riot trained officers were put on standby, including myself. Eventually, one incredibly humid July day, third-wave reinforcements were called for and I remember assembling with nine other officers in the back yard of Paddington Police Station. We were driven down to Brixton in the van with just our normal uniforms, helmets and a simple truncheon, nothing else.

What followed totally astounded me in its ferocity and violence. On the way, the main radio channel was crackling with calls for urgent assistance from fellow officers in various parts of Lambeth. One call has completely stuck in my memory. A police inspector was calling from inside a police vehicle which was being attacked by a JCB digger. This had been stolen and was being used to attack the police lines. His van had been surrounded and the digger had pushed it onto its side and was now attempting to ride over the officers inside. Clearly an attempt to kill as many as possible. Desperate attempts were being made to reach the unit in time. We arrived outside Brixton Police Station at about 7pm and all seemed completely quiet. Nobody was in the street, but the police station was completely shuttered – almost like a medieval castle with the drawbridge drawn up. We then noticed crowds of young people in the side streets peering out, huddled together. Just as we stopped the van, there was an enormous explosion as the front windscreen was shattered by a stone and the driver was caught full in the face by the debris. With blood pouring out of several facial wounds, we helped him out to the refuge of the back yard of the police station. As we did this, the front doors of the station opened and ranks of riot clothed officers emerged with long shields pacing slowly towards the street. It felt completely surreal to me, almost like a Bernard Cornwell depiction of Agincourt. After leaving our driver with the medics, we were then directed to the back of the station where a full scale hand-to-hand battle was taking place. The crowds, sensing a breakdown in police lines, were attempting to release the prisoners being taken off police buses before they could get into the Brixton police station building. With absolutely no time or resources to make further arrests, we were literally fighting for our lives and my truncheon became lost in the various struggles to beat off machete and knife-carrying rioters. The use of police dogs seemed to push the crowds back and I used the time to climb a nearby tree. With my Swiss Army pen knife I cut a branch off to act as a stave. It was that bad – requiring emergency measures of the most dramatic kind.

Looking back, what really affected me was the sheer brutality of that crowd as it gained in confidence. There was clearly every intention to kill as many of us as possible. What was more, we were clearly ill-equipped and trained to deal with this level of violence. The only piece of equipment on show that some Level 1 riot officers had, was the green army riot helmets used in Northern Ireland and which had been rushed to mainland Britain the week before.

Violence of this level has been seen several times since, most recently last year. This should be a salutory lesson to all people and politicians as to how near to the surface criminal elements in this country exist, causing complete anarchy, on a 'Mad Max' film scale.

Dealing with the Regent's Park Bombing

In July 1982 the Provisional IRA were mounting an extensive mainland campaign in the UK. One summer's day, as the Band of The Royal Green Jackets Light Infantry played to a large crowd of deck-chaired onlookers in Regent's Park, London, a device hidden beneath their bandstand exploded. Seven out of a band of twenty-five were killed, a further eight were seriously wounded and dozens of onlookers were injured by shrapnel. The bomb, planted weeks earlier, had been timed to detonate at that precise moment.

The carnage and trauma at the scene as we arrived from Paddington Green was indescribable, with men dead and dying. Trying to apply first aid in such circumstances was futile, so many of us spent the time holding the hands of the fallen just to give them caring human contact at their last.

I accompanied injured and traumatised soldiers to St Mary's Hospital in Paddington and will always remember the stunned silence of the survivors as they looked blindly forward in the waiting room, shaking and huddled together. The memory of that day has stayed with me ever since and has given me many sleepless nights, but also a great sense of fortitude in facing such evil with determination. What else is more important in life than that?

Dealing With a Series of Violent Deaths

In 1990, while serving on the All Saints Road Drugs Unit in Notting Hill, a succession of events occurred that had a particularly devastating effect on me. I was no stranger to violence by then, but a combination of things ground down my morale and confidence.

The first deaths happened one autumn Sunday on a night duty. We had been quietly getting on with neglected correspondence when we were called to a block of flats off Golbourne Road in North Notting Hill. As we arrived, all was still except for barking dogs and the eerie wailing and screaming from a group of Arab women outside the main entrance. On the ground lay two bodies. One was a man, the other a small boy. The bodies were still warm. While some of my team set about to trying to determine what had happened, others secured the scene or gave first aid, though the casualties – a father and son – were clearly dead.

Both had died from multiple injuries to the head and body. The boy, aged nine, had been thrown out of a fourteenth floor window by his father, who had then jumped out himself and all because he had failed to gain custody after a marriage dispute.

My entire team was clearly distressed by the scene, though totally professional in getting on with their job interviewing witnesses and securing the flat above.

What made this episode much worse was listening later to the 999 phone call from the boy as he pleaded with his father for his life. I think what got to me was what right had the father to take the life of his son, just because he could not be with him at that time? This selfish act of brutality really bit into me.

The next death happened nearer to Christmas when I heard on the BBC that two of my colleagues, Detective Constable Jim Morrison, who had been one of my probationary team at Bow Street police station for two years, and Sergeant Graham Melhuish, who had served with me at Notting Hill, were both dead.

Jim had been killed while off duty and waiting for his fiancé in Covent Garden, where he'd chased a bag thief running off with someone's property. Eventually he caught up with an Algerian youth in the Aldwych, who stabbed him through the heart, killing him instantly. His death had a profound impact on me and brought home to me even more the human cost of policing and the selfless courage of others.

Graham, an incredibly intelligent officer – a member of the high IQ society MENSA – quiet, calm, a consummate professional and a great character, had been killed going home from work on his motorcycle on the A40 at Northolt.

Against these events was set the relentless daily grind of incidents and work arising from the security difficulties in the All Saints Road.

All these events had an effect on both my values and beliefs. They made me feel the need to live in the moment and to treasure human relationships with colleagues and friends because they may not be there the following day. It also reinforced my belief in the sanctity of life and our duty to protect vulnerable children from the malevolent actions of adults. It was also a time that taught me the value of full debriefings after traumatic incidents if all the issues and feelings are not to fester and do damage.

The Breakdown of My Marriage

I married someone with no connections to the police and I think the unique pressures and demands on time, emotions and attitudes are difficult to understand for someone without that experience. This, combined with a high degree of incompatibility in our personalities, made for an increasingly difficult relationship.

But feeling understood, supported and valued is essential to a good marriage, because when the going gets tough, having a great home life is essential to keeping your morale high.

We doggedly persevered for twenty-five years and had two fantastic children but eventually came to a mutual decision that it was time to go our separate ways. The lesson I learned here was significant. A successful marriage must be a based on a combination of physical chemistry and compatibility of nature. Once you've done all you can to improve a poor situation, to stay with a relationship just out of habit is futile. It will suck the life out of both of you, diminish you as people and submerge your true identities.

Coping with Injury and Depression

If policing is your career, then injury and depression go with the territory. No matter how tough and single-minded you are, there will inevitably be periods when you have to recover from an injury sustained on duty, or to cope with the stress that comes from human tragedy and policing tensions.

I have been injured a few times, including multiple injuries from a car accident, back injuries from a violent prisoner assault and broken ribs sustained while arresting a mentally disturbed man. Each involved difficult periods of treatment and rehabilitation with sometimes years of physiotherapy. I have also been affected by episodes of depression resulting from pressures at work and home.

But I have discovered that you just need to accept that these things can happen and not to be surprised when they do.

To help prepare you for the occurrence of such events, this book describes methods and techniques for maintaining good physical and mental wellbeing as well as other 'tools' to help you recover and reconnect with friends and relatives during times of crisis.

Completing My MSc in Management

In 1991 another moment defined my future. I was becoming increasingly restless and bored with the monotony of operational policing. It was not stimulating me intellectually and my latest attempt at promotion had failed. I knew I wasn't right in myself because my mind and body started to rebel. This is something that can happen just as easily through boredom as it can through excessive mental pressure, as they are two sides of the same coin.

I was seriously considering leaving the police even though I loved the people I was working with. I felt things were coming to a head and I needed to give myself some space. So, I successfully applied for a police educational bursary to study management at university, receiving half my fees and a study allowance to attend the University of West London Business School.

There followed four years of study towards my Diploma and MSc in Operations Management. The course was a revelation and I loved it. I felt a completely new and revitalised person – an example of how important continued training and further education can be in remotivating you.

As well as allowing me the company of intelligent people from different industries, the course also provided me with the theory and practice of being a modern manager, giving me skills that I could then apply to my police work. This made me a much more effective manager.

Constant Knockbacks

My career in the police lasted thirty-three years. I retired as a chief inspector but had been a sergeant for two decades, promoted to that rank at the age of twenty-three after just five years' service.

I passed my inspector's theory exam in 1990, but failed the following selection board twice. My other attempts at applying for specialist roles in Special Branch, Royalty Protection and the Accelerated Promotion Scheme were equally unsuccessful. Lack of experience, confidence and preparation, were variously given as reasons for my lack of progress.

By 2003, I was beginning to realise just how selfish you have to be with your time, putting all else aside if you want promotion. I started to apply the same efforts to my personal progression as I did to my work.

The results were startling.

I was promoted twice in three years in what for most officers is the twilight of their careers. I was finding my stride as a late developer, but the operational and management experience I'd gained at the coalface as a junior manager really made me a much more effective senior manager. This enabled me to complete some quite extraordinary projects and operations involving millions of pounds and multiple partners, not because of my rank, but based on my abilities.

The lesson here is simple – value yourself and invest time in your own progression. This is not a selfish act but a necessary one if you are going to be sufficiently prepared for any selection process.

Increasingly Important Projects

After graduation from business school in 1995, my confidence and ability grew exponentially. Carried on this wave, I volunteered for, and was selected to lead, various projects of increasing complexity and importance to Scotland Yard.

This included establishing one of the UK's first business improvement districts as part of the new Crime and Disorder Partnership requirements. I relished this work and enthusiastically rallied, motivated and organised partners from the public, private and voluntary sectors to help put in place a range of projects along the pedestrian corridor that connects Piccadilly with Leicester Square and Covent Garden. This included engaging the genius of international students at *Central Saint Martins* College of Art and Design to help establish an entirely new centre of research and development for furniture, public space and product design to prevent crime. This was followed by projects such as setting up a new West End CCTV system and command centre in the Trocadero entertainment complex. After this, I was selected to join Scotland Yard HQ to develop the commissioner's new charity, The Safer London Foundation. I then went on to a succession of projects involved with controlling and managing violent crime across London more effectively, many of which I discuss elsewhere.

All of this showed me that I really loved being given a blank sheet of paper and making something happen. By setting things up from a standing start, I was continually testing my new skills and really enjoying the engagement with other partners.

But without throwing myself into these ventures and educating myself further, I would never have discovered my latent potential and abilities for doing this.

What Are Your Strengths and Weaknesses?

'Feel the Fear and Do it Anyway' by Susan Jeffers is a great self-help book with one simple message – just let go and get involved in everything around you. Without doing this you will become frustrated and cling to your comfort zone, just as a child has its comfort blanket, never taking on new experiences or challenges.

You cannot grow without doing this. I strongly believe that young people don't truly know what they want or what they are good at until they are in their mid- to late-twenties. Until then, they need to throw themselves into as many different experiences as possible. Having a broad-based career structure at first is desirable as it allows for specialisation later, when you have a complete understanding of yourself and what you want.

But often we don't take on the new for fear of failure and rejection and it is this that holds us back as individuals, something I know from my own life and career which has often seemed to be one long catalogue of apparent failures and rejections.

However, it has only really been in the last twelve years that I have come to realise that rejection and failure are *my* problems, since I'm the one responsible for my own success and progression.

Before this, I had allowed the great cogs of the police service to control my life by assuming that as an institution it would look after me by recognising the potential I knew I always had.

It was only when I accepted that my destiny was in my own hands – a eureka moment that probably came after my return from university business school – that I really began to organise and take control of my career.

By then I knew that through proper and thorough preparation the chances of failure in anything are dramatically reduced, and from that moment success just kept rolling in with commendations, performance awards and promotion.

The Need for Personal Awareness and Basic Self Analysis

I think I became aware at a very early stage of my career that my personal judgment in any given situation is normally very good. Intuitively I seem to sense what's needed in terms of the action required for any given circumstances. Call it a combination of common sense and heightened personal awareness, if you will.

You cannot afford to be too subjective initially as you must have the ability to identify and assess the root cause of an issue and factors contributing to it. From this point of understanding, you can then be far more subjective and assertive about your course of action and then start using your other attributes, such as tenacious determination, to achieve a solution.

However, what often held me back from doing what was right was my low self-confidence and a damaging degree of self-consciousness. This often meant that I was silent or too diplomatic to be taken seriously. So, inevitably I would get to the end of the incident, event or activity thinking – 'if only I had done that in the way I first thought and not allowed others to cloud my judgment'. Does that sound familiar to you?

Later in my career, once I had done an initial appraisal and formed an opinion about what was required for a particular situation, I used to stick to my guns and would not be swayed by anyone, often to the complete frustration and fury of my line managers however senior. But almost invariably I was vindicated.

Obviously, this can work both ways as someone who is arrogant with poor judgment can just as easily have a very damaging influence on the organisation and those around them.

It's also important to not just rely on your own assessment of your strengths and weaknesses because often what we do most comfortably is what we perceive as being the thing that we do best.

For instance, I have always considered myself to work best on my own as I have the self-discipline and focus to do this for long periods of time. Yet feedback from staff through 360 degree surveys, situational judgment tests and self-profiling, indicates that I'm a very strong leader and team player. This is because I allow others to contribute, encourage personal development and possess managerial judgment that others think is sound. I may not be comfortable in what is to me a 'stretch zone', but when I have to play this role I'm very good at it.

Your Personal SWOT

You have already read how by allowing your 'inner voice' to speak and through examining your own values and core beliefs you can better understand yourself, but now it is time to look at some of the tools you can use to further add to that understanding.

It's useful to periodically conduct a SWOT analysis of yourself, as this lets you monitor your development in different personal and work skill areas. Just before your annual appraisal interview is a good time. A SWOT will help you:

Identify Your Strengths – by listing what you think you are good at under skill categories such as communication, organising, analysis, project management, dealing with HR issues, teamwork or strategy. You can also include personal traits that set you apart, such as tenacity or tact.

Identify Your Weaknesses – by doing the same for areas where you are weak or less strong.

Identify Your Opportunities – by listing the things you can do to exploit your strengths. For instance, by undertaking new work, seeking greater responsibility or strengthening your weaknesses through further training and specialisation.

Identify Your Threats – by listing things in your environment, such as a poor relationship, travel constraints, care responsibilities or changing policies, which could impact negatively on your personal situation.

With a SWOT done, you can then discuss your assessment with a trusted line manager so as to get an independent view of each area, but don't show them the lists you have made. What they say can sometimes be very surprising, forcing you to reappraise what you thought you were good at and your professional situation.

A SWOT doesn't take long to do, and should never replace a detailed assessment of your competency, something I discuss in greater depth later.

360 Degree Staff Feedback

This is a modern self-appraisal tool that if used carefully and correctly will give you fresh perspectives on your ability by asking:

- Your subordinates under your line management
- Partners you work with outside your line management or organisation
- Peers who work alongside you and
- Senior line managers above you

   ... to anonymously comment on your behaviour and skills.

Not surprisingly, this takes courage to do. It worked particularly well with one manager I knew who could be very negative and pedantic, always finding fault with his team. The 360 degree feedback forced him to reappraise attitudes towards his staff that he was not even aware of. It also gave his superiors a vital insight into his effectiveness that otherwise would have remained hidden.

Amplify Your Strengths, Minimise Your Weaknesses

I repeatedly told my staff, 'always play to your strengths', by which I meant that they should be aware of the things that they are good at, along with the valuable traits and skills they possess. With that knowledge, always try to use those skills in the most effective way.

As a team leader, you have a responsibility to identify the strengths of individuals in your team and to make appropriate appointments and delegate tasks based on that knowledge. 'Horses for courses' as I always used to say.

The sheer variety of challenges you are likely to face as an operations manager means the profile of each project team will differ as the requirement for different skill sets changes. So, someone who is leader for one aspect of work will take a back seat during another, when different attributes are needed. The real trick is to bring the right people in at the right time with a total focus on the outcomes you are seeking.

Any weaknesses in your own 'quiver of skills' can sometimes be overcome by responsible delegation and co-ordination. However, key skill areas that are essential to your management and leadership role, must be patiently developed through training and hands-on experience or through intense preparation.

What is Your Leadership and Management Style?

Before you can apply your own unique style of leadership and management to the workplace, you need to analyse and understand the different aspects of your values, beliefs and natural traits.

There are some excellent profiling tools around for doing this and I have used them all during the course of my career to assess myself and my teams. Some of them are fully accredited by professional bodies, while all use robust methodologies of psychometric testing that have revealed some things of which I was already aware and which, at other times, were a surprise and gave me a new perspective on why my performance and attitude fell short.

With the new understanding and knowledge they give you about yourself, you can then consciously 'dial' up or down those traits that are helping or hindering your performance. I commend the following tools to you:

DISC Profiling

I came across DISC Profiling in 2011 while retraining as a professional coach with the UK Coaching Academy. Bev James, the Chief Executive, is the UK licensed operator of this system on behalf of PeopleKeys, who are based in Pittsburgh. She runs the European outlet for the technique through her training business, Elements Consulting. I have now been trained and licensed by her to administer and analyse the test through my own business, Standing Start Solutions.

This profiling tool was developed in the early 20th Century by William Marston, the inventor of the lie detector test, and is based on four primary personality groupings - D. I. S. C. These are found in all people and assess the intensity of different traits and how they blend together in both normal situations and under extreme pressure.

So, Marston's DISC method classifies individuals as being either task *orientated* or *people orientated* and then either as *outgoing* or *reserved.*

D Style individuals are dominant, mainly outgoing and task orientated. They take charge of a situation and are motivated by results, power and authority. They enjoy problem solving while their greatest fears are failure or being taken advantage of.

I Style people are outgoing and very people orientated. They interact well with others. They are highly influential and tend to be creative and inspirational characters. Their greatest fears are rejection and loss of popularity.

S Style individuals are reserved and people orientated. They like to maintain the status quo. They have a strong balancing effect on teams and groups being very stable in nature and supportive of others. Their greatest fears are loss of security and sudden change.

C Style people are reserved and task orientated. They are very detail-focused with high competency standards and an analytical approach. Their greatest fears are criticism and conflict.

The test takes seven minutes to complete and is therefore a very practical and efficient way of getting a good evaluation of your traits in both calm and pressurised situations. The results are best analysed by computer so as to give a very detailed profile which, when combined with the examiner's interpretation, provides a very powerful tool for management.

An interesting feature is that the results seldom change over time, unlike some of the methods below. DISC Profiling shows that my predominant personality traits are a heightened level of dominance followed closely by compliance. These are not at excessive levels on the scale and, in pressurised situations, I seem to fall back on more influencing traits. I was therefore a DC type person with a propensity towards action and attention to detail. For me, the complete profile was a very accurate reflection of myself.

Myers Briggs Profile

The Myers-Briggs Type Indicator (MBTI) is a psychometric questionnaire designed by Katharine Briggs and her daughter Isabel Briggs Myers. It is based on the typological theories of Carl Gustav Jung, which were first published in 'Psychological Types' in 1921. Myers and Briggs then adapted these to create a personality inventory for women entering the World War II industrial workforce, so they could identify wartime jobs where they would be 'most comfortable and effective'. This developed into the Myers-Briggs Indicator, first published in 1962.

The method is based on the premise of a split between two cognitive functions:

- The rational (judging) functions which are thinking and feeling.

- The irrational (perceiving) functions, which are sensing and intuition.

Jung's initial typological model regarded people as being either left or right-brained, traits they were either born with or developed as their preferred ways of thinking and acting. Author Daniel Pink later adapted this theory, analysing people's creative or functional strengths.

The MBTI sorts these different traits into four opposite pairs, giving sixteen possible combinations. None of these are better or worse than others, but individuals naturally prefer one type of combination to another.

The sixteen types are typically referred to by the initial letters of each of their four type preferences (except in the case of *intuition*, which uses the abbreviation *N* to distinguish it from Introversion). For instance:

- **ESTJ**: extraversion (E), sensing (S), thinking (T), judgment (J)

- **INFP**: introversion (I), intuition (N), feeling (F), perception (P)

My profile test revealed an INTJ combination indicating a preference for introverted thinking and judgment together with high levels of intuition. This seemed a very accurate reflection of my comfort zone behaviour traits. What must be emphasised though is that other tests demonstrate that when under pressure I perform well in a team situation and in a more extrovert way, which is against my natural tendencies.

The other factor to be borne in mind is that research has found that these test results *can change over time* when measures are taken to modify behaviour through self-development.

Results take slightly longer to come through than for the DISC profile as they are sent away for analysis, but the report that comes back is very thorough and contains good explanations about the technicalities. It does however need a trained person to interpret the results and help adapt the findings to an individual's particular situation.

Finally, you should note that this test is not an indicator of future success, as factors such as motivation and determination aren't assessed.

The Business Leadership Profile

The **Business Leadership Profile** (BLP) has been developed by Andrew Priestley, an Australian executive coach. Based on the Minnesota Multiphasic Personality Inventory (MMPI), the Hogan Personality Inventory (HPI), and the Five Factor Model of Personality, the BLP is a hybrid indicator that assesses strengths in the Task and Relational aspects of leadership in a commercial context.

Task
- Ability to get results; and
- Ability to sell

Relational
- Attitude
- Interpersonal skills

The BLP is designed to determine your strengths and weaknesses under five main business leadership principles:

1. Awareness – This is an awareness of situational and environmental circumstances; and an awareness of your internal responses to those circumstances (EI). Have you identified the critical issues and are you working on the right problem areas in the first place?

2. Assertiveness – This relates to your ability to communicate your awareness to your staff in a clear and effective way to direct the response.

3. Agreement – This relates to your ability to negotiate agreed levels of co-operation. Reaching clear agreements is a skill often overlooked in leadership training.

4. Accountability – This is where once agreement is reached the parties are held to account for their performance; and adjustments made if necessary to keep on track.

5. Acuity – This relates to your ability to reflect upon your own strengths and behaviours and self-assess whether you as the manager are being effective or if, in fact, your behaviour is inhibiting the effectiveness of others and contributing non-optimally to the situation.

The BLP profiles 36 traits linked with high performance in a business context. Specifically, it tells you what's working and what isn't. It clearly identifies coaching targets and generates practical recommendations about what to do next.

I took this test and have the following comments:

- It took two hours to answer the 400 questions, so there is a big time commitment to its completion.

- The results were very revealing and illustrated subtle factors such as my patience with other people's behaviour due to my high level of tact and interpersonal ability. This was a strength in terms of personnel management but could also be a disadvantage when I was driving high performance targets and needed a quick staff response.

- The questionnaire has a big focus on business leadership and your ability to be influential in your capacity, ie sales (the latter is an area in which I am not yet particularly experienced or proficient as a public sector operations manager). This highlighted areas where I needed training and practise to overcome these difficulties.

The Kolb Learning Style Inventory (KLSI)

David Kolb, currently Professor of Organisational Behaviour at Weatherhead School of Management in Cleveland, Ohio, is an American educational theorist who specialises in experiential learning, in other words, learning from doing things and then reflecting on the experience to identify what you have just learned.

He is renowned in educational circles for the Learning Style Inventory (LSI), a model on learning preferences he developed in the 1970s.

Using the KLSI will help your staff:

- Understand how their learning style impacts upon their problem solving, teamwork, conflict handling, communication and career choice.

- Develop their learning styles so it better fits with their roles.

- Find out why some teams work well together and others don't.

- Strengthen their overall learning approach so that they make progress faster.

Though everyone has their own way of learning, the KLSI identifies four *types* of learner (The Converger, The Accommodator, The Assimilator and The Diverger), and four phases in the learning process.

- The Experiencing Phase: learning from experiences, being sensitive to feelings and people

- The Reflecting Phase: reserving judgment, taking different perspectives, looking for meaning

- The Thinking Phase: logically analysing ideas, planning systematically, using concepts

- The Acting Phase: showing an ability to get things done, taking risks, influencing

These phases can be placed on two 'learning continuums' which, if applied to a familiar learning experience such as riding a bike, might be described as:

Active Experimentation through to *Reflective Observation* (just jumping on the bike and having a go through to thinking about riding and watching someone else doing it)

Abstract Conceptualisation through to *Concrete Experience* (understanding the theory and having a clear grasp of the concept of riding a bike through to receiving practical tips and a demonstration from a bike riding expert)

Given all this, it's obviously crucial for you as a manager to tailor your style to the learning methods of each team member and the KLSI is a useful tool for doing this. You can get the KLSI from the Hay Publishing Group, which specialises in management leadership training products and it takes about twenty minutes to complete. See the resource section at the rear of the book.

How to Apply Your Style of Leadership and Management

Some practitioners say managing and leading are the same because the skills of each are so intertwined with the other. However, thirty-three years of policing in some of the most difficult and demanding situations has clearly shown me that there is a difference, though the two areas are inter-dependent.

Leadership to me is not only about having a clear vision of where you want to take a department or organisation, but also being able to instil this into the minds of your staff with such clarity and inspiration that they feel they are integral to achieving your objectives. As a result, they will redouble their efforts because they are engaged and enthused.

Good management on the other hand, is about the efficient and effective use of functional skills to complete a task. This could mean undertaking quantitative analysis, optimising IT usage, project planning, HR training, staff deployment or resource allocation.

I have witnessed some excellent managers who are good at organising and planning, but who lack the charisma, vision and inspirational connection needed to be leaders. The jobs get done, but the people involved just tick along, doing what's required and no more. I have also witnessed very eloquent and inspiring leaders who have no managerial skills whatsoever. People are enthused by them but then, lacking in the direction or organisation they need, fail to perform at the highest level. Invariably projects and jobs don't get done properly and eventually staff become disillusioned.

So, you have to be a good manager as a minimum to be effective but to truly excel and develop a high synergy team, your leadership ability needs to be manifestly evident. On the other hand, to be effective you cannot rely on powers of leadership alone without having basic accompanying management skills.

Being Yourself vs Adapting Yourself

I have watched some extraordinary senior police officers in action over the years, some of them very engaging and entertaining. I remember one superintendent at Notting Hill who always had a willing smile and droll comment to make about any situation. I just couldn't help chuckling when I was with him and felt a real loyalty and sense of affection toward him. However, he was prone to inconsistency so sometimes officers who thought he was joking discovered to their cost that he was not and instantly felt his anger. They came out of such encounters bruised and confused having mistaken his comment for another comic observation. His behaviour became legendary.

Whilst at Scotland Yard HQ he served as a staff officer, to DAC Dennis O Connor (later to become the HMIC Inspectorate Head). Their management styles were completely opposite leading to a lot of tension. On one occasion, it was told that on hearing Mr O'Connor's Irish tones approaching down the corridor, he clambered into his uniform wardrobe and closed the door to avoid detection.

He would also stand by the window looking out onto The Broadway below Scotland Yard, giving an analysis of what passersby did for a living by how they behaved and dressed. This was akin to the TV actor Jeremy Brett's brilliant portrayal of Sherlock Holmes at his Baker Street window, who made similar observations using his powers of deduction. Absolutely hilarious.

The lesson here is that staff who appreciate your sense of humour will repay you with increased loyalty and possibly better performance, *but* you have to be consistent and create boundaries so others know when the laughing has to stop and the serious business begins.

It's impossible to *act* the part when it comes to managing or leading. The pressures are too intense to switch masks according to the situation. However, while you cannot be someone you aren't, you can adapt to the circumstances by being aware of and using your strengths appropriately. For instance, this could mean adopting a more conciliatory approach at moments of team tension, allowing others to have their say on what needs changing. At other times, you might use humour to defuse a situation or break a deadlock by demonstrating the absurdity of the moment. Sometimes you will need to act quickly and decisively by taking immediate action in a crisis.

Hands-on vs Hands-off Management

As I became more confident and skilled in my career, I began to realise that there were moments and opportunities when a hands-on or a hands-off approach to managing was more appropriate. I allowed specialists on my team, who had an expertise and experience level far above mine in certain policing skills, to take the lead on key projects, trusting their judgment and delivery capability. I would take a back seat and just support them with logistics and advice when asked.

As long as I was clear about the outcomes and objectives, putting in place clear parameters for the operation such as budget, deadlines and quality expectation, I left the path clear for them to direct and manage the process.

The knack in doing this is to set the framework and then monitor the situation for signs of distress, both obvious and subtle, from those involved. By allowing a team member to give you regular progress updates you can elicit and discuss problems, as long as there is an atmosphere of trust between you.

To create that atmosphere, and much to the dismay of my line managers, I used to take my project leaders over to the comfort of the lounge of the St Ermin's Hotel opposite Scotland Yard, where we would have afternoon tea or coffee. There, 'far from the madding crowd', feeling relaxed, valued and respected, my team always gave me the full picture, so I could then problem-solve with them.

Each tea party cost £8 but over the six years I did this, I must have saved the organisation hundreds of thousands of pounds in litigation and reputational costs by avoiding a number of catastrophic situations. As a result, the St Ermin's Hotel technique became legendary and the head waiter and I got to know each other very well, so much so, that he would always whisk us off to a private area where we would not be disturbed, and then serve us on the best silver.

There is a clear boundary though between delegated authority and abdication. I witnessed this frequently during my career, as some police managers would 'dump' issues and problems on others expecting them to solve them without being given their support or even showing interest. I hated this and was myself a frequent victim. My regard and respect for such line managers always dissolved rapidly. Many of them were eloquent and forceful characters and were promoted rapidly, much to my dismay and disgust.

Forewarning Your People

At the start of a new managerial role, there is always an opportunity to set the tone for the team members under your control and one of the best ways to do this is just to sit down with them socially and informally.

This enables you to get to know them as individuals and to learn what motivates and interests them. If you are to get the best from them, you need an intimate knowledge of every aspect of their lives including family, hobbies, sports, their temperament, sense of humour, skills and competencies, as well any personal issues that may affect their performance and finally, their aspirations and dreams.

This also gives you the chance to set down the minimum standards you expect from them in terms of dress, behaviour, attitude and work quality as well as detailing your own management style. By clearly telling your team your directional style, how approachable you are and your take on discipline, they will know what sort of person you are.

By doing this, your team will appreciate you and not be surprised by your style of management or the expectations you have of them. When I took up a post at Hayes Police Station, West London, I remember telling my team a few simple things, such as my pet hate – not wearing a uniform cap when getting out of a police vehicle to deal with an incident or investigation. I explained that this was not some petty point on my part, but a desire to portray a professional appearance and to avoid any misconceptions by the public that my officers were just private security guards.

Always spend sufficient time examining and assessing the current situation without changing things for change's sake. If you move too quickly in an unconsidered way, staff will lose respect for you and see your actions as just a facile way of making your mark.

Arming Yourself for Success

Looking After Your Health and Wellbeing

If you do not look after yourself, you will not be able to manage your department or your staff properly. This must be your top priority as nothing else can be achieved without your health.

With that said, it is incredible how, even today, many managers neglect this simple principle. Work pressures overtake common sense so their days get longer as they try to keep up with an endless stream of issues and demands. This in turn, leads to ever increasing levels of exhaustion, frustration and a lack of clear headedness that can quickly lead to illness and absence.

The key thing here is to maintain and develop a strong physical and mental condition as this in turn will give you a state of calmness, resilience and energy. A lot of people concentrate on either physical exercise or just relaxation techniques, but the mental and physical work best in tandem so there should be a balance between the two, otherwise you can end up being very fit but without the clear sense of direction and motivation you need to avoid lapsing into a state of depression.

So, to have both physical and mental wellbeing you need to adopt some fundamental daily strategies.

Managing Your Diet

As most managers are largely sedentary, sitting at their computers and in meetings or planning at their desks, there's no need for the high calorie diet that's essential for physically demanding jobs involving manual labour.

To make sure I don't put away too many calories, I've dramatically reduced my intake of potatoes, bread, butter and fatty food. This has seen a slow but steady decrease over the last three years in my waist size and BMI readings and weight loss of 8kg. At the same time, I have started to eat much greater volumes of:

- high protein white meats, such as turkey and chicken;
- fish;
- eggs scrambled, boiled or in omelettes;
- steamed or lightly fried vegetables in unsaturated cooking oils;
- fruit with bio yoghurt;
- porridge and low sugar muesli cereals.

The other startling discovery I have made is that simply by drinking at least two litres of water throughout the day to keep levels of hydration high, my energy levels seem to have increased exponentially. If I neglect this, I soon notice a physical deterioration. I can't just drink straight water though, so I mix it with assorted low sugar juices to make things more interesting.

But with all this said, I still like to reward myself when an objective is achieved by eating out and having a good steak and chips. My other need is to start the day with a cafetière of good Arabica coffee to get me moving, but after that I try to avoid coffee or tea for the rest of the day.

Managing Your Sleep

Sleep is the subject of hundreds of books and hundreds of different opinions including Napoleon, who reportedly said that: "Four hours a night is ample, six is a luxury and eight hours is for laggards".

I'm with the laggards on this, because in my experience, a good sleep of at least eight hours has many benefits, allowing the mind to relax but still tick over issues in a subconscious state, and the body to repair and re-energise itself.

Yes, you can function on six hours, but your levels of concentration and energy will waver half way through the day in a way that can only be compensated for by the enormous adrenaline boosts that come from dealing with crises.

This is an unhealthy routine to get into, as research has clearly shown that it's in the second four hours of sleep when there is a shallower level of unconsciousness that Random Eye Movement (REM), a phase that indicates dreaming, is at its highest. It seems that it's this second four hours that gives us the increased energy levels the body needs through the day.

I have also discovered the benefit of sleeping during periods of stress and depression, as it has an enormous healing effect when accompanied by other health improving strategies.

But the problem with sleep is that when we most need it, it eludes us.

When the pressure at work is full-on and the number of issues needing to be managed increases, inevitably we wake too early and start mulling over things. There are things you can do about this including:

- Good organisation and planning which means that issues are faced and managed rather than being hidden and avoided.

- Developing a sense of detachment at the end of the day that comes from the knowledge that you have completed all your priority tasks and have a plan of action for the next day.

- Having an overall sense of purpose, direction and self-belief in your life.

- Relaxing by reading, listening to music, exercising, meditating, watching comedy programmes or just winding down by talking with family or friends before you go to bed.

- Discussing the day's events with your coach or mentor, who is independent of the situation and can give you encouragement, insight and a fresh perspective to calm your anxiety.

Your Physical Fitness

This is a major cornerstone of your health and wellbeing, and one that needs constant maintenance. Getting fit can be a major challenge to many people, but when you get into a routine and pass through the 'pain barrier' you soon realise the benefits.

What's often forgotten is the sheer variety of ways to get and keep fit. It does not necessarily mean trudging off to the gym four times a week, but can include dancing, swimming, golf or other sports of choice played with other people, so you combine exercise with socialising. A win-win situation.

During the course of the last six months, I have used the 'Cross Fit' training regime. This is a high intensity programme that mixes cardio, endurance, strength and speed exercises in an hour-long session.

These different elements ensure a full body workout that uses different muscle groups while increasing stamina levels. I complete two sessions a week with flexibility exercises as 'homework' in between. This method of training is used very successfully by the US and UK military to get combat-ready.

My other recommendation is simple walking. This is a low impact activity that exerts limited pressure on the main weight-bearing parts of the body like the knees and lower back, but which over time can have a profound effect on your weight and fitness. I use walking in two main ways:

- As a practical means of going to meetings rather than using public transport or a car in gridlocked central London. You can also use this walking time to think about the agenda and talk through issues with a colleague on the way. Just schedule in some extra time to get where you're going.

- I have also spent several ten-day expeditions in the last two years walking the UK's National Trails in Cumbria, Northumberland, Wales and Scotland. Long-distance walks of over 100 miles are an incredible way to lose weight, exercise the entire body and witness some of Britain's glorious variety of landscapes that surround us but which often go unseen.

In my own case, I have also found great benefit from employing a personal trainer, a benefit which far outweighs its cost. You don't need to use a trainer continuously, but on an as-and-when needed basis to:

- Assess your baseline condition – weight, Body Mass Index, blood pressure and general health – you can then monitor your progress regularly from a known start point.

- Give you a structured training programme which you can then do on your own at home or in the gym.

- Support you directly through a series of structured sessions in or outside the gym to accelerate your fitness to new levels, which you can then maintain on your own.

- Support you in developing a tailored programme that will help you recover from injury, stress or depression.
- Give you dietary advice to go alongside your exercise programme.

I have used the gym, personal trainers and physiotherapists at various times in my career, and so can testify to their value particularly after sustaining serious injuries on duty.

In dangerous operational work, injury is an occupational hazard, the consequences of which can be devastating and long-lasting. Getting over these events needs personal discipline and commitment because the pain, stress and anxiety of being away from work and coping with the pain can be very debilitating.

In 1990 I was seriously injured arresting a very drunk woman. But, while the circumstances of the arrest were amusing to some, the lower back injury I suffered was certainly not, and is something that's affected me since, so that even now I have to doggedly maintain my core strength to support my lower back.

The injury happened while I was on night duty, supervising my team on the streets of Notting Hill. There was no police van that night due to mechanical failure, and I took a call to Colville Square where a woman was reported to be screaming hysterically. I was on my own driving an unmarked police car.

When I arrived, sure enough there was a women screaming, well-dressed and wearing high heels, but clearly drunk and unsteady. I asked her what the matter was, but she just kept on screaming and then tried to hit me as I reached out to stop her falling.

I decided that the safest course of action was to arrest her for being drunk and disorderly and get her back to the safety of the police station so as to sleep off the drink.

As all other officers on my team were on other serious calls for assistance at the time, I decided to handcuff her and put her in the back of my car to await assistance. But as I was doing this she somehow got on her back and lashed out with her high heels into my groin. I instinctively shot back and as I did so, actually heard, as well as felt, a popping sound at the base of my back, before wrestling the woman onto the seat. There, the car keys, still in my hand, got caught in her stocking top. The ensuing saga of my prisoner shouting: 'Get your hands out of my knickers', was witnessed by several cheering nurses who lived in the square and my late-arriving police colleagues.

With the woman finally in a police cell, I went off-duty and home. But later that day I woke up with my back in a complete spasm thanks to the herniated lumbar discs which I'd torn. Totally unable to move, I was eventually taken by ambulance to hospital for treatment. That episode ultimately cost me several promotion opportunities as I suffered from numerous back seizures that needed extended physiotherapy at the police convalescent centre and periods of sick leave.

Having a Sense of Purpose and Direction

Of equal importance to having a good level of physical fitness is having a clear sense of purpose and direction, because this helps you to maintain your morale and develop an overall sense of wellbeing.

The work and training that you need to go through to achieve this is equally demanding as it requires much self-analysis about your personal goals, aspirations and circumstances, as explained earlier. However, once you clarify your purpose and direction, the heightened sense of motivation that results will also boost your physical fitness, as the two work hand-in-hand.

Dealing with Stress and Depression

However careful you are over your health and wellbeing there will inevitably be periods when the onslaught of different challenges both at work and home will have a serious impact on your morale and state of mind.

Both high-octane activity and boredom can easily create stress that creeps up on you unnoticed. You must be able to identify its signs and symptoms in yourself, team-members and even your family. If these warning signals are acted on early enough you will be able to avoid illness and absence.

Let's be clear though, as so much has been written about stress, it has become something of an obsessional fad that's all too easy to dismiss. Of course, we all need some stress in our lives to get our adrenaline flowing and deadlines, a sudden crisis or a big event can all play their part in helping us perform to a higher level.

While stress is fine for short periods and is something humans have dealt with throughout the ages, it is detrimental if the pressure is unrelenting and comes at us from all sides so we are overwhelmed and, over time, ground down.

I'm sure you know exactly what I mean and can think of your own examples. If this happens then there is a very real danger that depression can be triggered.

The First Signs of Stress and Depression

Changes in behaviour can signal coping difficulties and as these alterations can be slow and subtle, they are often easier to spot in others than in ourselves. Therefore, it's imperative that your husbands, wives, partners and colleagues operate in a 'buddy' capacity, watching out for telltale signs in you such as:

- A failing sense of humour and fun.
- A gradual withdrawing into yourself and the shunning of social contact with colleagues, family and friends.
- A sudden loss of self-confidence in managing people or talking to others.
- A sense of high anxiety and nausea at the prospect of going to work.
- Feeling constantly tired even at the start of the day.

- Growing levels of anger and frustration at small things that would not normally bother you.

- A feeling of lost control over your daily life.

- An inability to get even the smallest of jobs done.

- A feeling almost of paralysis when moving around at home and work.

- A loss of sleep, being unable to rest and highly anxious about a situation on waking.

- Increasing alcohol, smoking or drug intake above your normal levels.

- Constant headaches, nausea, agitation and frustration.

The first step is realising you even have a problem in the first place. You need to listen carefully to yourself, your partner or your work buddy for the signs listed above. Be honest with yourself and take action.

Applying First Aid

At this point, I would emphasis again the importance for any operations manager of having an independent professional coach or mentor. Someone who can calmly, objectively and professionally help you analyse the situation and identify the factors that are putting you under pressure, stress or undermining your effectiveness.

When this is done, you can then start to address the issues full-on and make the changes needed to control the situation.

Using a Coach and the GROW Model

Unless, because of hereditary or for physiological reasons, you have a tendency towards depression, 'things' are probably the cause of your problems.

So as soon as you identify the early signs of stress, take a few days out to calmly and objectively assess your situation.

Again, I highly recommend you do this with a professional coach or mentor, or at the very least a friend who can act as a robust sounding board and give the objectivity you need.

If you are looking for coaching, then one of the best models is GROW. Widely used in the UK and elsewhere, it combines a variety of methods in an analytical process for goal-setting and problem-solving. See reference section at the end of the book.

Treating Serious Stress and Depression

If your symptoms reach a point where you are absent from work because you just can't face the day, then it is clear your situation is serious. You may, for instance, have reached a point where you are literally sitting at home or in your car almost in a state of mental and physical paralysis, staring forward, feeling sick with a sense of having lost control over your situation.

However, it is important to remember that these are not signs of some inherent weakness on your part, but signs of stress that can all too easily occur when you are in a highly responsible and pressurised role.

These are signals that you need to make changes so you can adapt and regain control. This may mean a radical change of direction or even moving from a department or organisation.

During my own career, I remember driving past the entrance to Notting Hill Police Station where I was due on an early shift and carrying on instead into central London, stopping in the underground car park at Covent Garden. I sat there for eight hours, not able to move. This occurred after the series of violent incidents I mentioned earlier and led to five weeks on sick leave from which I emerged successfully, thanks to the fantastic support of my team.

Understanding what's happening to you psychologically is half the battle because forewarned really is forearmed and, if the worst happens, at least there are a range of methods and techniques you can use to help yourself recover, these include:

- Seeking medical assistance from your GP. This is essential as they can help you in many different ways for instance by:

  o Referring you for counselling or Cognitive Behavioural Therapy (CBT), which may even be available at your GP's surgery.

  o Monitoring your general health while you recover.

  o Prescribing anti-depressant medication, if appropriate. Serotonin is the main ingredient of these. This is designed to lift you over the feelings of paralysis and to get you moving again

- Gradually building the momentum of your recovery by planning each day down to the most microscopic detail. For example, by making a list of non-taxing domestic jobs that you can do and then rewarding yourself with a treat when you've done them.

- Watching your favourite comedy shows on TV or DVD. Humour can have a major impact on your sense of wellbeing as laughing releases endorphins which will lighten your mood.

- Listening to your favourite music can have the same effect.

- Moving your body. Just putting one foot in front of the other is beneficial, so get out of the house and take a long walk along one of your favourite routes.

- Take more vigorous exercise. Going to the gym, cycling, swimming or taking some other sport will all help the body control the harmful stress oxidants in the bloodstream.

- One of the worst side-effects of serious depression is that it can make you very reclusive. This inability to communicate effectively with friends and family only makes matters even worse and reinforces your sense of isolation. Those around you will pick up these signs and will sometimes even avoid you due to your state of agitation, gloom or even bad temperedness. So, it's essential that you explain to them simply and plainly what you are going through and that you need their support and encouragement to get through it. If they don't understand they can't help you.

- Use Skype or Facebook to start reconnecting with other people by messaging best friends and keeping them posted about your situation. This is not only effective but also free and by using the written messaging service first, you can give progress reports, without having to speak or be seen. You can always use voice and video communication later when you feel stronger.

- Make sure you sit with your family once a day and tell them what you have accomplished. Then get them to tell you about their day in return, so the conversation's not all about you.

- I have also found that listening to inspirational speakers and personal development experts, such as Brian Tracy, helps tremendously in building the momentum that you need to overcome the inertia. Brian Tracy has a free email newsletter service that provides daily self-help advice and many invaluable video links. You should also search online for the free TED video presentations on an assortment of topics, delivered by some of the best speakers around the world. These have had a truly remarkable, positive impact on me.

- Sleep is another profound aid to recovery and getting as much as possible can help energise the body and give it time to repair itself. This does not mean staying in bed all day though. So after a maximum of ten hours you must get up and start applying yourself to your preset routines and job lists.

- Simple meditation at heightened moments of anxiety is also very helpful as by concentrating the mind on a single factor, such as your breathing, it helps blot out other thoughts and so brings a sense of calm and balance.

Combining all these methods will help give you a sense of 'positive momentum', just as a very heavy stone rolls downhill from a standing start, it slowly gathers pace as it goes.

Again, I recommend having a coach or mentor to help you here, as they will be able monitor your progress daily, weekly and monthly both encouraging and refocusing you towards recovery much quicker than you would alone.

Acquiring the Right Mindset

Even when you are in the best of physical and mental health, you still need a clear head to face each day's challenges. This comes from having the right mindset.

To be at your most effective, you need to cultivate this mindset to ensure that you develop the following strong, positive habits:

Drive and Determination

As a manager you will experience times when the world appears to be conspiring against you, thwarting your best efforts whatever you do. Other departments won't respond to your requests. Authorisations won't be granted, business proposals will be rejected out of hand and staff performance will suddenly deteriorate. At these times, getting things done each day will feel like walking into a gale-force wind head-on.

If you are to overcome these obstacles, your drive and determination will be constantly tested, so it's essential to maintain your energy levels and not sap them unnecessarily. This requires a high degree of dispassionate engagement, so you can keep chipping away at problems and driving through to completion without personalising any situation.

The Ability to Build Momentum

Just as having positive momentum is important to your personal wellbeing, it's crucial for your work as well, as knowing when to increase a project's tempo will help you achieve the 'critical mass' that makes things happen all the sooner.

The best analogy for describing this is to imagine a large jet airliner taxiing slowly and carefully, making final checks before it's ready to take off. On reaching its designated runway, the pilot waits for clearance from the control tower before bringing the engines to full power and accelerating until the plane takes off. This takes enormous effort and it is only when fully airborne and at cruising altitude that the pilot throttles back and relaxes. He knows the hard work's over. Exactly the same sort of effort is needed in your own work to get any project or operation off the ground. Careful planning and checks are followed by a slow gathering of pace through to the implementation phase (take-off), as momentum and focus are increased.

Tact, Diplomacy and Assertiveness

Some managers roar round like a bull in a china shop, seemingly oblivious to others. But good managers motivate and sustain loyalty from their staff by speaking to them politely and displaying understanding of their situation, a process Steven Covey brilliantly describes in his book 'The Seven Habits of Highly Effective People'.

By seeking to understand the opinions of your staff member or partners and the constraints they face, they will be much more likely to engage with your requests or instructions because they will sense your concern and appreciate it.

Thinking of others in this way is not a sign of weakness on your part, and doesn't mean capitulating to a contrary view or objection. Rather, gathering views that take into account another's needs wherever possible, shows a mutual respect that will invariably make that person want to do a good job without any need for coercion. If your role involves partners, and especially if it involves volunteers, cultivating this habit will be critical to your success.

Of course, in an emergency or other crisis, there is always a need for clear directions as there is not the time for all the niceties there would be normally. But, if you have good relations with your staff they will generally pull out all the stops under these circumstances often displaying dedication far above the call of duty.

Having a Clear sense of Direction and Purpose

Nothing motivates a team more than having a manager and leader who articulates their mission clearly and then assigns specific roles to each member so as to achieve it. Particularly if their skills and aptitudes are recognised in the delegation process and they have played a part in the planning.

Knowing When to Manage or Lead

To make sure a job is completed well you need to demonstrate many different qualities. A good manager must be skilled and competent in using a variety of tools and methods, such as quantitative analysis, through to project planning and budgeting.

But operations and projects invariably involve people – staff, associates, partners and suppliers – so motivating them into heightened performance is an essential 'habit' to acquire. This requires an altogether different set of qualities such as outstanding communication, inspiring vision, caring for others as individuals and overcoming adversity by determination and an unblinking focus on the outcome sought.

If you are to be as good as you can be, you must recognise when it is time for leadership or management.

Being Well Organised

If you are to succeed, you will need exemplary organisation skills for all aspects of your work and personal life. If you don't do this your mind will be untidy and cluttered and you will be unable to think and plan clearly. To help me stay well organised I use a page-a-day diary, which I use to capture and review my yearly, monthly and weekly goals and activities.

My personal organisation is based on a combination of two methods.

First, I undertake a yearly assessment of my situation and determine goals for the next three years. To do this, I highly recommend that you use the 'Wheel of Life', a tool that's used in coaching to explore what is important to you in key areas such as work, finance, relationships, health, community and family. The Wheel of Life helps you set clear objectives of what you *want to do*, what you *want to have* and what you *want to be*. This will then help you start to plot out the actions you need to take to get there. You can read more about the Wheel of Life in the 'Developing Your Skills and Awareness' section.

Then I apportion my time to job priorities. This is a good habit to get into, so, I always aim to apply Steven Covey's time-management matrix principles. This really makes you think about why you are doing something by forcing you to assign each potential action to one of the following categories based on urgency and importance:

Urgent/High Importance. Actions in this category top the bill when it comes to justifying the time you spend on them.

Urgent/Not High Importance. These actions require your attention even though they aren't your top priority. Most of us have many of these items calling for our attention every day. They include responding to emails and answering phone calls. However, because they are non-priority, they need to be managed ruthlessly. One of the best ways is to say 'No' to requests more often and to generally protect your time selfishly.

Not Urgent/ Longer-term Importance. Here actions don't need your immediate attention but they are in key areas that will become increasingly important. I call this my forward planning zone where I need to be very proactive by putting in place resources and working towards priority objectives. If you don't do these things, then the danger is that the nearer the deadline gets, the greater the pressure and stress as items suddenly become urgent.

Not Urgent/Not Important. Such actions may be of interest but are not essential or urgent. These include activities such as reading a newspaper or watching television. Use these items at the end of the day as rewards for getting through your schedule. They are a good way of relaxing and important during periods of stress.

Knowing How to Solve Problems

As a manager, problems and challenges are certain to rush relentlessly at you, so it's important to adopt and practice a very positive mindset in dealing with them. This means you need to learn how to enjoy unravelling each and then putting it back together like a jigsaw puzzle. As you become more skilled and experienced, finding the right solutions will become easier, which in turn will prevent more issues and problems occurring down the line. Then your operations will move ever more serenely through the water as they won't be constantly buffeted by sudden storms. Having a mindset that tackles each situation calmly, also gives your team enormous reassurance about your unflappable nature and great leadership capabilities.

Remaining Resilient

Your resilience to the daily pressures and frustrations, as well as the bad events and crises that are bound to happen in your personal and professional life, will be critical to your survival and success as a manager.

Fortunately, through practise you can develop a mindset that will allow you not just to accept knockbacks and disappointments but also to learn from them and not see them as a conspiracy against you.

Remember, those managers who are properly tested in the furnace of operations, and who experience failure and adversity generally come out stronger and go on to become outstanding performers. The 'steel' you develop in the face of such challenges will be respected by your staff. More importantly, it will give you belief in your own ability to overcome all that is thrown at you.

By keeping a healthy mind and body, you will improve your resilience levels.

Developing your Skills and Awareness

To ensure your skills and awareness constantly develop and expand as your career aspirations change and circumstances alter, you must concentrate on four areas of your development:

Your Professional Qualifications

Your credibility and competence are built on the foundation stones of your professional qualifications. This is not to say that you cannot be good at something without paper credentials. Many entrepreneurs have made it to the top and amassed a great empire without them. However, they employed the other qualified people as needed.

In a highly competitive and regulated world, there is a need for most of us to show competence by taking professional courses that demonstrate knowledge and standards. This provides regulators and selection boards with a recognisable baseline from which they can judge a person's relative skills.

The key to selecting the most appropriate and cost-effective courses is to focus on those that reflect your long-term goals rather than on ones that have little relevance to your needs.

The cost and quality of training providers are obviously issues, so you need to balance both with the benefit you'll receive. This does not mean that you have to attend the London Business School or LSE to get a course of real value and in many instances, your organisation may offer sponsorships or a bursary towards all or part of your course fees.

The important factor is to know exactly what is included on a course, the quality and experience of the lecturers, the opportunities to practise what you learn outside the classroom and the range of organisations your fellow students are drawn from, a point that is often forgotten.

On my MSc course in Operations Management, I learned as much from my fellow students as I did from the course itself because they were practising managers in other sectors and companies such as British Airways, British Telecom and DHL. Their insights into different aspects of management were based on experience and demonstrated just how many similarities there were between our operating realms. Seventeen years later, I still refer to my notes and course materials, which are as relevant to me now as they were then, even if some of the terminology and methods have moved on.

For students like me who do not have a first degree, returning to education as a mature student can be both motivating and career-enhancing. This is particularly relevant if you are a part-time student, as you can apply your new-found knowledge to a broad range of real-time situations in the workplace each week.

Any course you choose should be sufficiently broad-based so you can specialise in the future based on a foundation of general knowledge and awareness.

My Diploma in Management Studies (DMS) gave me a two-year generalist grounding in the key aspects of economics, marketing, law, quantitative business analysis, human resources and strategic planning. This has since enabled me to incisively question other practitioners in these areas to test their responses and monitor their work.

Professional Training

Throughout your career you will need to update your knowledge and skills in areas that have undergone regulatory, technical or policy changes. It's said that a manager who has not participated in such training for over two years becomes largely redundant in terms of effectiveness – an astounding statement but probably true in our fast-moving world of innovation and change.

As training is very expensive in terms of time and cost, just as with yourself, the courses you select for your team must meet robust criteria for relevance, timeliness, cost and quality. In appraisals of staff, my key training considerations were:

- What training did others need to help them complete their specific role effectively?

- What training did others need to improve an aspect of their soft skills such as communication, public speaking or giving presentations?

- What supporting skills, such as IT and analytical methods, did others need?

I also used tenure in post as a factor in my decision-making to ensure training was put to best use in support of the department and not lost too soon as people moved on to another role.

By employing this approach, I could assess connections between role, performance and staff progression rate within the appraisal process in a very joined-up way, something my staff could understand and respect. Training as a 'jolly' day out is just not practicable or acceptable in modern management.

Current Affairs Awareness

It is extraordinary how many times in the police and in my career since, my awareness of current affairs has affected my work at a number of levels by:

- Highlighting external factors that are or will affect my sphere of professional operation. This might be a crime problem on the other side of the world that had relevance to my area of policing. Feudal, political, ethnic and even family disputes in the Indian sub-continent or in the Baltic could quickly manifest themselves on the streets of London in a spontaneous outbreak of serious violence. So, keeping a close eye on the international news was a prerequisite in a capital where 260 foreign languages are spoken and where there are almost as many ethnic groups.

    I recall an occasion in 2004 when on a relatively quiet Saturday afternoon in Green Lanes, Haringey, London, there was a massive gun battle between rival Turkish organised criminals about a trade dispute, the origins of which lay in the Baltic but led to many being seriously injured by machinegun fire here in the UK. This highlighted a gap in our intelligence awareness and led to the setting up of a new intelligence-gathering cell and going to enormous effort to identify potential informants.

Bringing new ideas and theories to my attention from watching and listening to key television and radio programmes about science, management, innovation and project management.

Providing inspiration and insight. There are many BBC programmes that broadcast personal stories of those who have overcome hardship and adversity to achieve a personal or business goal. These can be very enlightening and have often resonated with my own experience or given me reassurance that others are facing the same dilemma.

- Suggesting business leads. In 2010 I was listening to the BBC Radio Today programme and heard the CEO of NCL Technologies being interviewed on the 'Friday Boss' section. His remarks about apprentice shortcomings led me to contact him directly and to present an entirely new training concept based on the competency framework I had used at Scotland Yard.

Obviously, the time spent doing this should be proportionate and I have found that by listening to BBC Radio 4 and The World Service I am able to do other things at the same time, thereby remaining productive. The main threat is when you become a compulsive cyclical news observer, watching repeat news items or reading newspaper stories about non-relevant topics. This can swallow up the day very quickly.

Professional Coaching and Mentoring

As mentioned earlier, I am a very strong advocate of employing a professional coach or mentor as I have experienced the incredible benefits this has brought to me and others.

However, during most of my career the only people I could talk to about work-related issues were my line manager, friends or relatives. The degree of objectivity, skill and concentration each could apply to the problem varied enormously. But, having a coach or mentor who could analyse my situation and help me formulate a personal plan of action often saved me one hell of a lot of stress, particularly when there were many things I did not want to share with a line manager, as the issues often involved them anyway. While friends are sympathetic, they often tell you what they think you want to hear, while relatives often have many issues of their own they want to discuss and look to you as a source of solace and not of grumbling.

There are distinct differences between the role of a coach and a mentor. Simply put, a coach is trained to elicit answers from you about your current situation and future direction but they are not allowed to give advice or draw from their own experience. They work by using deep questioning techniques, questioning that helps you dissect the issues for yourself so you generate you own solutions and identify your own goals.

A mentor, on the other hand, acts as a sounding-board and *is* allowed to give advice from their own experience on particular topics, though they have a key responsibility to listen closely to ensure a complete understanding of the situation. Both approaches can be used at the same time.

Coaching and mentoring are very well established in North America but have only taken hold in the UK and Europe in the last ten years.

With no recognised formal accreditation in the UK, there is a wealth of providers all using different techniques. I have had the pleasure of being trained by the UK Coaching Academy and must say that their trainers and my fellow students have been the source of some of the most enriching personal development knowledge and inspiration I have ever experienced. The Coaching Academy has a range of skill programmes for NLP, corporate, small business and youth and they offer a foundation diploma that uses the GROW model of coaching.

Setting Your Standards

Inconsistency in standards is a trait of bad leadership and I have witnessed many examples of contradictory and even hypocritical behaviour by police managers in the past. So, before hitting the factory or office floor you need to think extensively about the standards you are going to set for yourself and for others, most particularly with regard to:

Existing Situations

Certain roles require a quick-fire reactive response that is immediate and effective in controlling a situation. Here detailed long-term solutions may not be required.

Your Personal Behaviour

Personal behaviour encompasses a broad range of areas. Yours should be exemplary in areas such as: being dressed appropriately, being sober, being courteous to others and acting with integrity in all matters. Your core reputation – always hard won - will be based on these things and can quickly be tarnished by unseemly behaviour.

Your Quality of Communication

All your reports, emails and messages must reflect who and what you are. So, if your use of English is of a very high standard this reflects well on you and is much more likely to lead to clarity in your instructions and advice.

The Standards You Expect of Others

Your expectations must be clearly set out to your staff through daily reminders about their role and responsibilities in daily briefings, project review meetings and in other ways. A baseline standard for each person can then be monitored and periodically appraised. If you expect a high standard of behaviour, staff will respond. However, if standards fall short in certain areas, further training or coaching may be needed to raise individuals to the right level.

Your Personal Commitment

Once you have decided on your goals and priorities, your personal commitment to these must be total if you are to progress because it is very easy to become distracted and to lose focus. This same commitment must also be displayed by your staff whether they are sitting at a desk in front of you, outside the office or even at home. They need to be selflessly applying their time, skills and effort to the department's objectives within their delegated areas. If they are, then the evidence will be there in the quality and timeliness of their work outputs.

Resisting Compromise

There is a tendency in any endeavour to look for shortcuts to success. This can mean that at the first sign of difficulty, the white flag of surrender is raised and a compromise is reached. In my experience, one small compromise leads to another then another until, before long, the outcome you had designed and into which you had already poured hundreds, if not thousands, of hours of research and development is diluted to such a degree that it's largely ineffective.

As an operations manager, there will be many pressures on you to do this, and from all directions. For instance, your line manager may want you to divert time onto another initiative, or to come up with a 'quick and dirty' solution. End-users may want you to deliver the product or service more quickly or cheaply than before. While, your proposals, if they pose a perceived threat to the vested interests of another department, may soon see you immersed in a secret lobbying war as others try undermine your position behind your back.

Resisting such compromise is an art form and is strongly connected to the standards you set yourself, as discussed earlier. However, the need for large-scale compromise should never arise if the standard of delivery and outcome has been properly agreed at the outset. With the best will in the world, the attitude of line managers and end-users is fickle at best and it is you who will eventually be held to account for the success or failure of an initiative.

With this in mind, you must clearly predetermine the standards you are going to set. This largely depends on the type of situation you are facing. If there is a need for an emergency patch then thought must be given to its effectiveness in the short-term. If the situation will have far-reaching consequences for others in the future, then more thought must be given to finding a far more durable and sustainable approach.

Several times during the latter stages of my time as a chief inspector, I was responsible for all proactive prevention work in the Specialist Crime Directorate (SCD) at Scotland Yard. This is the department that investigates all serious and organised crime on behalf of the

Metropolitan Police, including homicide, kidnaps, armed robbery, gun and gang incidents, economic crime and child abuse.

Historically, the directorate had been largely reactive to reported crime but the assistant commissioner, Tarique Ghaffur, wanted to get ahead of the curve by dealing with the source of problems before they escalated.

To help him and the management board make better key decisions about human resource allocation, prioritisation and long-term planning, I was asked to conduct a review of each department's capabilities and capacity for proactive prevention work that would reduce crime in their areas.

I immediately realised that this was a potentially pivotal moment in that it created an opportunity for the entire effort of 3,000 detectives to be refocused in a way that would make them more effective and productive, rather than just judging performance on the basis of reported crime clear-up.

But, to my astonishment and alarm, I was told by my head of department to do a 'quick and dirty' report that could be rapidly put before the management board. I resisted this compromise and wrote a short and concise project initiation document setting out my proposals. These included desktop research and department interviews at different role levels. I put forward a three-month schedule, but was then asked to condense the time dramatically to just two weeks' worth of work.

I explained that the mechanics of organising interviews and properly evidencing my findings using a semi-structured question format needed more time than this. I also emphasised the far-reaching consequences of the report and the need for care if false assumptions weren't to be made that would damage the reputation of our unit.

I expended much time explaining this methodology to my head of department and eventually won the day. The subsequent report was acclaimed and most of its 24 recommendations were eventually implemented.

As I remarked to my chief superintendent: "I don't do Skodas sir, only Rolls Royces."

He laughed, and understood perfectly why I had taken the stand I had and that his reputation had been enhanced in the eyes of the assistant commissioner because he had tabled a credible well-researched report which could be used to make sound management decisions.

You will also find many occasions when you have a line manager who is not well organised and is constantly flitting from one priority to another. This disorganisation can be the result of competing pressures coming from above as well as their own lack of assertiveness. But whatever the reason, this can have ramifications for you as the operations manager and so you must be steadfast, and continue to firmly explain the consequences of moving too rapidly from one programme to another without achieving completion of anything.

Such changes can have a substantial demotivating effect on staff, as well as wasting resources and budget with timelines having to be continually reconfigured.

Sometimes you are the one who must make a clear judgment call on which initiative requires continuity of sustained effort and which should be assigned just enough resources to keep a line manager off your back. The way in which you do this is critical and sometimes requires some 'smoke and mirror' tactics.

In my own department, I relied heavily on a monthly tasking and co-ordination meeting. This included a very tight quick-fire update from lead officers about objectives, milestone completion and obstacles that needed overcoming with all the details set out on a concise spreadsheet. All the department managers were expected to attend, including the head. This then gave everyone an awareness and appreciation of work rates and the combined investment of staff time against outputs and outcomes. In many ways, this disciplined the minds of vacillating line managers and reduced some of their programme flitting.

I encountered sustained pressure to compromise on one initiative that had far-reaching consequences for Scotland Yard. Between 2004-6, as a consequence of the SCD review I had conducted into proactivity (see above), I was asked to audit and appraise all the structures, systems and personnel requirements for the identification and management of London's most dangerous violent offenders.

In my review, I had already discovered signs of a wholesale unco-ordinated approach, as different departments dealt with different crime types and then failed to properly communicate with each other about the offenders they were managing. As a result, there was a significant threat that cumulative risk factors were not being identified for particular individuals, which led to them being given a lower threat rating.

For instance, there is a strong correlation between burglars and rape, based on factors such as violation of, and power over, victims. However, these crimes are dealt with by separate units and so an offender's behaviour across these crime realms is not always picked up. This problem is compounded by the different legislative and process frameworks that exist for each crime type, borne out of separate laws and major reviews that have occurred after a public protection scandal such as Victoria Climbié or the Baby 'P' case.

My work culminated in a full report as part of Sir Ian Blair's Service Review of 2005 (which became somewhat blurred by the overhanging cloud of the Stockwell shooting enquiry). This report recommended a new Public Protection Command at the centre that would oversee local Borough Public Protection Groups. This was designed to bring separate units under a combined intelligence, risk assessment and management system for all violent offenders.

But as my research, report and recommendations developed, I became aware of a great deal of lobbying going on behind my back. This was being done to the Metropolitan police authority by my own SCD Command, who wanted to protect the independence and autonomy of the Child Protection Command, which fell under its auspices. So, they were making a concerted effort to ensure their department would fall outside the remit of the new structure and system.

I later discovered that the rationale for this was to protect the brand identity of what was a relatively new department born out of the Climbié child abuse enquiry. But there was absolutely no logical sense for this and, what was more, all that was being proposed was a new line command for co-ordination purposes with the underlying identity and position of investigating officers remaining untouched.

But, with the service review perceived by senior commanders as a threat to the independence of their assets, what should have been a straight question of improving effectiveness and victim protection was being compromised by wanton power politics.

Regardless, I carried on, repeatedly presenting my findings to the different commands, assistant commissioners and the Metropolitan Police Authority Challenge Panel.

When the cold, simple, logic of my research findings and recommendations could not be refuted, the only remaining issue was where the new central command should be positioned. Should it be under the Territorial Policing or the Specialist Crime Directorate? Seven years on, this has still not yet been finally resolved.

The pressure on me at that time was intense, but having conducted the groundwork thoroughly, I was probably the only person in the Metropolitan Police who had a full appreciation of all the different departments and how they could be made to better work together. As on so many occasions, decision-making becomes much more difficult when asset power politics get in the way of objective thinking. Without my research, the management board would have found it almost impossible to differentiate fact from vested interest.

On another occasion, growing political interference in operational policing saw me being directly pressured to make a compromise.

In 2003 I was asked by the then commissioner, Sir John Stevens, to head up a pilot project to counter small business crime in the Asian community as a result of strong lobbying from the London Chamber of Commerce Asian Business Group.

I spent several months on secondment to the London First organisation, conducting research with an American intern that led to the development of the first integrated small business crime pilot project in Brick Lane. This was done in conjunction with my main partner BT and together we formulated a new IT infrastructure for business members, a risk-management plan, a CCTV network and a new police response unit.

The entire project was monitored and evaluated by Alan Mackie of MHB, a highly credible small-business crime consultant.

I negotiated a substantial grant from the Government Office for London for operational work, which was agreed with the board. However, I was then directed to dismiss my appointed evaluator and to instead put in place a preferred Home Office consultant. After making it clear that the partnership board had already agreed the appointment and that it would be very difficult for me to renege on this, I received two personal phone calls from a senior civil servant directly threatening me and my promotion prospects as well as indicating further line management sanctions if I did not obey the Government Office for London. I was quite astounded and informed my line management immediately. The promised grant was then rescinded, which substantially weakened our efforts, leaving only ourselves and BT to push forward.

The growing and alarming politicisation of the police was further illustrated to me in 2005 while I working with the Head of Scotland Yard's Homicide Command, Commander Andre Baker. He had courageously and systematically developed a series of Homicide Prevention Working Groups involving victim representative groups, practitioners and analysts in several key crime categories such as knife murder, domestic violence, sex crimes and mentally disturbed attackers.

The purpose of this was to introduce a much more scientific approach using predictive and preventative techniques to identify fascinating and revealing patterns of crime between areas such as burglary, animal abuse, sex predators and domestic violence. The aim was to stop killings by using first class analytical techniques and prevention strategies. Anyone who saw Tom Cruise in the film 'Minority Report' will have a slight flavour of what we were trying to do. After asking for additional resources, Commander Baker was confronted by a senior Home Office civil servant who said: "Mr Baker, why are you doing all this work on prevention? We're interested in your murder clear-up rate and that's the bottom line."

This was yet another example of Home Office expediency, with statistical targets driving the agenda rather than fundamental life saving measures that stop murders in the first place.

Promotion and Selection

A major part of arming yourself for success is your approach and attitude to promotion and selection. Many selfless managers neglect this area, something I once did myself. There is almost a self-delusional expectation that as you are giving 120 per cent effort to an organisation, it in turn will look after you by recognising your work. Sadly, experience tells me this is often not the case and that your efforts will just be taken for granted, regardless of your ambitions and aspirations.

So, my early career was littered with failed attempts at promotion and specialist role selection interviews, as the demands of normal work meant late preparation, with me going to interviews in a state of near exhaustion.

It was only in the last ten years of my career that I suddenly realised that it was incumbent upon me to literally force myself to set aside time for preparation and to apply the same level of effort in the run-up to an interview or assessment that I gave to my work. You have to be ruthless, almost selfish, about the need to do this as the competition is invariably fierce and the degree of focus and applied effort needed to come out on top is enormous.

In 2006, I entered what was to be one of the most testing and comprehensive selection procedures ever developed to promote and appoint new chief inspectors. With 450 candidates out of a force of 35,000 officers putting themselves forward for just 20 places.

I was told afterwards that I came in the top five. The selection process used the most contemporary senior management appointment tests from around the world, including a situational judgment exam, structured interview, an in-tray exercise and a presentation. In preparing for this, here's what I learned.

Are You Even Suitable for Selection?

There periodically come moments in your progression as a manager when the prospect of promotion or application for a post with increased responsibility and salary seems attractive. But before you 'just go for it' you need take a very level-headed approach and ask yourself whether your interest is driven by raw ambition or by a true belief that you have the competence, confidence and aptitude to do that job right now. So, you need to consider the following points:

- Your performance appraisals will give you an indication of whether you are capable of doing the job, *if* they have been conducted in a thorough and effective way. This is something that can vary enormously between departments, organisations and the ability, or interest, of your line manager, something I will discuss in more detail under *Team Development* in section 3. But if appraisals have been based on an objective assessment of your core competencies across a range of managerial activities then you will have a good overview of your progression over time.

- Your line manager, as long as they are not part of the selection system, should also be able to give you their thoughts on what corporate skills will be needed for the position, now and in the future, based on what they know from strategic management meetings. If your profile is ideal for a given position or promotion, they will then also be able to make a judgment as to whether your character fits the role, as they hopefully know you better than most.

- I highly recommend you also go and see someone who is already performing the role and respected for it, as they will be able to give you realistic feedback on the implications and demands of the position. You can then use this information to better inform yourself and to test your suitability and resolve.

- Other work colleagues, either subordinates or those at your level, may also offer a valuable insight into your future managerial capability, especially if this is done anonymously using 360 degree staff feedback, as mentioned previously.

- You should also consult your partner about the promotion, as the role may involve increased responsibility and time commitment, which could have a serious impact on your relationship. If there is no support and understanding from them, this can seriously undermine you over the long-term and even lead to your relationship breaking up.

- Thorough self-analysis with your coach and mentor can identify your goals, strengths and weaknesses at any given moment. You can also use this process to test your suitability for the role and manage any limiting self-beliefs.

Once you have made a decision to apply for promotion or a position, you must totally dedicate yourself to its pursuit. You cannot be half-hearted, so watch out for things that will throw you off track such as:

- A lack of confidence and negative thoughts along the lines of: 'Oh well I'll give it a go but I doubt anything will come of it'.

- Overwhelming work demands that deflect your effort and attention away from the application process.

- Discovering that as you make an effort, you do not have the resilience or the other characteristics that you need, but then, rather than steeling yourself and battling on, your effort just wanes and withers.

All this means that the application process requires a particular mindset, just as your general management approach does.

The Need for Space and Time

Determination and drive are not enough in themselves if you are to do your application justice. You will also need enough time and space.

This means that you have to:

- Agree with your line manager a proportion of the day that can be set aside for preparation over a given time.

- If you can't agree the above, then negotiate a period of compressed hours so you work longer on some days and less on others.

- Book short periods of annual leave or take accrued time off in lieu at crucial stages of the process when concentrated effort is needed.

- Delegate team members to cover non-critical meetings and obligations.

- Clear your home office space ready for the materials you will need, such as flip charts, revision timetables and a digital camera set up with tripod for interview practise sessions.

- Download reference materials onto your laptop and MP3 player for playback while you are travelling.

- Identify colleagues and friends who will support you in conducting practice interviews. These should include a coach and mentor if you have one.

- Select periods of the day when you are at your optimum strength and energy for your preparation rather than leaving it until you are at your weakest. For instance, if you are a morning person then get up two hours earlier and do your preparation then. This will mean reorganising your bedtime and making sure your household is aware of this change.

- Get the support of your family and friends so they give you space and consideration during this preparation phase as the application process can be as demanding as the new post itself. To thank them for their co-operation you could agree to go on holiday at the end somewhere great, something that everyone can look forward to.

Have a Preparation Plan

Any serious application needs to be based on a thorough plan which, once formulated, you must stick to. This plan can take the form of a timeline or Gantt chart up to, and including, the interview day. This will plot what you need to do down the left or Y axis, against time (days/weeks) along the bottom or X axis. You can then use this highly visual format to sequence activities into blocks of time across the chart. The main items you should include on your timeline or chart are:

- Key milestones or deadlines for the application submission, test days, assessment centre days and, of course, the interview day itself.
- Research time for topic areas on which you will be tested.
- Written applications and draft completion.
- Progress monitoring sessions with a trusted colleague or coach.
- Practise interview sessions.
- In-tray exercise practise.
- Presentation practise sessions.

To contain all collected research papers relevant to the process, you will also need a ring-back binder with many clear plastic A4 holders that give easy access, viewing and reference during your revision.

I also highly recommend buying a dedicated one page a day diary for the application process, albeit much of it will not be used, and then using it to flesh out in detail the activities you have summarised in the Gantt chart. In effect, you will be creating for yourself a daily action list for each milestone. Unused diary pages can then serve as additional note making space.

Collecting Work Performance Evidence

Whatever the type of application process, invariably the selection will be based on your work performance and aptitude for the position.

You therefore need to collect a range of evidence that shows this and which you can bring into your written application and the interview itself. But before you can do this, you need to scrutinise and analyse the requirements of the role so as to identify and confirm:

- What skills and competency behaviours are required for the position?

- What level of operational experience is required and of what type?

- If the application requires references and referees to vouch for your competence.

Once these are determined, you can direct your efforts to collecting the evidence you need in support. This can come from:

- All relevant line management appraisal reports over the last three to five years. There is no need for anything earlier than this as most selection boards give recent evidence a higher value than old evidence, which may not take account of changes in effort, aptitude and development.

- Any commendation or performance awards, together with the citation and subject description.

- Emails that demonstrate key aspects of your competency behaviours, such as managing change, strategic awareness, respect for diversity or planning and organising. Include instances when you have dealt with staff conflict situations or work-based problems.

- Any reports, memos or presentations you have completed that do the same.

- Any problem-solving reports on work-based situations that are evidence of your skill in reductionist analysis.

- Review your diary for previous events, crisis or work-based problems that you have encountered and overcome. As a deep test of your competency, many interviews and application processes prefer to test HOW you overcame adversity rather than WHAT you did, so if you have kept a diary of conversations or daily actions this can be an invaluable source of evidence.

- Collect together all the profiles that have been conducted to assess your managerial, personality or leadership qualities. These could include among others those previously discussed, such as:

  o DISC personality profile

  o Myers Briggs assessment

  o Business Leadership profile

  o Meredith Belbin profile

  o Learning Preference profile

  o Staff 360 degree feedback questionnaires

- Collect corporate reports that describe the organisation's vision and business plans for the future. This will enable you to show your awareness of them during your interview and how you can help achieve them.

- Gather any regulatory inspection reports on your organisation that are relevant to your sector. These can be a very important source of assessment centre questions and may give you an early indication of issues that are of topical importance.

Your Written Application

Most modern selection procedures use a competency-based criteria framework to assess an individual's suitability for promotion or appointment. Scotland Yard in 2006 was doing this extensively and in many cases to great effect for both selection and general staff appraisals.

The competency test allows an assessor to analyse how the candidate performs in key areas of management activity such as communication, leadership, strategic awareness, managing change and customer focus.

The role being advertised will have certain intrinsic skill requirements and normally the application form will reflect these, so it will be your challenge to match your proven performance with these areas as closely as possible. Whatever organisation you belong to there will also be some general needs that you have to meet in your application. For instance:

- The examples you select will normally have to be describable within a word limited box on the application form.

- They will also need to clearly demonstrate your potential to operate at a higher level by emphasising degrees of responsibility, effectiveness and leadership you have already shown, for example, by deputising for a senior manager or volunteering for a particularly arduous and important job.

- You will need to cover competency behaviour indicators and in particular show HOW you conducted yourself or overcame obstacles, and not just what you did. This is a particularly difficult challenge as the two can easily be confused with one another.

- Each description needs to be in excellent English. I highly recommend building up a bank of descriptive, action and connecting words to help make the content flow and so be highly readable to an assessor. This word and phrase bank can also be used when practising interviews in the way described below.

The purpose of the application is to test your managerial skill and ways of thinking and NOT to provide an opportunity for you to tell your 'war stories' of the great feats you have accomplished. This means that your first task is to match your collected examples of work performance to the job's requirements. This needs to be done carefully as you have to cover as many positive indicators of competence as possible, even if your collected examples are limited and on the face of it only relate to a few.

The police use a standard way of structuring such work examples that I think is equally applicable to other industries and organisations:

Situation

Describe the context and circumstances that you had to manage.

Objective

State your objectives as you started to tackle the situation. These should be based on the SMART model for goal setting.

Actions

Describe HOW you managed the situation by drawing out salient competency indicators. This is where 80 per cent of your example content should lie.

Result

Detail the outcomes of your actions and relate them to the objectives you had earlier set yourself. These ideally will show such things as organisational learning, high performance or meeting crucial commercial needs and not just something ordinary.

It is highly likely you will need to complete several drafts before you arrive at a satisfactory final version. I got to about eight drafts on mine. While this is incredibly time consuming, it is essential as assessors will use your written application as a way to sift out inferior candidates.

If you are not an excellent written communicator yourself, you should find a trusted colleague who is, especially if they have previous experience in the application procedures of the organisation, they might even have been an assessor themselves, though obviously not involved in your current process. This person should be rewarded (a bottle of something special always seems to do the trick) for reviewing your drafts and commenting on their strengths and weaknesses.

Make sure your line manager's section of the application is completed by them PROPERLY and refer to my comments in *Getting Your Line Manager into Position* below for help. This is very important as sometimes their evidence can add greater weight to your words and give you a greater opportunity to promote yourself.

Assessment Centre Tests

At the assessment centre you are likely to be given a number of tests to evaluate your skills and competencies. These are likely to include:

The Situational Judgment Test

Some modern processes use situational judgment tests to filter out large numbers of applicants. These tests ask the candidate to read through a series of different work situations, probably in unrelated sectors, and then consider a series of different responses to each. The candidate is then asked to place an appropriate score – possibly from 1-4 against each. This judgment must be based on their own particular style of management and there is no completely right or wrong answer. The responses are then scored according to the competency being tested. This type of test is very hard to prepare for but my advice is:

- Work with a fellow candidate using the examples provided in the selection guidelines to develop a bank of scenarios for each other, then you will have a broader range of response choices.

- Create a system of marking the situations with different colours or symbols to differentiate the characteristics of the scenario and the component parts of the responses. Once you decide on a method for doing this, stick to it so you consistently analyse the different work situations set.

- Practise working against the clock so that you get used to responding to all the situations and managing your time

- So you get the best score possible, leave difficult decisions to the end and don't waste valuable time when you could be answering easier questions.

The Structured Interview

It's almost inevitable that an interview will form at least one important component of your assessment, so you need to be clear about what an interview is for.

- It gives a panel the chance to observe your skill and ability in verbal communication. In particular, how articulate you are, whether your pronunciation and diction are clear and if you are able to engage and command through the spoken word. These are all fundamental management skills if you are leading a team. However, it's all too often forgotten that communication itself is being tested at an interview in addition to the other areas.

- It considers the quality of your work performance examples and checks that they are in alignment with the competencies sought. The panel will test this by asking deep searching questions about why you took the actions you did in any given situation.

- It assesses your confidence and competence, which can help predict your response to a stressful work situation. Some people are better at this than others.

- It reveals the candidate's awareness and understanding of current corporate strategy and policies that could relate to the role they are applying for.

In some cases, the interview panel will not have read your application form so they can then test your verbal communication skills without being influenced by the quality of your written evidence.

To prepare for an interview panel I would strongly recommend:

- Undertaking a series of practise interviews with a trusted and able colleague, coach or mentor in as close to interview conditions as possible and to do this at least once a week during the six weeks prior to the selection centre.

- Recording all these practise interviews on a voice recorder and preferably using a video camera set up on a tripod in your home office. This not only adds to the pressure but the recordings can then be used to analyse content and delivery afterwards.

- Building up a long list of interview questions that could be asked to test the required competencies in depth.

- Starting with short practise interviews of just one to three questions, then analysing these as you go along using a template that's designed to assess:

  o The depth and breadth of your answers in terms of the quality of *how* you achieved results and the occasions when you demonstrated these skills.

  o The clarity, speed and cadence of your speech and how you use emphasis and dramatic pauses, as well as body language to communicate.

  o The level of your corporate awareness and understanding of such areas as policy, strategy and competitiveness.

- Developing your interview stamina by gradually extending your practise sessions until they are as long as the interview you expect on the day. This will give you a clear sense of the mental demands required and help you deal with a greater variety of questions, Always analyse your answers after the practise not during it, so as not to break the flow.

- Putting on the smart clothes you will wear for the interview as the day gets closer. This will help make you feel comfortable and confident wearing them.

- Doing hour-long personal practise sessions each day speaking into a voice recorder. You will be amazed how difficult this is at first, so it may mean coming out of your comfort zone and stretching yourself. You just have to go through the pain barrier and sustain your effort but it does get easier with practise. You will be grateful for the effort on interview day when the pressure will be ten times greater.

- Practise using what I call the 'funnel technique' to answer questions. This consists of:

  o Pausing to consider the question. If it is not clear what is meant, ask for clarification.

  o Begin with broad points that answer the question and relate these to the broader corporate situation.

o   Start to funnel down to specific work examples from your own experience that demonstrate the competency indicators needed for the role you are applying for.

o   Give both sides of the argument if asked for an opinion, *but* make sure you offer a clear personal view that is strong and well thought through. Don't sit on the fence.

When you finally go into the real interview, exude a quiet, strong confidence but not arrogance. This is your chance and you should treat the room as your territory. Take command by addressing the panel clearly at the start and even shaking their hands. As long as you don't perspire heavily, even take off your jacket and put it on the back of your chair so they can see you mean business. Keep eye contact with the panel, even if they are scribbling notes frantically.

The In-tray Exercise

To test a candidate's speed of assessment and decision-making, many assessment centres use an in-tray exercise followed by a presentation. Together they demonstrate that you possess good organisational skills, clear thinking and confidence, and that you can identify major issues correctly and set out a rational plan for dealing with them. Both should be planned for and practised.

The in-tray exercise often simulates the first day in the new role by putting a bundle of items of varying degrees of importance, type and priority – email hard copy, letters and reports – into your in-tray.

Most bundles will have a few main themes that cover key managerial aspects such as HR issues, critical incidents, operational management problems, threats to corporate reputation and inter-departmental co-ordination.

In practising for this test, the first thing to do is design a template you can use to scan and analyse the bundle. One way is to draw five columns on a piece of paper in landscape format. Starting from the left, head each column as below:

Theme *(the general subject under which the issue can be put)*

Grouped Issue *(other issues that are related to the theme)*

Short-Term Actions *(immediate actions needed to stabilise the situation)*

Longer Term Actions *(medium to long-term actions needed to eradicate the problem completely)*

Delegation *(issues that can be delegated to others)*

Practise drawing and laying out this template carefully as you can often leave it behind at the end of the exercise to show the assessors high quality evidence of your planning and organisational skills.

Managing the In-tray Bundle

At my assessment centre, 50 minutes was allowed for assessing a bundle of 30 separate pieces of information that included in no particular order, a myriad of minor and major issues. Often the key pieces of information were submerged beneath the minutiae of other content. I used a ratio of 30 minutes for scanning and 20 minutes to write my actions down. This is about right but means there is no time for sentences, so one word and short phrase bullet points *must* be used.

The key to getting through the bundle is speed reading and then using a pre-planned approach that groups issues together with associated actions. This is the method I used.

1. If you know the in-tray exercise is to be followed immediately by a presentation on your findings and actions, create a general process diagram using flip chart paper first. This should be generic so it fits all scenarios and so can be adapted to your particular bundle. This is VERY important as it gives you a lifeline if you have run out of time in the in-tray exercise. It also demonstrates good order and clear thinking, qualities that are invaluable whatever the position or organisation you are in. See below for more on presentation formats.

2. If you are allowed, take out the staple from the bundle to make sorting into themes easier.

3. Draw your template grid on the paper provided, perhaps with one theme on each sheet.

4. Scan each item in the bundle quickly for key information and note down under the relevant theme what the issue is using one word or a short phrase. Your task is to get to the end of the bundle quickly as the biggest priority may be on the final sheet. There may well be dozens of issues but your aim is to pick up on only the major issues and discard the minor ones. If you don't do this you will be penalised heavily. Write down the major issues under the respective themes.

5. After scanning the entire bundle go back to your grid sheets and complete the short, long-term action and delegation columns. Again, use bullet points given the time pressure.

6. Write up the main themes on the presentation schematic diagram you prepared at the start.

You can practise for in-tray tests by using examples from other assessment centres.

Dealing with Presentations and Questions

I have already mentioned the importance of having a general schematic plan on flip chart paper. This should be in the form of a circle on which there are the following process areas:

1. At the top, place a squared title 'Where I want to be'. This forms the first base of your presentation and sets out your short and longer term objectives.

2. Going clockwise on the circle put a squared off title 'Where I am now'. This describes the main themed issues you are faced with in the scenario.

3. Another squared title is 'The key issues'. This describes the main issues under each theme together with the short and long-term actions needed to solve each.

4. Under 'Communication', you can describe how you are going to direct, delegate and communicate your intentions to staff and end-users.

5. 'Monitoring and review' is about how you are going to monitor and adjust your approach as it develops.

6. This brings us back to 'Where I want to be'.

7. Inside the circle down the middle, you can then place titles such as:

   a. TQM (Total Quality Management)

   b. Leadership style

   c. The main corporate priorities for the organisation in the scenario

In the actual presentation, you can then exude an air of authority and organisation by starting at the top of the circle and explaining each process area in turn. As time will be tight, summarise everything and group interconnected issues quickly to show your short and long-term responses. Do not try to deal with each issue in its entirety or you will run out of time.

Often you will be asked to return after a short interval to answer follow-up questions on your presentation and to clarify information you have given. This is a perfect opportunity to cover things you were unable to address in your initial presentation.

As your flipchart process diagram will probably stay with the assessors during the interval, you can also use it as an ongoing tool for developing your thoughts on areas not previously explained.

Health and Wellbeing

If you are to succeed at your interview, you will need to maintain your energy and concentration levels throughout what will be a stressful and nerve-wracking time. This means making sure that you stay fit and healthy in the run up to the assessment as well as on the day itself. So, as well as using the methods and ideas previously described, you also need to take special measures in the lead up to selection day. This is my advice.

- As minimising energy-sapping disruptions is crucial, develop a daily routine and keep to it, using your deputy to cut down your workload and to cover for you at meetings when possible.

- Don't 'cram' your preparation, it's far better to stick to a plan over a sustained period to retain energy levels rather than working in 'sprints', which can exhaust you and lead to illness

- Make sure you eat good food with plenty of vegetables, fruit and protein.

- Remember to drink lots and lots of fluids to keep your body hydrated.

- Think ahead to the day itself and plan it in microscopic detail. You don't want to eat a lot of fatty foods that will send blood to your stomach instead of your brain, where it's needed. So, eat slow burn energy foods like porridge, oatmeal bars or nuts and raisins. These contain complex carbohydrates that will keep you going for hours. Make sure you take a high glucose sports drink for periods between tests and interview. When I attended my 2006 Chief Inspector's Assessment Centre I was so exhausted after the first fifty minute structured interview that I didn't know how I was going to complete the following stages, but I drank a sports drink and in ten minutes was completely energised again. It's small things like this that can give you a competitive advantage over other candidates.

- Getting plenty of undisturbed sleep is essential. You need eight to ten hours of REM sleep to top up the banks because the power of good sleep is extraordinary.

- Meditation can also help focus the mind and help you calm down in the run up to selection or immediately before tests. Just sit somewhere quiet and listen intently to your own breathing for five or ten minutes. Blot everything else out from your mind.

- Stay exercising, but not too much. The aim is to increase

the circulation to your brain, calm the body and release endorphins, not to exhaust yourself. Walking, stretching floor exercises or a short fifteen-minute jog each day is fine.

Getting Your Line Manager into Position

I cannot emphasis enough just how important this is. Sometimes you will have a very conscientious line manager who will, if they support it, approach your application enthusiastically. On other occasions, this attitude will be completely absent, which will weaken your supporting evidence and make preparation more difficult. If you have given your heart and soul to your work under their command, you are entitled in return to their due diligence and support when it comes to appropriate applications. This is a two-way process of respect and professionalism, so don't let them shirk their responsibilities.

Once they have agreed to support your application and you have discussed your relevant merits for the position with them, you need to:

- Negotiate the space and time you need to prepare each day, either by using compressed working hours or getting your deputy to provide cover as appropriate.

- Seek their encouragement and maintain their interest through regular progress review meetings. If you trust and respect your line manager they could also get involved in practise interview sessions.

- Book diary appointments before application submission deadlines to ensure all the technical requirements have been met and relevant boxes ticked and filled in.

- If you doubt your line manager's commitment in support of your application because they are just too busy or uninterested, do your best to make their life easier. In some cases this might mean setting out the bullet points that can go into their section of the application or even writing the section itself and then agreeing the contents with them. They may even welcome this and be relieved by your proactivity.

- Use them as valuable sources of intelligence about how your application will be managed within the organisation. In my case there was a key issue of physical disability, the result of injuries I had received on duty earlier in my career. This had limited the range of operational duty options open to me. Consequently, there was a rumour that my application for superintendent in 2008 would be hampered. However, my line manager and I made very strong representations to the selection board for my rights be upheld under the new 2006 Disability at Work Act.

Appealing an Adverse Decision

If your application is rejected at a key stage, it's likely that there will be an appeals process based on either evidence of process abuse, transgression against employment law or, when the evidence is so strong as to make the decision questionable and open to a second opinion.

Although rare, a few of my staff have won promotion appeals and gone on to be selected. If you feel a need to appeal I would suggest the following could increase your chances of success:

- Research any appeal process and make a point of understanding the relevant criteria for doing so and how they will be applied.

- If you think it is likely your application will be rejected, get any necessary forms beforehand so as to save time. There will be a submission deadline for appeals so the turnaround will have to be quick.

- Make sure you collect *all* emails from line managers or the selection committee members in answer to questions you have raised about the process. I used this technique myself to demonstrate partial discrimination under the Disability Act in 2008 and which could have been used against them at a future employment tribunal.

Position Yourself for Success

The Need for Clear Roles and Responsibilities

From the very outset of your period in a new managerial role, certain vital factors need to be negotiated and agreed with your new line managers. Ideally, this should be done before accepting the position but after selection, so you can assess the fit between your individual leadership and managerial style and the degree of latitude you will be given to do the job.

If the gap is too wide to be acceptable then you may have to walk away. This is far better than being forced to conform and then to find yourself in a continual state of misery, frustration and confrontation.

To do this takes great courage and fortitude. However, as you gain experience you will realise just how necessary this is for your future success and that of the department.

Normally your application for a role will have been guided by a published specification and applicant profile provided by the organisation. This should be used as a baseline in discussion with your new line managers as to how you propose to apply yourself to meet these requirements. To do this you will need to clarify a number of areas.

1. You must clearly explain your leadership and managerial style to line managers so they know your traits and are not surprised by your style and approach when you start your work. This prevents many misunderstandings and possible concerns as others will understand your way of doing things when it comes to communication, dealing with personnel issues, being hands-on or hands-off, your attention to detail, the standards you set and the general tone you want to establish in the department.

2. You need to know exactly where your responsibilities start and end, which business areas you are accountable for and what parts of the inbound logistics, operations and outbound

logistics you will oversee. If there are key areas you do not have control over, will these be fundamental to the effectiveness of you or your department? What's more, is this lack of control to be a permanent state of affairs or could it be changed at your request? What are the expectations on you to deliver results and is this to be judged against a quantifiable target or a quality description of the outcome? Are these realistic and achievable?

3. Your line manager also needs to set out the standards they expect from you in the same way as you will set them out for your team. These should cover the same areas – communication, dress, behaviour, work quality and any other key areas they think important. Obviously, if there is something that concerns you this needs to be discussed, addressed and agreed.

4. For clarity, points 2 and 3 above could be incorporated into a written statement of expectations and attached to your final contract.

5. How much room will you be allowed for day-by-day managerial decision making? Do certain things have to be passed by a separate committee or your line manager? You will have to make a judgment call about the answers you get to these questions as to whether there is a very pedantic bureaucratic system in place or acceptable latitude for managerial decisions. The budget given to you together with expenditure ceilings could be good indicators of this. However, within the parameters agreed with your line manager, you will want a position of minimal day-to-day interference from them.

6. You need to be clear as to which areas, issues and budgetary factors must be referred up to a higher authority for approval and then to make another judgment call as to whether this is satisfactory or not. For instance, the selection, training and appointment of personnel within your department or unit is a crucial area of control for you, as your future performance will be largely dependent on the quality, motivation and discipline of your people. You may need to draw some red lines as to what is acceptable in terms of deferred authority.

7. As a manager, you must be allowed to contribute your views on strategic and tactical elements, so as to help shape the annual overall budget.

8. Another key area will be agreeing a way of resolving disagreements with your line manager without undermining their authority. If parameters are clearly agreed, the occasions when this is needed will be rare. Obviously, they will insist on ultimate decision making but you should be allowed an opportunity to put your case and draw attention to any incursions into your areas of responsibility or agreed decision making.

9. It may be very appropriate and valuable to agree to have a regular private meeting with your line manager, outside the formal tasking and co-ordination forum, when you can talk through your thinking on current and future developments involving work or staff. This can be an incredibly useful way of clearing up misunderstandings and creating a greater appreciation of the competing pressures on both of you. Armed with this knowledge, decision making in formal forums can be guided and more informed. This can be a terrific way of getting to know each other and bonding more effectively through mutual respect and understanding.

10. As well as your line manager outlining the parameters and their expectations for you, there is a need for them to also:

    o Agree to thorough staff appraisals using objective evidence, peer and subordinate 360 degree feedback in all the required competency areas.

    o Provide you with necessary training and education in skill areas that are relevant to your responsibilities.

    o Take an interest in your development and in nurturing your potential for further development and progression.

    o Set aside sufficient time to complete the line manager's assessment and administration for any applications, if you wish to seek further promotion and advancement.

o Support you as far as possible when dealing with personnel issues by offering advice and guidance from their own experience.

o Give you constant encouragement, support and guidance where appropriate. This should be in the form of solutions not negative criticism.

o Recognise your good work openly and unconditionally.

These things will take time to discuss and agree, but are a wise investment for both parties, as it can save a great deal of aggravation and disruption in the future. I give this advice after having accepted many new roles without preparation or discussion with my new line manager on many occasions in my career. In some cases, this was borne out of my inexperience and lack of confidence, and was invariably a serious mistake.

Becoming a Key Person of Influence

In performing effectively as operations manager, there are several areas that you need to be clear about in your own mind. Operations management is pivotal to the entire success of the organisational enterprise. It's not a bolt-on and should not be viewed as a 'necessary evil' to get product or services out to end-users.

As an operations manager you are at the interface between the customer and the higher echelons of the business and as such are in pole position to reflect and adapt to changing needs. The degree of influence you exert over future strategic decision making should be substantial, as your view will be based on real-time experience and dynamics. Similarly, you will also be the conduit through which management board decisions are turned into action on the ground.

This is a two-way process. So, the importance of your role needs to be recognised throughout the organisation. Ultimately this makes you a person of key influence both inside and outside it, but for you to be recognised as such, certain foundation points of influence need to be established.

Department Representation at Meetings

There are certain times when the operations department needs to be represented and given an opportunity to inform, influence and sometimes vote on corporate management decisions. So, you must be seen to be actively participating in areas of direct and indirect interest, although in some cases it's better for a briefed representative to attend meetings rather than you, but this will depend on their degree of importance and priority.

Meetings for the Tasking and Co-ordination of Operations

You or your deputy need to chair these meetings as they are at the core of the monitoring and progression process. Project and team leaders should all be present to report on their respective portfolios. Here your role should be highly visible, holding the leaders to account for their speed of progress and being supportive when it comes to finding ways around obstacles. By chairing this meeting you will gain a clearer perspective about the actual details of milestone completion and be able to assess leaders' performances and attitudes through body language and tone.

This is important, as you need to pick up on warning signs, which are sometimes subtle, that things are going wrong. Knowing actual operational detail is vital too because 'the devil is in the detail'. This is why I always encourage a hands-on approach for any operations manager as your success depends on it. Your interest in them, will also be noted by the team leaders, and this will push them to be even more thorough. I would suggest these meetings are held at least once a month to a tight agenda with succinct reporting required on key aspects of each work stream. More on this in the next section.

Team Leaders' Meetings

This type of meeting allows you to gain a deeper insight into development issues in your department in terms of future operational calls on resources, changing end-user needs and major obstacles that need to be overcome. These meetings also give team leaders an opportunity to explain and discuss aspects of their work streams in more depth and to engage more fully in the management process so they gain a greater sense of belonging, ownership and value. The meetings can be focused as needed around an agenda that is specialist, thematic, generalist or problem-solving in nature

Research and Development Meetings

As operations manager, you have a lead role to play within the organisation when it comes to commissioning and informing further research and development into a particular product or service. Apart from the marketing department, you have the most contact with end-users and so can observe what does and doesn't work so well. This is vital intelligence that will guide future products. So, you, or a well-briefed deputy, should always be at this type of meeting as it often requires someone with a high degree of pragmatism and a close understanding of what is required and what can be produced cost effectively to meet that need. You will be the only person in the organisation who can do this in a truly objective and constructive way.

Strategic Development Meetings

Any main board meeting that considers strategic changes requires your presence, as strategy should be guided by end-user dynamics and need. You are also central in being able to offer a view on the relative merits of directional changes and to give the likely cost and managerial requirements for achieving them.

Senior Management Meetings

Operations should normally be represented by you at these meetings so you can give a first hand report on major aspects of your department to the board. It also gives you an opportunity to gauge the constraints affecting other departments and to identify any opportunities that could be used to your advantage. Getting alongside your counterparts is also essential for unity and so as to form good, sound relationships with them. It can also indicate small power struggles or favoured departments – things you need to be aware of and to work into your positional planning.

Marketing and Sales Meetings

You or a representative should, if possible, be at such meetings as vital market information from surveys and sales data will be discussed that could affect operational requirements. These meetings also give you an opportunity to inform the meeting about the reasons for customer behaviour changes. They are also vital in planning campaigns for new products and services, as these will need to be realistically anchored so as to prevent false expectations and ensure future activities are founded on facts.

For example, in 2008 I was involved in the planning of a London-wide campaign to encourage the handing in of real and imitation firearms to secure areas at police stations. The Scotland Yard marketing department, who I have a highest regard for, commissioned design work that led with a message of anonymity to all people participating – the radio and poster advertising showed an image of an invisible person walking into a police station wearing just clothes and a hat. My input was canvassed too late as the campaign had already been signed off with no one spotting the obvious problem that there is CCTV at all police stations. Anonymity couldn't be guaranteed, something known to everyone on the streets.

Budget Development Meetings

I was constantly staggered while in the police about how little contribution was expected of departments and individual team leaders when it came to planning and agreeing the yearly budget. Instead, this was normally a top-down process in which the finance department told the organisation what percentage of saving was required and then forced each unit to squeeze its feet into this new shoe, regardless of priorities or circumstances.

In my department, I expected a bottom-up approach with a report from each leader about forecasted events and the resources needed to meet planned work schedules. A lot of this could be accurately predicted with a contingency put in for emergencies and unforeseen events.

Using such a methodology, once again positions you as an engaging and involved leader who allows staff to articulate the relative merits of their position. However, as each report came in I rigorously assessed whether there were potential cost savings or the opportunity to share resources between work streams.

HR Selection and Deployment Meetings

The success of your department will be based on the quality and motivation of your people, so how you select and use your people should be one of your top considerations. This means you must be involved in any HR initiatives to rebalance your department's staffing profile or selection procedures for any posts advertised.

The profiling of team requirements, described later, together with your intimate knowledge of team dynamics should guide this decision-making and give a clear view about sustainable levels of staffing. To do this effectively you will need to be able describe and explain the skill, aptitude and personality mix you are looking to create within your department.

Becoming a Key Person of Influence (KPI)

My career brought me into contact with an extraordinary family of Australian entrepreneurs. They came to London seven years ago first with Daniel, the youngest son, setting up a new enterprise called Triumphant Events. Starting with no network here whatsoever, he has now built what is a multi-million pound business. At the heart of this is an initiative called 'Becoming a Key Person of Influence'. This uses a five-step development process to help small entrepreneurs in the digital age become highly effective in their niche area of business. This can be used by any operations manager in any sector who wants to become highly influential and successful.

So, I highly recommend his book, 'Become a Key Person of Influence', as it simply and practically describes how managers can work smarter and position themselves in an organisation as a respected and influential person by using the resources available to them in an internet age.

1. Developing a Perfect Pitch

You need to be able to describe what you do in a succinct and powerful way to others, both inside and outside the organisation, in a way that creates a lasting impression. You use this 'perfect pitch' at business, networking and social events to make sure everyone knows what you do, while making you sound intriguingly interesting at the same time.

To create your perfect pitch, you need to prepare a few lines on your role and what you actually do. This should be something you can deliver in no more than three minutes, and which creates insight, clarity and interest in what you do as an operations manager in each of your department's work areas.

Each summary should therefore:

1. Clearly describe what you do and your area of work in a conversational style that you would use when talking face to face with someone in the pub. This is not a moment for insider terminology or jargon.

2. Add to your personal credibility by encapsulating your experience so as to demonstrate that you are a person of substance who knows what they are talking about. You can do this in a quietly confident way without bragging or showing any arrogance.

3. Emphasise that you are very solution-focused in all you do and give an overview of what you are trying to achieve or overcome.

2. Publishing Your Work in Books and Journals

The world today wants to learn from others and, as a manager with a growing portfolio, it's important that you should look to add to the operations management knowledge pool because you can contribute a unique perspective. You have insights and information that would be of value to other managers in ways that they would not otherwise be able to learn about.

As such, it's important to set down what you have learned in books and articles for professional journals. This adds to your credibility and identifies you as a selfless manager who is willing to share their successes and failures to further management understanding. If you write a book, it does not even have to be a best seller to mark you out as a clear authority in your field.

3. Extending Your Reach through Online Products

Intellectual property is fast becoming the most sought after commodity in today's world, something that has become possible through the digital power of the internet.

Knowledge products, such as training programmes, self help courses and video and audio recordings can all be placed on your own department's website, while free channels like YouTube, allow you to present your unique take on topical areas of management, leadership and innovation.

As well as influencing your peers, senior managers and end-users by portraying yourself as a dynamic and progressive individual, these channels can also give your organisation the opportunity to extend its reach commercially twenty-four hours a day.

What's more, with the wholesale movement towards online shopping showing no sign of abating thanks to the sheer convenience and time saving it offers, the internet also gives you ample opportunity to reduce costs by cutting out the intermediaries.

4. Raising Your Profile

Another key aspect of raising your levels of influence is by proactively increasing your personal profile both inside and outside your organisation. This isn't about bragging or posturing but rather an essential component of operating the brave new world of digital communication. It will help increase people's understanding of you and what you can do for others in a modest selfless way. And, with personal capital increasingly important, social media now give you the perfect opportunity to do this by presenting you as a contributor not just a taker. Here's how you can do this:

- Become a member of the LinkedIn Group Forums for management institutes, such as Operations Excellence, The Institute of Management and Leadership and the Chartered Institute of Personnel and Development. Contribute material to the groups and comment on the online debates so as to get yourself known.

- Advertise to specific target audiences using Facebook, LinkedIn and Twitter. All offer very low cost directed messaging to social and occupational segments of the community. This is something old style newspaper and magazine advertising cannot do with their expensive blunderbuss approach.

- Start your own blog using the Wordpress platform where you can summarise your daily challenges and present any insights you have gained. This is a form of diary which you could use as a source of information for your own future promotion or selection attempts, as well as a mass communication tool. Obviously, the main difficulty here is giving out too much personal or confidential data, but there will still be many topic areas where you could comment without opening yourself to a writ for defamation.

- Share your management presentations on the SlideShare site. Here your work, methodology and messages can be presented to a much wider audience, especially if you 'tag' using key subject words to make searching and researching easier for others.

Getting Noticed by Accident

There are other very unorthodox and surprising ways to raise your profile too. In1984, I was on uniformed security duties at the G7 Economic Conference in London. This was hosted by Prime Minister Margaret Thatcher and most of the western heads of state were present. I was attached to Bow Street Police Station in Covent Garden at the time and was leading a small detail of officers inside the National Portrait Gallery in Trafalgar Square, where a high-level dinner party had been arranged in one of the sumptuous art galleries where portraits of UK historical heroes and persons of note were displayed. This was a typical gesture of PM Thatcher, who was always ready to promote our historical heritage to her visitors.

I was standing just inside the main gallery entrance wearing my number one uniform, white gloves, and as a sergeant, the tall traditional helmet so characteristic of the British police. The guests gradually arrived and I stepped back out of the way of the close protection teams as they swept through with their principals. I was intrigued at being close enough to observe their behaviour.

First came President Francois Mitterand of France, who looked very sullen and morose, possibly pondering some of the latest revelations about his private life. Next through the door was none other than the beaming face of the US President Ronald Reagan. Tall, confident and looking very affable, he passed through waving to everyone in sight, then suddenly spotted me. "Hey a London bobby!", he shouted and strode across the gallery and reached out his hand for me to shake. I felt somewhat shocked but really enjoyed that moment and the memory of it, which I've carried with me ever since. I always think of him each time I visit the gallery now in a private capacity.

5. Joint Ventures and Partnerships

My entire police career, but particularly the latter half, has been substantially influenced and shaped by partnerships and joint ventures. I have naturally inclined towards working with other agencies and organisations to overcome crime problems as I learned very early on the benefits of operating this way rather than flying solo.

At this stage it's enough just to say that connecting with others in this way marks you out as a person of true leadership quality, someone who is willing to harness the resources and strengths of other bodies with common interests and concerns so as to get a job done. In my case I forged these partnerships to:

- Problem-solve an issue.
- Enable consultative and city centre regeneration programmes.
- Facilitate good research and design.
- Establish neighbourhood policing forums.
- Set up business improvement districts.

- Initiate new furniture design and manufacture.

- Develop crime prevention product design and manufacture.

- Undertake social research and analysis.

For me this has meant working across the public, private and voluntary sector with a wide range of organisations that have included retailers, landowners, community groups, design and educational centres, local authority departments and manufacturers.

Conclusion

Being the best you can be requires you to consider, plan and action all the factors described in this section. Keep reminding yourself that unless you invest in your own development and wellbeing, your effectiveness in the workplace will diminish proportionally. You owe it to yourself to do all you can to make yourself stronger and more capable of delivering the results you deserve.

Section 2

Making Things Happen and Work Successfully

Introduction

This section is at the heart of what makes operations management so exciting and fulfilling – translating an idea, concept or strategy into something real and tangible that leads to a successful operation.

But to achieve that you need to do two things.

First, immerse yourself totally in the dynamics of the situation, the issue or the need to allow you to gain a full understanding of its characteristics. This requires careful research and analysis from different perspectives, and will often involve people from other organisations who can help you acquire the level of insight that's essential for developing an appropriate response.

Second, the subsequent planning, organisation and implementation of your chosen response needs to be exemplary, something that requires management of the highest order together with exceptional people skills.

Both these elements are affected by factors that include:

- Having to work with other departments or even outside organisations. This requires a 'partnership mindset' to identify areas of common interest, best use of resources, delivery agreements and accountability.

- Organisational politics. These are very likely to get in the way and can seriously undermine your efforts, if not properly identified and planned for.

- Sudden emergencies and crises that interrupt planned work. These can take many forms and include natural disasters, terrorism, key staff illness, injury or industrial action. Despite their unexpectedness, much can be done to prepare your department for these as I describe in more detail later.

- 'Hidden obstacles' that hinder implementation and for which adjustments need to be made after monitoring and review.

- Ongoing adjustments that are needed as part of a continuous improvement process to make your product or service even more effective.

Awareness

Your first need is to have a complete understanding of the different challenges facing you either in terms of end-user requirement, the operational problems or organisational constraints. This understanding can be helped by using the following techniques.

Environmental Scanning

Environmental scanning is used in modern business management to create a thorough awareness of internal and external factors that could affect your organisation, department or specific work area. Such factors might include:

- Changes that could affect the behaviour of customers, clients or end-users.

- Changes that could present a new development opportunity.

- Changes that could limit or threaten your operation altogether.

In my view, this requires a systematic and organised approach that is far more than just reading newspapers and journals to keep abreast of current affairs and professional topics.

In my experience, thorough research and predictive analysis have been of enormous benefit to Scotland Yard in determining its three-year cycle of strategic planning. The now disbanded environmental scanning unit in the Commissioner's office played a major role in forward planning for events, such as the Millennium Bug, Hong Kong immigration issues after Chinese re-incorporation in 1997, and numerous technological advances in innovative crime prevention and policing.

For environmental scanning, I recommend that you use three principal techniques:

- PESTLE, to look at external factors.
- Value Chain, for examining internal processes.
- SWOT analysis, to consider a combination of internal and external elements.

In using these three methods, one key point to understand is that they are interdependent. I have witnessed on many occasions managers attempting to employ them independently in a subjective quick-fire way. As each relies on the other, this totally defeats the object of the exercise.

It's best to complete the three methods using a small group of analysts who can individually list the factors they perceive to be important and which can then be compared, aggregated and combined for prioritised consideration.

PESTLE Analysis

PESTLE is designed to systematically evaluate key areas of external influence on your business by auditing potential changes and developments and then matching these to your operational circumstances. The degree of impact each is likely to have now and in the future can then be scored to measure its importance and relevance. PESTLE Analysis can be completed quickly to give a snapshot, or developed in more depth as tool for ongoing review. It is particularly useful in making you think more broadly and in a more predictive way about the interaction between your operation and the outside world. The PESTLE mnemonic stands for:

P – Political

Political influences on your department and operation cover all forms from organisational and local, through to national and international. It also includes individual beliefs that influence others through persuasion, lobbying and even coercion. For instance:

- The policies of representative trade and professional associations in your sector.

- The individually held beliefs of partner organisations and their representatives.

- Those who are, or will potentially be, lobbying local MPs, central government or even regulatory authorities, whether they are for or against your operational work areas.

The underlying motives and behaviour of individuals need to be closely monitored for the indicative signs of 'politicking' because, as I have learnt to my cost, there is wide variation between what people say and what they actually do in terms of delivery, voting on committees, operating agreements, terms and conditions. This is infuriating as it often smacks of total hypocrisy as it is done to achieve position, authority and influence, which means the clarity and integrity of the designed outcome is lost in a fog of political manoeuvring.

E – Environmental

This refers to the natural environment that surrounds your operations and the influences arising from it. So it considers:

- Environmental sensitivities, such as delicate ecologies and protected fauna and flora that your operation will need to take into account.

- Operational outputs that will impinge on the local environment and attract criticism or even positive comment.

- Environmental controls, policies or laws that need to be factored into business planning.

- Aspects of the local infrastructure that may impact upon your operations, such as policing, transport, energy, water and other utilities.

S – Social

Social demographics may be of key importance and require you to assess the following:

- The skills and experiences of the local population, as these could have a bearing on employment availability for your organisation.
- The social classes of people in the area, their level of affluence and shopping and leisure preferences.
- The state of security in the area as reflected by crime rates, antisocial behaviour and people's general sense of wellbeing.

T - Technological

In today's world, technology is increasingly important given our reliance on mobile communications and the internet, so several areas need to be assessed:

- The relative strength of fixed line and mobile broadband in an area. This can vary widely between rural and urban areas, a vital fact if you rely on selling online.
- The strength of mobile cellnet coverage in an area. A weakness could lead to lost signals and business traffic.
- The use of new technology, machinery, telecommunications or automated systems to improve production and service provision.
- The use of social media to funnel and channel business traffic, sales and customer feedback.

L – Legal

This area can constitute either a major opportunity or be a threat to your operation. During my career in the police, vast amounts of time and planning were taken up by legal changes for the Data Protection

Act, The European Convention on Human Rights and the Freedom of Information Act, as systems of administration and operation all had to be changed, demolished or built anew at massive cost. So, among the factors to consider are:

- New or planned local and national government policies and laws that will affect your operations positively or adversely.

- Decisions about whether to lobby local and national government for amendments, additions or deletions on key elements, either directly or through professional associations.

- The need to adopt legal standards of accredited performance, such as the ISO 9001 International scheme for management systems, as this may open up new business opportunities and give competitive advantage over rivals.

E – Economic

Macro and microeconomic factors will inevitably affect your operation through:

- Changes to the financial budget of the countries in which you operate which affect your local and national tax liability.

- Changes to the general economy and wellbeing of the population, which will affect sales and end-user behaviours.

- Decisions that will need to be taken in local, regional and international areas of operation to take advantage of economic conditions.

Value Chain Analysis

Before you can assess the combined relationship between internal and external factors, it's important to differentiate between **primary** and **support** functions within your organisation and the added value that each may bring.

By primary functions, I mean the entire operational process including:

Inbound Logistics (the materials, facilities, suppliers and people used in operational processes).

Operations (the actual process of manufacturing or providing the product or service. This uses resources arriving through inbound logistics).

Outbound Logistics (the storage and distribution of products and services after they have been created).

Marketing and Sales (how end-users are made aware of the product and services together with sale methods).

Service (how end-users are looked after on a continuing basis through repairs, maintenance and after sales care).

By support functions, I mean:

Procurement (how well the organisation gets the resources it needs for each primary function through negotiated contracts, trade agreements and tendering).

Technology (how well the organisation uses its IT infrastructure, intellectual property, research and development and human know-how).

Human Resource Management (how well the organisation recruits, selects, trains, incentivises and develops its staff to become more efficient and effective).

Management Systems (how well the organisation uses its planning, problem solving, finance and quality control systems to ensure all aspects of its capacity and capability are maintained).

Wherever primary and support activities intersect, you need to analyse and identify how added value is being created by listing and then quantifying where you are getting competitive advantage or gaining an improved reputation. This will give you a perspective about the relative internal strengths and weaknesses of the organisational infrastructure.

Although as an operations manager your focus will be on operations, you shouldn't neglect other aspects, especially marketing and service, as these can give you vital end-user feedback about the effectiveness of your product or service provision. Where possible, value chain analysis should be conducted as a corporate effort with every department involved.

SWOT Analysis

Having identified the main external influences that will have a current and future impact on your operations using the PESTLE methodology, the next step is to compare each of these factors against your organisational strengths and weaknesses so as to determine whether the external change will have a positive or detrimental effect on your operating areas. This can be done by a combined PESTLE and SWOT chart that plots using a plus or minus sign for a strength or weakness where a PESTLE factor intersects. The plus and minus scores can then be tallied to give an indication as to whether there is an overall opportunity or threat to the organisation. Figure 1.1 below illustrates the point.

	Political	Environmental	Social	Technological	Legal	Economic
Current Operational Strategies	+ or -					
Main Department Strengths	+ or -					
Main Department Weaknesses	+ or -					
Total + (Opportunity)						
Total - (Threat)						

The advantage of this method is that it gives you a more analytical approach to understanding the interface between external and internal factors. Some changes in the external environment may even strengthen a department function that's currently weak. For instance, new legislation may liberalise a commercial situation making it easier for you to trade.

Avoid just listing internal strengths, weaknesses and then the external opportunities and threats, as this will give you a somewhat distorted and shallow picture of the situation because it will be based only on your own view of things.

Understanding the Problem or Need

If you regularly use the three techniques above, you will have a more complete understanding of the current situation and possess a robust predictive measure of how future changes will affect your end-users. This will also make your peripheral awareness second to none, as it will enable you to monitor subtle changes in end-user behaviour, attitudes and needs.

The trick here is to get as close to the ground or operating front as possible because it's here and NOT in distant strategic discussion groups inside or outside the organisation, where you will identify future needs.

Having your ears and eyes so close to the end-user is another unique factor that makes the role of operations manager so pivotal. For me, when I was in the police, getting close to the end-user meant using consultation methods such as:

Neighbourhood Working Groups made up of residents, businesses, faith group representatives, voluntary community representatives, local authority personnel and home beat police officers on the ground. The attendance at these was normally very good as crime and safety is generally a key issue to locals. These groups are so powerful because they are living and breathing what's happening on the ground 24/7. This makes them acutely aware of incidents, vulnerable people and changing street dynamics because of what they see, experience and are told on the grapevine.

They continue to be a vital aspect of modern-day policing and intelligence gathering, as they were for Scotland Yard in the July 2005 London terrorist crisis. Then it was only information from a caretaker in the Peabody Estate, Notting Hill, that identified large numbers of peroxide canisters being disposed of in waste bins. This led to the identification of several fugitive terrorists from the second wave of attempted bombings who lived in the block concerned. No other intelligence was available to track down these dangerous individuals from central or national security departments, including GCHQ.

Partnership Working Groups create a working relationship between at least two departments or organisations. These relationships are formed to make maximum use of each other's relative strengths and skills in a shared or common interest. They require agreed deliverables and a high degree of trust and accountability between the parties if they are to work. What they give in return is fresh perspective and the opportunity to use the experiences, knowledge and intellectual input of people you would not otherwise engage with.

Between 1997-2000 I had the honour of leading a pilot project that created an improved pedestrian corridor between Piccadilly Circus and Covent Garden. As part of this, I formed three working groups to consider and develop separate projects on spatial street design; risk management in crime hotspot locations; and a new community justice approach to reflect local concerns and fast-tracking justice procedures and local payback projects. This involved bringing together practitioners from many different agencies including retired judges, the local authority, police crime prevention officers, St Martins College of Art and Design, London Underground and local universities. The diversity of experience and knowledge was breathtaking and gave me access to the combined wisdom of dozens of people from different backgrounds and perspectives.

Multi Agency Problem Solving Groups bring experts, designers, end-users and researchers together in structured problem solving sessions that accelerate awareness and understanding of the issues facing you. As you dissect the situation systematically and logically from all angles, matters you were not even aware of come to your attention. This makes the services and products you provide much more effective.

I used this to great effect in 2004 when I held a gun crime problem-solving day for industry, research and victim groups, as well as police practitioners. We examined the entire chain of supply and use of illegal firearms and created a continuum along which we could identify intervention points where we could control, prevent or minimise the criminal use of guns on the street. For this we went into great detail, even as far as the component parts of a bullet and how these could be better regulated to prevent unauthorised sourcing.

Practitioner Interviewing. Sometimes interviewing individual practitioners, experts and end-users is better than forming a group, as confidential and sensitive matters can be discussed with less fear of possible leaks. It also gives those who are more reserved the opportunity to speak without having to compete against more extrovert individuals.

This is the method I used in 2003 to appraise all the Scotland Yard Serious and Organised Crime Departments for their capacity and capability to prevent serious crime as distinct from their traditional detection role. To do this, I used a semi-structured format to interview eight heads of department and individual practitioners who had operational or strategic roles. Their candid answers were detailed and gave me a realistic insight into the issues they faced. This made my final report much more telling and effective and led to the introduction of several long-lasting reforms.

Problem Solving

This is an area where rolling your sleeves up and getting your hands dirty is essential as this may open up cans of worms and uncover unpalatable truths you would rather not know. However, this is an integral part of your role if you are to become a true operations manager of value and someone who gets to the source of a problem, need or issue, achieves understanding and then develops a solution. To do this you need to bring together a small team of people who can focus on both general and specialist aspects.

General Considerations

- What type of problem needs to be addressed?

    o A functional one that involves a product, system or facilities, such as access for disabled people?

    o A social situation or trend that may be very complex in nature, such as a community that is being affected by an outbreak of crime?

    o A technical issue that involves the law or regulatory authorities?

- What are the main constituents of this issue or problem? This will guide you as to who to invite onto your team and from which agencies.

- Does the problem involve high level macro issues, low level micro issues or a combination of the two? You may need a mixture of strategic and operational practitioners if both are involved.

- What is the scale of the problem and can it be defined on a narrow front or is it multi-faceted? This will give you an indicator of the likely time implications of dissecting the situation and creating outcomes.

- Who with an interest in solving this problem can you call on to help? Or will you have to pay consultants if this is a purely commercial issue?

- Where will the problem solving team meet, how often and for how long? The venue needs to be adequate with white boards, flip charts and possibly break out rooms for segmented problem solving. To guide, enthuse and channel participants, one or more suitable facilitators will be needed who are appropriate for the task, skilled and available for the time required.

Specialist Considerations

- How are you going to manage the outputs and outcomes from the problem solving sessions? For instance, will you have a parallel development team to work on the detailed progression of the solutions coming out of the process, or will this be integral to the problem solving team itself?

In the case of my gun crime work, the findings of one problem solving day were further researched and then developed into a full tactical manual for the Metropolitan Police that involved strands of prevention, enforcement and intelligence work by a team of three over a six-month period.

The Problem Solving Process

I have used three methods in particular to solve the policing challenges I have faced: the Metropolitan Police's Nine Stage Problem Solving Process, GAP Analysis and Process Mapping.

The Metropolitan Police's Nine-Stage Problem Solving Process

This has allowed me to use a solution-based framework to logically and systematically pull apart an issue and analyse what is going on from different perspectives. The nine stages are:

1. *Where is the problem or need and who is flagging it up?*

It is important at the outset to determine exactly where the need for change or improvement is coming from, as this will give you an early indicator as to which parties should be involved in generating solutions and describing or defining the issue.

The need or problem may be flagged up anywhere by an individual or a monitoring method. This may be a production issue or a more complicated change in user behaviour, driven by a fashion fad or technical advance, for instance.

This may also uncover hidden agendas and ulterior motives for change that need to be managed if they aren't to distort the operational situation.

2. What is the perceived problem?

The key parties to the issue need to be contacted individually and questioned carefully as to their observations on what is causing the situation. If there is evidence to suggest that there is real substance to the issue, particularly something that could present a threat or even opportunity to operational delivery, a **joint action group** needs bringing together. This should be as large or small as the scope of the situation requires and can include personnel from inside and outside the organisation.

In forming a JAG, you need to consider:

- Who should be invited for their expertise, experience and aptitude for problem solving? Individual personalities should also be assessed so they are in tune, as you will need highly collaborative effort, not destructive conflict and confrontation.

- Who will chair and facilitate the group's work? Someone trained in structured problem solving with a high Belbin co-ordinator's team profile would be ideal.

- Where will the group meet and with what frequency? The facilities will need to be good and the venue accessible.

- What will be the broad terms of reference? Though the group should be encouraged to develop its own set of specific aims and final report.

3. What is the aim of the problem solving process?

The joint action group needs to decide what outcomes it is aiming to deliver and their scope and type, as these are likely to define the duration of the group's life and its work outputs. The outcomes sought should be described at the first meeting with the following areas agreed and further explained.

- The structure, purpose and process of the problem solving needs to be clarified carefully by the main facilitator.

- The issue for which the joint action group has been brought together must be described in terms of its scope, type and importance.

- The group needs to decide on what further research and analysis is required to fully understand the issue from various perspectives. See below.

- The group's roles and responsibilities should be determined. This might involve listening and contributing verbally, through to research and report writing outside the sessions. In addition, the role of process facilitator and chair also needs to be established. A first class chairman who does not necessarily have problem solving process skills may be best suited to this role. If the problem is complex, then there may be several strands that have to be each led during break-out sessions.

- How will the team interact with other groups and individuals who are using their findings or supporting the team through research and analysis? When people are giving their time, either voluntarily or professionally, they will want to know that their efforts have a real purpose with valid outputs and outcomes at the end. This is really important.

- What will be the likely time commitment inside and outside these sessions, for doing background work and liaising with other key people?

4. Further analysis

At Scotland Yard, our analysts supported the problem solving group by developing an intelligence product called a 'Problem Profile' taken from the national intelligence model guidelines. This gave a quantitative and qualitative appraisal of the current position using crime and police source statistics, other intelligence, demographic and public survey information. The problem profile focused on three key perspectives: the victim, the offender and the locational factors. This gave a rounded picture of the interconnected dynamics and numerous variables as these three paradigms interacted with each other.

However, while the report was useful, I often found it flawed because the analysts hadn't actively participated in any live research but instead were taking their data from existing computerised indices. This 'sedentary approach' has many drawbacks:

- As with all automated systems, the data quality is only as good as the information inputted and I saw ample evidence of weak and inaccurate data collection.

- Large swathes of intelligence about offender, location and victim behaviours were not even inputted as the officers and detectives concerned kept this knowledge to themselves and didn't share it. Although this was against the guidelines, it was a practical reality because of the chance of large-scale leaks to unauthorised people and even criminals. This posed a real and well-known threat to operations.

- The problem profile gave just one perspective on an issue and so it lacked input from many other related agencies or individuals with an interest in a situation.

This is an essential factor to keep in mind with this type of work. In my partnership work for Capital Link in 1998, improving the safety and design of one of the UK's busiest pedestrian corridors between Piccadilly and Covent Garden, I discovered that most crime incidents outside Leicester Square Tube Station on Charing Cross Road were being listed as Leicester Square. This led to a misconception that the crimes were occurring in the square itself, which in turn meant extra local authority and police effort was put in to patrol this area. However, in reality the problem was actually caused by congestion at the pedestrian barriers in Charing Cross Road which attracted pickpockets and robbers who preyed on static crowds at this busy street corner. The implications of such flawed data for planning, response and wasted resources can obviously be enormous.

This also highlights the fact that it is possible to identify the underlying reasons for an issue or problem prematurely, so great care needs to be taken to unwrap the situation so as to really determine the dynamics of what is going on. To help do that I would make the following research and analysis recommendations:

- By all means list the group's early opinions about what is happening and why, but then apply strict test criteria such as:

  o Is the opinion based on personal experience or gathered data?

  o Is the data being used, reliable, and how can it be tested for accuracy and quality?

- Then list question areas that need further research and analysis. For any manufacturing or service issue, you should consider these broad areas:

  o What are the indicators of change for any given situation and what are the relative strengths of each? Are there any strong correlations or causal relationships that can be identified between the indicators? For instance, are end-users' circumstances changing or are there supply issues?

  o What are the environmental factors (PESTLE) affecting the situation? See above.

  o What demographic factors to do with population, ethnicity, wellbeing and cultural influences could be affecting the situation?

  o Then apply assessment methods, such as SWOT, Value Chain, GAP Analysis and Process Mapping, to evaluate the interaction between the internal capacity and capability of your enterprise and changing external environmental factors.

- Make full use of individual and focus group type interviews, as these will give you a lot more qualitative information about changing behaviour and dynamics. Make sure you include a mix of interviewees and design a set of semi-structured questions to elicit deep thinking about the issue among:

  o Practitioners who have different levels of tactical and strategic responsibility in the area. For example, from 'tactical' street cleaners through to the 'strategic' head of local authority environmental services.

o   End-users of the product or service. These may differ depending on times of the day or week, with each having an entirely different experience.

o   Academic and industry observers, who may hold quality data on the issue from different perspectives.

I will give you a small example of what I mean. In 1979-80 I was assigned to the 'Beat Crimes' unit at Paddington Green, whose aim was to investigate minor crimes such as cases of low value theft, criminal damage or assault. I really enjoyed this work as you had more time to speak to the victim and collect evidence in contrast to a quick-fire emergency response. The area was experiencing a spate of bicycle thefts, which over several months amounted to hundreds of incidents.

As part of the problem solving process, to help assess the scale of the problem and to get a geographical picture in my mind of the proximity of theft locations, I asked the police helicopter to pass over and take photos of the area. The result was staggering. The helicopter crew reported seeing hundreds of bicycles on the roof of one of the residential blocks on the Lisson Green Estate. This led to a major enquiry after which an entire local family was implicated in what was the industrial scale processing and distribution of stolen bikes. We would never have known about this otherwise as no maintenance engineers normally went onto the roof area.

5.   Defining and describing the underlying problem or issue

Once research and analysis comes back, it needs to be sifted, sorted and interpreted. So, I recommend that you:

- Delegate each piece of research to particular joint action group members or strand leaders for review and summary of:

  o   The quality of the underlying research methods and data collected. This needs to be scored so its relative strength is understood.

  o   Any clear trends, correlations or causal links identified in the research.

  o   Any recommendations for further investigation.

- o   A summary of the main findings arising from the research and relevant implications.

- Once this is done, the resulting reports can be circulated to all group members for reading and thought outside of their sessions.

- The team then needs to be brought together to determine:

  - o   What is the scope and type of issue being faced?

  - o   What are the principal external and internal factors.

6.   Options for change

At this point, a series of sessions should be arranged to consider the options for addressing the issue. This can be done by:

- Using a flow schematic diagram to plot the entire inbound, operations and outbound chain for a pure manufacturing or service situation. The group (or sub-groups, if preferred) can then consider where points exist to either exploit an opportunity or control a threat.

In a more complex social situation where issues are interlinked and one factor often knocks on to another in a domino effect, the best course is to take a more holistic approach. This will assess the dynamics of interdependence based on environmental changes and behaviour controls, something that often requires a high degree of lateral thinking.

For example, in 1990 at Notting Hill Police Division, I was in charge of a specialist unit combating drug supply to the All Saints Road. This was, and to some extent still is, a notorious area for the supply and use of controlled drugs like cannabis and crack cocaine. In effect, there was an internationally known street market to which hundreds of punters came each day to buy their fix.

On the periphery of this market, and living on one of the estates north of the area, was a family all of whom had been involved in violence, intimidation and drug supply at one time or other. In 1990 the youngest son who was causing most problems by using pit bull terriers and various bullying tactics to intimidate local pub managers into allowing him to trade inside their premises. He and his cohorts were quite prepared to use extreme violence and were genuinely feared.

Given the growing evidence against them, my team decided to take a strong position and spent much time stopping and searching him, generally disrupting his daily life with 'in-your-face policing'. On one particular Sunday afternoon, he confronted my uniformed officers with his dogs and threatened to kill one of them.

I decided that enough was enough and that we would stamp our authority on the area. Together with various other enforcement agencies, we undertook a full raid on his home and that of his brother. We seized several pit bull terriers from both addresses.

From that moment, nothing further was seen or heard of the younger brother on the streets of the area. All his activities changed to other parts of London, unfortunately one being near my home, where he became involved in burglaries.

I later discovered from contacts on the ground, that it was the older brother who had proved to be the key to this. Not only had he hated having his pet dogs seized by us but, more importantly, he really resented being raided because of his brother's activity. He was a married man and the raid had upset his wife and children. He made it very clear to his sibling that he would not tolerate this happening again.

Though I'd not planned it, this family pressure then became the principal lever in changing the young criminal's behaviour. It was a valuable lesson and in the late 2000s, I was also able to apply the same principles to gang crime control.

I discovered that arrest and even imprisonment is of little concern to gang members when their life expectancy is only 25 years or so. But what does have an influence over their behaviour and reaction to police enforcement are 'softer' factors such as the withdrawal of sexual contact by their girlfriends, the seizure of their favourite caps and trainers, along with their high value cars.

Using the Proceeds of Crime Act, I developed 'seizure tactics' that included transferring their BMW and VW cars to the police commander's vehicle pool. Drug dealers hate seeing their prized cars being driven by uniformed senior police officers as it 'disses' the respect afforded them in the community.

7. Option appraisal and selection

Once you've generated options you need to go through a process of careful selection using robust selection criteria based on questions such as:

- Is the option practical in terms of time and financial costs? You may also need to consider what the cost of NOT doing anything will be.

- What is the likely impact of this option on the problem either directly or through the types of leverage discussed above? For instance, will you just move the problem elsewhere?

- Is the option appropriate in terms of the likely reaction to it from interested parties? This could be very negative and damaging if there is a regulatory backlash or negative end-user impression. For example, using sexual inferences in advertising can undermine an organisation's reputation as a serious and responsible player.

- Is the option feasible given the organisation's current capacity and capability?

A number of separate options may need to be applied to different parts of the problem, so these will need to be graded and sorted according to their purpose. Always be mindful of the law of unintended consequences as certain options you choose may have unexpected knock-on effects.

One of the best examples I know of this comes from Canada and involves the British Columbian Hydro Electricity provider. Every winter they faced the very real problem of power pylons and cables collapsing under the weight of snow.

They applied a problem solving process to the situation, generating and selecting options:

1. How can we shake the snow off the lines and pylons regularly without massive cost or getting engineers on the ground to manually shift the snow?

2. Can we use natural means to clear the snow? For instance, encouraging bears to climb the posts, who will shake the snow off as a side effect.

3. How can we encourage them to do this?

4. Why not place meat regularly at the top of the pylons to encourage the bears to climb?

5. How can we get the meat into position affordably?

6. Why not use a helicopter and winch meat onto the pylons?

This solution was tried and with unexpected results that should, in retrospect, have been obvious. As it hovered close to the pylons and lines, the helicopter's downdraft displaced the snow. Problem solved with much time and cost saved in buying meat and getting it into position.

Now all that's needed is to fly along the lines at an appropriate altitude and speed to achieve the same effect. This is the law of unintended consequences as applied to problem-solving and illustrates the need for lateral thinking in any problem-solving process.

Sometimes the use of decision tree methodology may be more appropriate when considering the different possible outcome scenarios. By applying options to each scenario branch, a decision making route is created that's appropriate for the circumstances. In other words, ask a 'what if' question followed by 'I would do the following in this circumstance'.

8. Implementation of best option

This part of the process overlaps with operational implementation, which is discussed in the next section.

While serving on Notting Hill's All Saints Road drugs team in 1991, my officers were faced with a growing threat from dangerous pit bull terriers. Criminals were keeping these for intimidation and personal protection. I had already lost two officers who had suffered very serious bites from which it took them months to recover.

Pit bulls have extremely powerful jaws and are very tenacious in character so when they latch onto the calf muscles of your leg they literally rip out the soft tissue and muscle. The only way to get them to release is to deny them oxygen by discharging a CO_2 fire extinguisher into their face. Hitting them with a police truncheon over the head has no effect whatsoever, no matter how many times you do it.

After thinking through possible tactics for dealing with this developing scourge, I decided to use the RSPCA's new Dangerous Dogs Unit on our police raids. Their team was trained and equipped to control and capture aggressive dogs and interestingly, they were also authorised to carry firearms so they could shoot a dog as a final solution. The police don't have this authority and in extreme situations have to call in a tactical firearms team, who are not specifically trained to kill a dog. This is a specialist task, as the shot has to be positioned to a particular part of the skull for an outright kill. This can be particularly difficult to do as you seldom get a clear shot on a fast moving animal and are far more likely to shoot one of your colleagues instead.

I remember with affection and some amusement the raids we and the RSPCA team went on together. They may have looked like Michelin tyre men with fishing nets, when dressed in their protective gear, but they were very brave and often went into a building first after we had blown the door off so they could control the dogs quickly before we conducted the search and arrest. I recall one occasion when their team leader said to me: "Jim, we love going on these raids with you but could we stop going in first as our health and safety advisor's having kittens."

9. *Evaluation and review*

Again, this also overlaps with operational implementation, which is explored further in the next section.

GAP Analysis

GAP Analysis enables you to establish with clarity your current position and where you want to be in the future together with the nature of the gaps between the two positions.

I've used this technique both for rapid appraisals and to achieve a more in-depth understanding of crime patterns. It's also very useful where a shifting environmental situation may have implications for public sector resourcing.

I used GAP Analysis in 2006 when assistant commissioner Ghaffur of the Specialist Crime Directorate asked me to research and assess the implications for London of being host to people from a variety of ethnic backgrounds and speaking over 260 different foreign languages. Each ethnic group was vulnerable in its own ways to serious crime, either as a target or perpetrator. These changing demographics presented a new and unique policing challenge to the capital.

I worked with the Greater London Authority's demographics office and two interns from Sam Houston University in Texas to evaluate data from the 2000 Census and recorded police crime incidents. This identified specific crime patterns involving minority communities that clearly needed to be factored into future police strategic decision-making.

Process Mapping

To the best of my knowledge **Process Mapping** isn't widely used, but it has been of great value to me in plotting a flowchart of existing systems or behavioural patterns so as to identify points of strength, vulnerability, inefficiency and opportunities for improvement.

By using it to develop a flow diagram, you can get a helicopter view of the complete activity journey.

I have found it especially useful to identify:

- Potential vulnerabilities in the process chain in terms of operational effectiveness, efficiency and threats from external factors.

- Opportunities for controlling, preventing and eradicating the vulnerability issues you have identified at different points of the process.

I used process mapping in 2007 at the Allied Bakeries factory in Orpington, Kent. This factory produces several million loaves of assorted breads every month and serves much of the south east England market. For several months, the factory had been plagued by criminal contamination of its products with customers finding metal objects such as pins, paper clips and assorted debris between their bread slices.

Because of the regional and national implications to the food chain, the Serious and Organised Crime Group of Scotland Yard were asked to assist in the investigation, with my department called in to help with problem solving and crime prevention tactics.

Working alongside members of the Food Standards Agency, we moved forward on several fronts, including the forensic examination of contaminated products, DNA testing of staff, and a wide sweep of associated incidents, staff grievances and customer threats.

It soon became clear that isolating the timing of any contamination would be a major problem as it required a lot of painstaking analysis.

Eventually I took the view that if we were to prevent contamination recurring, I should map the entire operations process from inbound materials, production and storage through to the outbound distribution chain to outlets.

Although this took time, it gave me an opportunity to plot the course of production and to identify vulnerabilities and likely points of contamination. I backed this up by surveying the production line, interviewing key practitioners and photographing the areas concerned. I then graded vulnerabilities and created a prevention plan to control weaknesses in supervision using natural surveillance, quality control, new management systems, factory layouts and product design. This resulted in some eighteen recommendations of varying complexity and cost that included:

- New packaging materials and coded seals.

- Greater control over staff clothing and new pre- and post-work decontamination regulations and methods.

- New overall clothing requirements.

- Deep cleaning of all floors and production areas.

- CCTV monitoring of problem areas.

- Storage pallet layout changes to allow for closer monitoring and better lines of sight.

- Access and exit controls to all production, storage and distribution areas.

Process mapping in this practical way, backed up by personal site visits, surveys and practitioner interviewing was invaluable in analysing the situation and determining how security could be significantly improved.

Consequently, over the next twelve months there was an 80 per cent drop in the number of incidents as more and more of these measures were implemented, as budgets allowed. No arrests were made but through our team's combined efforts, the opportunities for undetected contamination were largely choked off.

Managing Sudden Events and Crises

Looking back, sudden events and crises seem to have taken up an inordinately large part of my management life, with a stream of unforeseen emergencies constantly affecting my daily plans and business continuity. On reflection, I suppose this is the essence of policing, which is about managing complicated and unpredictable human behaviour.

The aim of the operations manager is to progress and develop business calmly and successfully with as few interruptions as possible. No matter what sector you are in, 'stuff' just happens, this is unavoidable. Factors such as an industrial strike, a terrorist incident that paralyses the transport infrastructure, a fire or even sudden illness or injury to a key member of staff, can all adversely affect operations suddenly and dramatically.

As such situations envelop you, normal activity slows to a halt. There's a grinding of gears and directional change as the management team struggles to cope. All of us have gone through these events and I truly empathise with those who are faced with such situations.

The good news though is that much can be done in advance to lessen the impact of sudden events by creating transitional steps that will help you meet the challenges more smoothly while remaining operational.

On the morning of Thursday 7th July 2005, just such a moment occurred at 0900hrs when, in an *al-Qaeda* inspired plan to paralyse the capital, four extremist bombers attacked central London by setting off homemade bombs on the underground and on a bus in Tavistock Square.

The ramifications were enormous.

The entire transport system immediately ground to a halt, mobile telephone networks were suspended and fear gripped the country as dozens of seriously injured people were seen being evacuated from tunnels and streets.

My life was turned upside down as the detailed work I was carrying out on reforming the police public protection systems for handling dangerous offenders had to be dropped immediately. Meetings were cancelled and all police officers and staff were called back to Scotland Yard to be issued with new instructions and roles.

Keeping Core Business Continuity

There is an art and science to coping with such challenges and it requires that:

- The core business of the operation is continued but temporarily on a narrower front. Some activities just have to go on regardless because to stop doing them could be catastrophic to your end-users or mean the termination of the entire enterprise.

- Sufficient resources and effort need to be redirected to meet the nature of the challenge and to stabilise a situation until matters are rectified or a new plan of operation is established.

That July, even though London was in the midst of a concerted terrorist effort to cause panic and mayhem, certain aspects of life and crime continued. People were still being murdered or assaulted in unrelated incidents. Fights still broke out and people were still being killed or seriously injured in road accidents. Policing couldn't just stop to hunt down terrorists and this meant core aspects of investigation, detection and response had to continue.

'Operation Theseus' was set up and my role was to help the Specialist Crime Directorate, move onto a transitional path, one of crisis management, business continuity and resource reallocation.

This directorate consists of 4,000 very experienced detectives working on serious and organised crime across both the region and nationally. Its main areas of responsibility are homicide, child abuse, gun and gang crime, kidnaps, forensic investigation, surveillance and commercial robbery. Some of the UK's biggest and most dangerous criminals are tracked and investigated by this command, so ensuring continuity of its operations was a high priority.

Already in place was the London Resilience Programme, which in the aftermath of the previous 9/11 catastrophe, was being developed by Scotland Yard and London First, the representative body that helps co-ordinate and lobby on behalf of big business interests.

This resilience work was designed to establish a communications system for improved security information exchange, and to provide specialist training for staff and management expertise in contingency planning through desktop exercises. The new channels of communication were already in use but as with all emergencies, plans can often only really be tested on first 'contact with the enemy' so the sheer enormity of the 7/7 bombings and the second wave attacks on 21st July had many unforeseen consequences.

Primary and Secondary Effects

- Certain police skill areas came under extreme demand and pressure as:

  o Forensic examiners were needed for different bomb site scenes.

  o More people were required for body recovery and mortuary duties.

  o A casualty bureau had to be staffed to take telephone enquiries and offer family support.

  o Surveillance teams had to be deployed to cover suspected terrorists.

  o 'Kratos' trained surveillance and firearms teams were required to intercept suspected suicide bombers.

  o General investigators had to be released from core specialist crime commands to join the Anti-Terrorist Command temporarily to help track outstanding suspects or follow up leads

- Police staff in these sections had to start working 24/7 to maintain cover because of skill shortages, which had serious welfare and performance implications arising from a lack of sleep.

- The bombings took place just as the summer annual police leave was starting, which meant that many units were already at minimum strength.

- All mobile telephone communications went down due to the sheer volume of calls as people who were stranded or seeking reassurance about the location of friends and relatives used their phones. This meant people had to use their own initiative, follow contingency plans or monitor TV and radio broadcasts for public information.

- With the railway network suspended, many had to walk or drive out to semi-inner areas of London to reconnect with the transport system.

- However, one positive short-term effect was that reported crime fell substantially even in the most serious of categories. It was almost as if everyone was watching their TV to see the evolving drama and were too enthralled to commit offences.

I give you this as an example, because although the situation was extreme, the lessons learned are applicable to many areas of business.

Contingency Response and Fallback Positions

Scotland Yard excels at this type of redeployment and crisis management. As an emergency service it's in our DNA. Staff with the required skills were released in substantial numbers across the department to join the Counter Terrorist Command. Many proactive operations had to be suspended as a result and objectives realigned to combat life-threatening situations and critical enquiries. But after five days, this had to be reassessed as core major investigation teams just could not sustain their efforts even at a minimal coverage level.

We took the view then that every command should plan for two fallback positions in the event of further atrocities:

Position 1 was to provide only enough staff to cover critical incidents and threats to life.

Position 2 was to provide only enough staff to cover immediate threats to life.

All other staff would be released for anti terrorist duties. Every command was then sent a template document on which they could detail the staffing requirements for each position, together with their rationale for providing that level of cover.

Monitoring and Adjustment

In parallel with this contingency planning, I introduced a weekly monitoring spreadsheet for the top SCD management team that detailed:

- An impact assessment from each command about suspended operations, the heightened risk levels resulting and any welfare issues.

- Statistics about the staff abstraction rates from each command.

- Statistics about reported crimes during the course of the crisis.

- The cost of releasing staff to the Anti Terrorist Command.

- Examples of outstanding work for Operation Theseus by department staff.

- A report on the next week's demands and their likely impact on planning.

By doing this, we kept adjusting and refining our approach which led eventually to the formation of a 24/7 operational support unit that became the main interface between anti terrorist resource requests and our specialist crime commands. Abstraction and skill requirements were plotted to ensure the core business standards set at each contingency operating level were maintained across the departments.

Team Skill Inventory

A key factor in contingency planning is having up-to-date information about the availability and skills of staff, as this enables any emergency co-ordination unit to match demand to supply much more effectively. This information, collected on electronic spreadsheets, should include:

- Full name and address of the staff member.

- Their current role and position of responsibility.

- All their contact telephone numbers and internet addresses (Skype, Facebook etc).

- Their ability to access their own transport (car, bike etc).

- The time it takes them to travel to their main base of work.

- Their special skills and qualifications, subdivided into categories. This should also show the current level of training attained.

- Their availability over the next time period (week/month).

Scenario Planning and Practice

An investment in time and resources for contingency planning is a fundamental management responsibility. And while guidelines can be produced centrally, the planning process must take place as close to the operating front as possible if all the variables that reflect the reality for each department and unit are to be considered.

The cost implications of not doing this type of planning are substantial, as operations will quickly become paralysed in a crisis if staff don't have the high degree of adaptability needed to interchange roles with confidence.

The use of scenario planning is now well established, having been used extensively in the 1980s by Dutch petro-chemical company, Shell.

The beauty of scenario planning is that it allows you to consider multiple variables that might result from an event and the 'ripple effect' they may have. Obviously, not all eventualities will happen at the same time or in the presumed order, so management needs to practise being nimble and flexible.

I think the other guiding principle in scenario planning is to look at the probability of certain events occurring. This is something that can be determined from historical information and through environmental scanning, as described earlier.

There are however, in my estimation, a number of levels of different emergencies that need to be anticipated and planned for.

Level 1 Emergencies are simple, single and internal events involving one member of staff or one system and without any knock-on effects. For example:

- Key staff absence due to injury or illness.
- Incidents of crime affecting operational security.
- Operational area incidents involving injury or damage (also Level 2).

Level 2 Emergencies are complex, internal events with multiple knock-on effects of increasing magnitude and which involve large numbers of staff, different systems and have substantial implications for other departments. For example:

- Communication system outages to telephone and mobile communication.
- Power cuts to electricity or other energy sources.
- Industrial action by staff either planned or spontaneous.
- IT software and hardware crashes.

Level 3 Emergencies are simple, single external events involving one isolated problem that affects operations but doesn't do so significantly. For example:

- Incidents that have a high reputational impact on the organisation, such as employment disputes, corruption, incompetence or neglect.
- Key supplier emergencies resulting in lost or stopped materials.
- Infrastructure problems affecting the supply and distribution chain, such as transport closures (also Level 4).
- Sudden changes of end-user demand, either up or down (also Level 4).

Level 4 Emergencies are complex, external events with multiple knock-on effects of increasing magnitude so that they have a wide impact on operations and affect substantial numbers of staff and systems. For example:

- External terrorist, natural disasters or public order incidents with a large geographical ripple effect on all supply routes, staff, materials and operations.

In responding to each you need to consider:

- If the situation can be controlled or stabilised by swapping or supplementing a staff role.

- If the operation can be re-routed through a contingency pathway or location.

- If the operation can be narrowed to core priorities if the emergency worsens.

Learning from 7/7

What I learnt from the 7/7 London bombing attacks was that as plans are exposed to the brutal realities of a real time situation, some fundamental things need to happen, so:

- Senior managers must have the latest data about their staff at all times and that this should be kept with them in a hard copy format.

- All senior managers need a deputy who is readily available at all times. This means automated email replies that say you are unobtainable are totally unacceptable.

- Staff must be trained and qualified in a range of interchangeable roles so that in a crisis they can move to cover and fulfil others' functions quickly and easily.

- A department's senior management team needs to have a continual understanding of those operations which are core and critical to survival. This may change over time and so needs frequent re-evaluation.

- Separate fallback positions need to be identified for each of the four emergency levels above, with managers constantly aware of the minimum level of resources (both in terms of staff and system requirements) required in response to each.

Practise, Practise, Practise

The other key factor with all contingency planning is practise, practise and more practise for managers and staff, both together and separately. Playing out scenarios either on location during downtimes as desktop exercises is crucial if people are to learn how to think flexibly and quickly. As humans, we all get into habits and routines that are the enemy of crisis management, as response effectiveness is dependent on people's ability to react fast and appropriately. If staff know what the response plans are, their preparedness will be that much higher. Even if their manager is unavailable, they will be able to take the initiative and show responsible leadership.

To help achieve this, the Metropolitan Police uses a first class simulation laboratory at Hendon Training Centre run by Jonathan Crego. Jonathan has analysed numerous major incidents of crime and disaster in the UK and abroad, along with the different management needs that were involved in responding to each. From this work, he has been able to recreate many different scenarios and expose trainees to a growing number of factors that need to be considered in their decision making. As these scenarios are based on what actually happened, the pressure on students is intense as they struggle to control real situations through good decision making and resource direction. Equipped with a number of computer pods, the simulation suite can be tailored to suit the specific needs of each department.

Advance Warning Systems

While trouble often comes out of a clear blue sky, if your personal awareness levels are acute, you can often identify or predict the signs of approaching trouble either by using internal monitoring processes or tools such as environmental scanning. These can provide both market information and advance warning of internal and external threats.

Armed with this knowledge, team leaders and department heads can then be put on alert to revise their contingency plans or even run practise drills with staff so they are familiar with any scenario, before it occurs in reality.

Team Re-deployments

The need for team and staff re-deployment in a crisis or emergency needs to be clearly set out in contracts of employment and job descriptions. There is no room for quibbling over details when the storm breaks, as there will be an immediate need in a fast moving situation for members of the operations teams to take on multiple roles. However, I have never found this to be a problem as long as there is clarity and good leadership at such times, with staff thoroughly briefed on:

- The nature of the crisis, its known scope, type and likely duration.
- The core operating priority for this new situation.
- The fallback positions *if* the situation deteriorates further, together with appropriate contingency actions.
- Their new roles and responsibilities.
- The capability and capacity status of all units under their command now and into the short and medium-term.
- How existing non-priority operations will be temporarily closed off safely and without being irreparably damaged.

The key here is to match resource needs to the situation so you can maintain a predetermined core operation. You can then release staff and resources to stabilise the crisis itself.

Navigating the Politics

Unfortunately, office and organisational politics are a fact of life and the sooner you recognise this and respond accordingly the better. It took me twenty years to completely acknowledge that many around and above me weren't actually interested in reducing crime or developing a more effective policing service to the public, but in protecting their own position or creating a power bloc.

Call me cynical, but to think otherwise is to naïvely blind yourself in a veil of denial.

Those driven by professional motives of doing the best job they can, rather than chasing self-promotion, will understand exactly what I mean. But sadly, this 'selfishness' has crept inexorably into public service over the last 25 years with deeply damaging consequences. Now decisions are often made not on the basis of what is the right thing to do, however difficult that may be, but on how it will affect a person's reputation, power base or prospects for promotion.

Office politics takes many forms and you will need to consider and be aware of each as you go about your daily business. So, develop your awareness levels quickly and your antennae will be much more sensitive to subtle changes around you.

Here are some underlying principles I think you should adhere to:

- Once you have settled on a strategy and tactics for getting things done, be true to yourself and your end-users and stick with it. To do this you will have to show courage, resilience and tenaciousness implementing difficult programmes of work. Remember continual compromise is the enemy of effectiveness. You need to know where the red lines are in your proposals and projects before they are diluted into meaninglessness.

- When you come up against internal and external resistance, try to isolate and identify the reasons for this. If objections have substance and are supported by evidence, then show humility and be ready change or adapt your course to incorporate sensible suggestions. If the resistance is driven by selfish motives, you will need to work out a path over or around the obstacle, using allies and the logic of your argument.

- As an individual, you will need very senior champions on the board and in end-user groups who recognise the quality and integrity of your work and are willing to stick their necks out for you when the going gets tough.

- You will need to display a high degree of selfless commitment to your work, which will inspire and guide your team to do likewise. So, always make it quite clear you will not tolerate self-promotion and selfishness, but be equally clear that good work will be fully recognised and promotion applications given your fullest support when appropriate.

Controlling Personal Agendas

Over the course of my thirty-three year long police career, I have worked with a wide range of people from many different social, cultural and ethnic backgrounds, values and beliefs. This was refreshing, stimulating and at times difficult and required sensitivity and high levels of awareness on my part as a manager to prevent misunderstandings and grievances from developing.

However, if you make clear your objectives and the rationale behind them, then often background differences become irrelevant, as doing the task in hand as well as possible becomes a common goal. Nevertheless, you soon realise that certain individuals have powerful personal agendas that are sometimes not compatible with your objectives or the work culture you are trying to develop. These agendas are pursued by those who can be categorised as follows:

The Litigator

The Litigator can be recognised as they lumber down corridors carrying a small suitcase overflowing not with project work, but the legal papers for their next encounter with a staff representative or their solicitor. They are in a vortex of continual grievance procedure and employment law litigation that takes over their life to the exclusion of all else. Consequently, they will not be able to talk about anything else at meal times or at the coffee machine. This is not to say that their claims of unfair treatment, or of other grievances, are not legitimate, indeed I've pursued a few cases of my own, it is just that their entire work life is so dominated by these issues they are in real danger of becoming a drag on their department's efficiency and morale.

Your Response

- As a line manager you will need to take an early, balanced but firm approach to these individuals before things get out of hand. If you do not do this, then a pattern of vexatious claims could develop as retribution is sought.

- You will need to be supportive when there are clear cases of discriminatory and unfair treatment, but also to dispel any illusions of persecution they may have, if after careful consideration you find their claims ill-founded. Though there is perhaps a natural tendency to take the side of the staff member, managers need to be scrupulously objective in their approach since I've witnessed on many occasions how a claimant's views have distorted the facts to their advantage.

- If there *is* evidence of unfair treatment, then the staff member must be supported and help given so they can present their evidence as strongly and clearly as possible.

- However, in all cases the line manager needs to be clear about the time that will be allowed for them to prepare the claim rather than getting on with their core work.

- Consider assigning them a coach or mentor so they can discuss the situation neutrally with someone else and get things off their chest.

The Pet Keeper

Single-minded and tenacious, the Pet Keeper will secretly pursue their own pet projects of interest when they should be doing other things. This means you will find yourself spending an inordinate amount of time sitting on their shoulder to ensure they are carrying out their allotted tasks.

Your Response

- Make sure the department's objectives and the roles and responsibilities of each team member are made as clear as possible at the outset. I used to set very clear deadlines for project and work completion for my staff as well as the quality standard I expected for each item. In return, I didn't sit on their shoulder or expect them to be at their desk continually. I was happy to sanction home working if this helped to remove travel pressures or meet domestic needs.

- However, if the work was not returned on time or to the quality I wanted, then I would take a dim view and make my displeasure clear. The individual would then be given a clear warning and a new deadline.

- In cases where a team member had a clear interest in or aptitude for a specialist area, I would give them a relevant work stream, if I could. Again, 'horses for courses' was my guiding principle here.

- If their area of interest was not of current relevance to the department I was encouraging, but made it clear that further work would have to be done outside their normal schedule although they could use work IT and indices.

- In some cases, you may be able to attach or second such a member of staff to a unit where their interest can be indulged, though normally this would have to be in exchange for another staff member.

Perpetual Victim

The Perpetual Victim has a continual chip on their shoulder about how they have been so badly treated by the organisation or their colleagues. They imagine that a conspiracy of Watergate proportions is continually trying to thwart them at every step.

Your Response

- These individuals need to be handled firmly but sensitively as they have grown into a habit of looking at things in a negative way and this can be changed with the right support.

- Assign them a qualified and suitable coach or mentor who can help them think more positively and pragmatically about the world around them. Gradually this will pay dividends as they gain a renewed sense of direction and purpose.

- Use humour in the office to challenge their negative statements and to get them to think sensibly about what they are saying or implying. Since the Perpetual Victim can quickly spread gloom in an office to a level I can only compare to that generated by the Scottish undertaker Fraser in the TV series 'Dad's Army', I would often put on his Scottish accent and shout, "We're all doomed!" This always got a laugh and gave some relief.

The 'Saatchi' Self- Publicist

These characters take every possible opportunity to promote themselves in reports, presentations and media events. Every waking hour seems to be taken up by the relentless pursuit of public recognition. They never think twice about swapping their name for a subordinate's on the front cover of a major report, or taking their place at the podium to talk about a topic they are clueless about. However, when difficult decisions have to be made they are nowhere in sight.

Your Response

- These people really used to irritate me. In a true team, there is simply no room for this type of behaviour, as a selfless commitment to achieving objectives should be the only game in town. In the final years of my service, Scotland Yard was riven by this attitude and I became increasingly disillusioned by the hypocrisy of senior officers who proclaimed a 'we're all in this together' attitude, but then showed their true colours by a thirst for blatant self-promotion. In the military they would quickly have been ostracised until they changed their habits.

- The use of 360 degree staff feedback on individual performance can have a dramatic effect in getting people back on track as the truth, when told anonymously by colleagues, usually hurts

- Authors of reports should be fully recognised on all materials that they have helped to produce. This does not mean they can't disagree with the findings or recommendations. So the senior management team should be encouraged to respond professionally with full written comments on the feasibility of a report and its relative merits and faults. This makes for a very robust and transparent management process.

The Abnegator

This character does not delegate responsibility but abnegates it by passing work they should really be doing themselves on to others within the department. They will often expect high and often unrealistic results but never provide the help or support that's needed to achieve them. In cases of failure they will deny all responsibility, but then claim all the glory for any success. The overuse of consultants in the public sector is a prime example of this, and an approach that I abhor as it is often used as an excuse to row back from taking responsibility for decisions.

Your Response

- Any staff member who receives such orders and instructions from an Abnegator obviously has a responsibility to carry them out to the best of their ability, especially in fast-time situations when there may be no room for discussion and hierarchical leadership has to take precedence. However, the recipient also has a responsibility to consider the brief and to feed back in writing any likely implications the instruction may have on resources. They should also make clear how other work streams may be affected if this new assignment is given priority.

- Sometimes staff must be resolute and brave and challenge the line manager if the support that's needed isn't on offer or there is an unfair expectation of what can be achieved. If necessary, the issue may need to be taken further up the line using grievance procedures.

- Your department's tasking and co-ordination forum can also be used to control bad delegation as it means the job will then be listed and scrutinised for its resource implications, progress and alignment with department objectives.

Asset Control Power Politics

I was frankly astounded by how much this played a part in Metropolitan Police management. Following what was contemporary management thinking in the 1990s, the organisation went through a sustained period of devolving power and control from the central Commissioner's Office. As a result, borough commanders and department heads were handed responsibility and accountability for delivering operational targets as well as a high degree of autonomy when it came to setting up their command and running it.

Many processes, structures and standards became highly localised as a result, with a high degree of disparity between different geographical areas. The relative strengths and skills of the local leadership were continually tested and policing quality turned into a form of 'postcode lottery'.

While there is nothing wrong with a tailored local approach, what were once common interests in training, risk management and deployment were now driven by local agendas set by a commander and local groups. Previously common standards were lost to 'localism'.

This was particularly evident in the way the organisation managed dangerous offenders and the systems for public protection, as mentioned earlier. Localism also encouraged a certain 'fiefdom' mentality where any central instruction or request was resisted or challenged on the basis of perceived operational interference. It also encouraged the 'Saatchi' problem with some police commanders creating their own 'brand identity' though strong self-promotion tactics.

By 2009 this was definitely not an organisation with an 'all pull together' value and belief system.

While serving on the Commissioner's Service Review Team in 2005, I had a first hand taste of how this was playing out on the ground as irrefutable logic and detailed research met a dogged and intransigent form of protectionism.

I had been lead officer in reviewing the various police units that managed aspects of violent offending. This work revealed that over several years when it came to the investigation and risk management of some of the most dangerous offenders and overseeing vulnerable victims, a bunker mentality had developed.

This had come about as legislation and government enquiries had centred on particular crimes such as sex offending, child abuse and domestic violence. As a result, there was a failure to recognise that numerous offenders were involved in many different types of violence, ranging from neighbourhood intimidation, animal abuse, through to GBH and murder. Consequently, there was little intelligence sharing between different squads and units, which meant a much lower risk rating for an individual and uncoordinated police approach to dealing with them.

My work led to over 40 recommendations for streamlining the entire public protection realm so as to create a consistent system of risk identification, assessment and management with all the units working under a unified public protection command. The units would work to different assistant commissioners and I also proposed a new borough and central public protection structure that would come under just one accountable assistant commissioner. The proposals were scrutinised by a multi-agency challenge panel and were very favourably received by most practitioners who operated on the front line.

However, behind the scenes and unbeknown to me, a massive lobbying effort was being mounted by the Child Protection Command and my own Specialist Crime DAC to omit them completely from the new arrangements.

Certain senior commanders had made great efforts to establish this new command after the Victoria Climbié child abuse scandal and these same individuals felt the changes would dilute their influence, be a direct threat to their independence and dilute their brand.

Consequently, they were directly lobbying various key members of the police authority to stop the reforms. What was extraordinary to me was that my detailed report made no attempt to abolish the command but only to make it work more effectively in a joint command system, alongside the other units under the territorial police assistant commissioner

As no one in the Child Protection Command appeared to have actually read what I had researched and reported, their objections seemed a knee jerk reaction to a perceived threat, with the benefits of improved effectiveness, greater efficiency and increased synergy seemingly lost on them.

A Suitable Response

- Once an organisation loses its sense of direction or forgets who it's there to serve, it steps onto a long and slippery slope of decline. When this occurs, major steps need to be taken to rectify the situation through a fundamental review of its purpose, structure and decision making. In the case of the police, this in my view should be through another Royal Commission on Policing that could assess what the UK needs in the future from its police, while at the same time preserving its constitutional independence.

- The centre of the organisation must reassert itself and define the boundaries and parameters of devolved decision making. Where there are common areas of interest, these need to be addressed by consistent systems, structures and standards. Policy and standards can be set at the top, but still allow for a tailored local response without losing the synergies of a unified system.

- Simplified performance indicators should be established to hold local department heads to account under a unified corporate management structure.

Personality Clashes and Alliances

In your work, you will operate alongside and manage many different people each with their own unique personality, values and beliefs. You will naturally be drawn closer to some than others because of a shared sense of humour and opinions. I have worked alongside many characters over the course of thirty-three years and felt a great affection for the eccentrics among them, as they seemed to be remarkable islands operating in a sea of conformity and conservatism. Equally, there were many individuals I did not feel at ease with, either as colleagues or line managers.

What's more, I discovered that in poor teams there were often cliques of people with a disproportionate influence. If your face did not fit, they could make life very hard for you indeed. Hidden alliances can also operate and these can take many forms from those based on sexual relations through to alternative leadership cells.

Every team has a number of natural demarcation points that set apart the new 'sprogs' from more experienced staff. For executive officers, team leaders and senior managers a certain separation is of course necessary to maintain objective decision making and ensure effective delegation and management.

But alliances will naturally spring up between those who are facing daily frustrations together. Understanding the dynamics of how these cells interact is vital for effective operations management because it's when these dynamics break down, become blurred and confused, that problems really start. This is an area I will discuss at length in the next section on team development,

Of course, your own position within a team can be greatly aggravated by inexperience, your attitude and lack of personal confidence. For a young and newly promoted manager this can be a real issue.

In 1983, aged twenty-three and after just five years of service in London, I was promoted to the rank of sergeant and joined a uniform response team of thirty officers based at Bow Street police station in

Covent Garden. Their average age was about the same as mine, with just a few more experienced constables and an inspector in charge coming to the end of his career. Operating between the inspector and the constables, this was my first leadership role.

At the time, a chronic shortage of sergeants meant that most of my time was spent with the only other and also newly promoted sergeant on the team. I had high standards and wanted to do a good job in my first management role, but on reflection, I was far too aloof. My inexperience made me seem remote from the team when in reality I was merely trying to preserve management distance.

However, I did discover a particularly unhealthy state of affairs, with constables often going over the sergeants' heads to the inspector for decisions about deployments and the prosecution of prisoners.

So, with my orders often countermanded and my briefings interrupted by his opinions, the inspector and I immediately got into a tense relationship which, as it deteriorated, saw my self confidence evaporate leaving me even more reserved and isolated from the team.

The growing weakness of my position was exploited by a senior clique on the team who tried to undermine me through defamatory remarks and even intimidation, with items left in my correspondence tray and criminal damage to my car. Eventually, the entire episode came to a head when the inspector recommended that I be considered for demotion.

To his credit, the chief superintendent fully supported me and went to great efforts to display his displeasure at the state of affairs. After an investigation, two team members were reprimanded and promptly transferred to other stations. I was disillusioned by the whole disgraceful situation, but after an appropriate interval, I was offered and accepted another team.

In complete contrast to my first team, here I was immediately accepted and respected and began working very effectively with a senior inspector who did support and train me. My skills, standards and character were absorbed into the team with very little adjustment.

What was the big difference between the two teams? It clearly was not just down to me as I had changed little in the time. Rather, the difference was in the tone of leadership, the support for junior managers and the lack of any damaging cliques in the team.

Response

- You need to be able to work with a wide range of people, some of whom will not be similar to you in character, attitude or nature. But, as long as you take an objective approach to the work in hand you can invariably combine your different aptitudes and strengths without personalising the situation. We are all different, and professional life is about getting the job done to a defined standard. All else is secondary.

- You must be true to your character and not try to act a part you think appropriate. You have a particular style and method of management and leadership. As long as you are consistent and fair, others will need to adapt to you and not the other way around.

- Team leaders have a duty and responsibility to support and train their junior managers, not to undermine lines of authority by unnecessary countermanding or intervention.

- There is absolutely no room for unhealthy cliques in a team. These damage authority by causing insubordination and alliance building that's based on personal agendas and preferences. If personal agendas arise, they need to be quickly challenged and removed by having a clear set of team objectives and ensuring that the lines of decision making are adhered to.

- A relationship with your line manager needs to be established at the outset with clear terms of reference between the two of you, something I discussed earlier.

- In situations where the line manager is unsupportive and hostile, this should be challenged and an attempt made to stabilise the situation, no matter how junior or inexperienced you are. If this proves impossible, a move to another team or department may be the only answer.

- As a junior manager, you must still have an intimate knowledge of your team members if you are to be able to support them in their work and aspirations. This does not mean becoming their friend but rather showing a close interest in them as individuals so they recognise you as someone they can go to for advice and direction. You can still keep your distance while showing them professional regard. This is part of your role and you have a responsibility to identify personnel problems early and manage them in discussion with your own line manager.

Dominions of Hidden Power

In many departments and units I have served in, there have been occasions when I discovered that to get things done you had to take account of individuals who had enormous influence who often were not responsible or accountable for the final decision making but merely administered the process.

Over time, these 'influencers' had been able to acquire a mantle of control that should have been beyond their reach, by using their knowledge, force of character, or because a more senior line manager had abnegated their own responsibilities. Sometimes it is even as a result of a scandal or serious case of mismanagement when those who should have taken decision making responsibility failed through incompetence or corruption.

For instance, in the 1980s when Dame Shirley Porter, the then leader of Westminster Council was at the zenith of her power and influence, Conservative voters were moved into particular residential areas under the council's control. This gerrymandering was on such a scale that it resulted in a criminal enquiry and forced the resignation of Dame Shirley. Thereafter, a culture of distrust pervaded relationships between councillors and the administrative officers in all departments. This led to new controls, some of which wrested decision making control away from elected representatives in an unhealthy way and gave it to those who 'oversaw the process'.

I call this syndrome 'dominions of hidden power' and having talked to many managers, I am convinced that all organisations suffer from it. How many times have you entered a new department to be told 'go and see so and so, they'll sort this out'? Or, 'don't get on the wrong side of Irene, otherwise you'll never get on.'

I have seen several instances of these dominions develop. In the Metropolitan Police during the 2000s a very strong health and safety culture arose that ultimately became damaging and self-defeating. The commissioner was prosecuted by the Health and Safety Executive for the infamous Menendez shooting at Stockwell station in 2005 during the al-Qaeda attacks on London; and also for neglect of care in two major cases involving officers who were injured chasing burglars across rooftops. As a result, officers were instructed that they could not climb above two metres in pursuit of suspects. Other ridiculous guidelines were also brought in as lead officers implementing health and safety came to hold a disproportionate hold over policing policy.

The power and influence of the procurement and contracting department can also be absolute as they can stifle decision making by referring you to European tendering legislation, or using their deep knowledge of the regulations to take an overly bureaucratic attitude to funding applications. Getting on the right side of such administrators was essential.

Department finance officers also hold enormous power and influence over operations as their knowledge and expertise about how much money is available and where contingency or alternative streams of finance can be accessed.

Any major application for public finance had to be approved by the Metropolitan Police Authority and, on several occasions, I applied to them for start-up funding towards the new Safer London Foundation Charity, the gang conflict management company and a regional imitation firearms operation. The level of report drafting, submissions and explanatory meetings with officers and members that this required was staggeringly time consuming.

Office managers and administrators were also of key importance as they had an intimate knowledge of systems and processes and so were often afforded an undue respect by senior managers as a result. They played on this influence to their clear advantage, in the case of middle and junior managers, by delaying or challenging requests from those who did not court their approval.

Response

- As a manager, you have to acquire a basic knowledge and awareness of several key areas of specialist expertise. These include finance, procurement, contracting, health and safety and other associated legislation such as data protection. Even as an operational police officer this is essential as you will have to navigate your way over many hurdles of regulatory control. If you leave this responsibility to others you will just add to the problems and issues discussed earlier. Obviously, you cannot and should not concentrate all your efforts on narrow areas of expertise but instead gain sufficient knowledge to test and challenge those directly responsible. This will help ensure you are treated fairly and that operations are facilitated without undue delays. None of this should detract from the status of administrators, but they do need to be held properly accountable for their actions.

- So, by all means, get on the right side of those who administer, but not in a sycophantic way. Rather, explain clearly what you are trying to achieve and the importance of a good outcome and make it clear that you need their help and advice to do this effectively.

- If you come across a profusion of hidden dominions of power you will have uncovered a story of abnegated responsibility by senior managers. You will need to make substantial efforts to rectify this by training and raising the expectations you have on your managers to use and control the administrative processes properly.

Response

What Needs Doing and How – the Four Steps

This section is about the very heart and soul of your work – making things happen – after all this is your core purpose as an operations manager. To my mind there are four key components to 'making things happen'.

The first of these is that **implementation should be outcome-driven** and not process-orientated. This is not to say process isn't important, it is, particularly in operations management, it's just that it should not be the overriding factor in decision making. In other words, process follows delivery and the 'tail should never wag the dog'.

Next come methods of **planning and organising.** I cannot overstate the importance of meticulous planning in achieving a successful outcome. Planning is something that does not come easily to a British manager's mind because as a nation we tend to prefer muddling through or getting things going quickly and then making lots of adjustments as we go along in order to make things work.

The Germans, on the other hand, plan methodically and precisely before any cogs of the machinery are created at all. As a result, the German economy is pre-eminent in Europe, turning out precision engineering with a huge industry exporting domestic luxury items of the finest quality. Something at which they have historically excelled, producing the best weaponry on the World War II battlefield by far.

We British, in contrast, are outstanding at generating ideas and being creative but this can never make up for the need to develop and exploit an idea's commercial potential. This is a lesson we are currently learning the hard way, yet again. But I am convinced we have the potential and ability if we had more leadership and drive. Just look at our proud record of achievements in past years with such notable pioneers as Isambard Kingdom Brunel, Alexander Fleming and latterly, James Dyson. We cannot just rely on the creative arts and service sector to get the economy going again.

My contention is that the UK has an astounding knowledge base and that the creative application of this intellectual property is the right route for us to follow. The internet is taking over and will provide a massive boost to the small entrepreneur who can use its potential for free marketing and sales. Online knowledge products for science, training, management, self-development and other, more niche sectors could be our salvation. This is something the UK can do brilliantly as it suits our mentality for individuality and small enterprise.

Whether you are managing operations or a project, there's a need for **close monitoring** to make sure you stay on track, and I'll discuss options and methods for doing this.

Lastly, there is a need for **evaluation** so that any operation continues to serve the end-user by giving them what they want and need at an appropriate quality and price.

So, let us consider in more detail the first of these components – knowing your outcome.

1 Design a Clear Outcome

"Begin with the end in mind," Steven Covey exhorts in his book 'The Seven Habits of Highly Effective People', a statement with which I'm in total agreement.

So, you must be able to answer the question, 'What is it that you are trying to achieve? This means that you must know the outcome you want, the 'standard' it needs to be and the 'price' you are willing to pay to make it happen. Only then will you have the true clarity of purpose needed to complete an operation or project successfully.

To determine the scope of your desired outcome, your need to ask yourself some further questions like:

- What is the end-user need the product or service is meeting? This must be comprehensively researched to determine such factors as function, form and feel.

- Will the product or service be used by a broad market, or will it meet a niche or even micro-niche need?

- What is the timescale for introducing the product and service? This may be very urgent as in policing, where an operational response needs to be jacked up quickly to deal with a crisis. In these situations, planning needs to be fast time and very functional. The process can be refined as you go to make the outcome more effective but action always needs to be taken immediately, even though this may be very costly in terms of human resources, overtime and disruption to other services. On other occasions, slow time planning can be used to design an outcome that is the most efficient, effective and least wasteful.

- What level of quality is desirable in the product or service? This is discussed in more detail below.

- How much is in your budget to meet the need? This is obviously important as it has a bearing on the effectiveness of the outcome. You may only be able to apply restricted resources to a situation, which in turn will shape the outcome's design. In slow time situations, I highly recommend this is not used as an excuse to hold you back from what would be the most desirable outcome. If the outcome design is first class and fully meets the intended need, investors will invariably be found to finance its achievement. Therefore, always make the quality of desired outcome your primary objective. You can reverse engineer from this later so as to take account of likely or actual resources available. You may, in any event, be able through a mix of cost saving efficiencies and venture capital, get the best outcome without compromise.

Describing Your Outcome

An outcome is more general than an objective because it concentrates on describing the effectiveness of a response in meeting a need or problem and details the benefits that the end-user will experience from doing this. By using the methods above, you can begin to define the outcome you want.

For example, in the case of a modern Dyson vacuum cleaner, the outcome description might look something like this:

'The customer will experience a deep clean to their carpets, surfaces and materials with a much higher dust extraction rate. The dust is collected in a uniquely designed cylinder that does not allow the collected material to escape.'

Describing Your Objectives

Every outcome consists of a set of objectives that need to be described using the SMART approach to goal setting. So, they should be:

- **S** – Specific. There can be nothing vague about an objective. You must be precise in what is to be achieved.

- **M** – Measurable. The results of an action taken must be measurable so you can monitor progress. If you don't do this, how will you know when or if you have succeeded?

- **A** – Achievable. The objective needs to be realistic and not so challenging that it cannot be realised with the resources available.

- **R** – Relative. The set of objectives need to be closely related to the outcome you are trying to achieve.

- **T** – Timely. There should be a clear time line for progress, with interim milestones for implementation and a deadline for completion.

Using our Dyson example again, a SMART objective for the new cleaner could have looked like this:

'By the end of March 1990, a prototype cyclone cylinder vacuum cleaner with a suction rate of 10-100 mbr and a 100 per cent non-leakage rate of collected dust will be produced for testing by a customer focus group.'

Determining Your Outputs

And output from an action plan is what is actually produced and so includes all items that spill out of a process as you move towards your desired outcome. So outputs could be physical units, project plans, business case, presentations, press releases or customer surveys

Again, using the Dyson example, an output description could be:

'Between January and March 1990, the following will be produced during the implementation process: a schematic technical drawing and photographs of the prototype, a press release, a project plan and a focus group assessment survey to detail feedback from prototype testing.'

Is It Worth It? – Cost Benefit Analysis

Cost Benefit Analysis (CBA) is all about determining what you get out from what you have put in. In other words, the ratio between the benefits of achieving something and the costs of doing so.

Once a required quality level has been established, the cost of achieving this can be estimated in terms of time, funding, materials and professional expertise. While it is a highly useful method for examining operations and projects, sadly, the technical aspects of CBA are beyond the scope of this book, but these are some basic considerations:

- Any plan for the development and implementation of a product or service needs to evaluate the length of time required to pay back investment costs. This can be calculated in terms of profits acquired, or perhaps more appropriately for public sector services such as policing, the savings achieved. Though it may not appear so, crime always costs money. For instance, the cost of a single murder to the state is an estimated £1.3 million in terms of the police, criminal justice, health and social welfare costs involved. Therefore any prevention work done can be a cost saving measure.

- What is the ratio between investment and the benefits

resulting? In the case of a cheap product that addresses a very expensive problem, this gearing can be huge. For example, in the West End of London, the problem of bag theft from bars and restaurants amounts to as much as 50 per cent of ALL crime (4,000 crimes a year) and costs the public millions of pounds annually. However, by convincing hotspot pubs and restaurants to install a simple chair back design that prevents bags from these premises being stolen, I managed to reduce levels of this crime by 60 per cent in just twelve months at only a nominal cost.

Set Your Quality Standards

Of what quality does the product or service need to be? By quality, I mean fitness for purpose. Let me explain.

Quality standards are fundamental to any management decision as they are intrinsically linked to durability, finish, aesthetic attractiveness, functional capability and other factors. That means you must decide if you just need to get the job done or whether you have to surpass a basic threshold in order to increase customer satisfaction and extend your market attraction. Such decisions have a massive bearing on the time, money and resources you apply to an operation. Sometimes 'just enough' *is* good enough, but at times the product or service must have exceptional qualities if it is to attract and retain the respect and admiration of the end-user.

Just consider the now iconic Apple computer. Its reputation has been built not just on its functional capability but the ease of its operation and the style of its design. It meets the end-user's appetite for visual and auditory communication in a highly original way that has been reinforced by the growing cult following of its late CEO Steve Jobs.

So, what will make the end-user satisfied?

For an operation this is a combination of both service and product. For example, a first class meal brought to you in a Parisian restaurant may meet all your expectations in terms of ingredient quality, taste and look but the entire 'operation' might be let down by a waiter who is rude or sloppy. This means most operational areas require a mixture of service and product provision, though in the past this interdependence has not always been appreciated.

So, while I used to enjoy the functional design of Vauxhall cars, I was constantly let down by the indifference and quality of their service garages. My loyalty to them eventually ended and I became a devoted Honda fan instead.

These same principles can apply just as well to policing.

In the 1990s, the Metropolitan Police went through an era when targets of response time were set for 999 calls but with little attention paid to the quality of policing effectiveness on arrival at the scene. I recall one hilarious situation in 1991 at Notting Hill when the chief inspector of operations, who later became a police commander, wanted to introduce the ISO 9000 accreditation scheme to policing, including response times for the area car. His dream was to see the ISO 9000 logo on the side of all his police vehicles!

What he and many contemporary managers failed to recognise however, was that the end-user is seeking a particular outcome and is not interested in the process of getting there. Therefore, when the police actually arrive they want the problem dealt with by an arrest, a robust stop and search policy, an injunction enforced or some other appropriate action.

Getting somewhere quickly is not always the determinant of success.

No wonder the chief inspector was infuriated when I once suggested that we should have a lion logo on the side of our police cars to indicate quality, just as they do on eggs!

Creating Quality

I have already discussed some of the general principles of designing quality into an outcome, but there are two more specific ways of looking at this – Total Quality Management and Continuous Improvement.

They are sequential in nature and both should be built into the planning and organisation of any successful operation or project.

Total Quality Management

Over the last 25 years, much has been written about the quality control strategies that were originated by the American theorists Deming, Juran and Feiganbaum and which were then adopted and developed by the Japanese manufacturing sector in the 80s and 90s. Of these, the most famous is Total Quality Management or TQM.

TQM is about getting things right from the very start so you diminish problems and save on cost because fewer expensive corrections and adjustments have to be made further down the line because you have already foreseen and allowed for them. TQM involves meticulous research, design and development and is something the Germans and Japanese are particularly good at.

It is a holistic philosophy that must be applied to all aspects of your management infrastructure so:

- External suppliers of materials and resources to your organisation must emulate your own high standards of operation and quality.

- Your management and production processes must be consistent and effective.

- Your staff must be well trained, motivated and led.

- End-users must be comprehensively consulted about their satisfaction levels through product and service feedback.

- The product or service being delivered must be exemplary in design having been reverse engineered from a desired outcome so that it incorporates not just functional capability but also ease of operation, maintenance, durability and aesthetic attractiveness.

TQM is a complete culture of efficiency and effectiveness for people, systems and management in which the attitude of 'getting things right first time' is ingrained. This means it can never be replaced by process systems like ISO 9000. Even though seeking such accreditation is to be applauded, any tick box system of operation that gives an illusion of efficiency will lack true effectiveness in meeting end-user needs.

Continuous Improvement

Another technique for quality development is Continuous Improvement, or Kaizen. This is based on the principle that it is always possible to incrementally improve the fundamental qualities of any organisation, any service or product delivery so that it better meets needs. For it to work to best effect, everyone, including end-users, staff members and observer experts, must be given the opportunity to contribute to this process of 'ratcheting up' quality through surveys, suggestion reward schemes, focus groups and evaluation studies.

For example, in 1982 I made a submission under the Force's suggestion scheme to issue and train major incident officers and their assistants in the use of Dictaphones. This was prompted by the Regent's Park bombing which highlighted the sheer volume of directions and observations that arise during the course of a major incident. These can easily overwhelm any attempts at written recordkeeping, especially in poor weather or under chaotic conditions when writing notes is particularly impractical.

A Dictaphone, on the other hand, allows an incident officer to record detailed observations and commands for transcription later into a more comprehensive and accurate written report.

2 Planning and Organising

If you are to be a successful planner it is important to understand what is the main difference between an operation and a project.

An operation is an ongoing process to create or deliver a product or service, whereas a project has a planned beginning and end and produces a specific, designed outcome in the form of a structure, product or system.

In modern operations management both types of approach are used constantly with a specific project often undertaken to enhance the overall operation. In policing for example, there is a 24/7 operational need to respond to 999 calls, investigate crimes and patrol the streets. Frequently however, there is also a need to plan and implement projects to deal with a specific problem, such as street robbery, in a particular geographical area. This requires additional resources, or expertise in the form of surveillance and phases of work, that culminate in the arrest and charging of offenders.

Both approaches have similar requirements including:

- Quality checks on the outputs to make sure they meet the standards set at the beginning.

- Timeliness of progression and implementation.

- Keeping to budget through exemplary planning and organisation of materials and human resources.

- Ensuring staff are competent, appropriately skilled and well motivated through training and supervision.

- Monitoring and assessment of end-user satisfaction to ensure they are getting what they want and need.

However, there are differences in emphasis between the two such as:

- The timeline of progression and completion is more important in a project, which requires tighter control and scheduling of activities and responsibilities.

- To ensure standards are maintained, consistency of quality is an ongoing feature of operations.

- More specialists are needed for projects, whereas operations require a larger pool of competent generalists.

The Organisational Action Plan

Once an outcome has been designed and quality standards for it set, concise and well thought out action plans are needed for both operational and project planning. These should have two main components:

- A **Summary Sheet** outlining the main elements of the plan which can be used as a quick aide memoir and explanatory brief.

- An **Initiation Document** giving much more detail about each of the summarised elements which has the following sections:

Methods

Each objective listed in the operation or project plan should be backed up by a list of actions needed to achieve it. This is very much about HOW you are going to do something rather than what you are going to do, which is contained in the objectives. So, the following elements must be precisely and concisely described:

- The specific actions needed to achieve each objective.

- A sequence for implementing these actions, some of which will be concurrent and others consecutive.

- The relative importance and priority of each action.

- Who is to be responsible and accountable for each action.

The use of critical path analysis in planning is very useful here, though it needs to be done as a separate, albeit linked, piece of work. You can find out more on this by referring to books that cover the subject in detail.

Timetable and Milestones

To ensure planned progression and effective monitoring, each objective needs a timeline with the interim milestones clearly set out. These milestones are often self-evident and easily recognisable points in the implementation process.

In our Dyson example, the milestones in achieving a prototype between January and March 1990 might have been:

'By January 31st main cylinder case and mechanisms to be designed and drawn up with a full specification of materials for assembly.

By February 28th main cylinder, electrical motor and hose components to be produced.

By 31st March all components to be assembled and factory testing completed ready for customer focus group.'

The use of Gantt charts is particularly useful for doing this and the action plan should display a summary of their contents. Gantt charts are discussed later in greater depth.

Resources Required

These should be linked to each objective and the following elements described:

- General and specialist personnel needed to complete an objective, such as a project manager, site surveyor, research and development team, mechanical or civil engineer, production managers or technicians.

- The materials and equipment needed to complete the objective.

- The finance necessary to pay for people and other resources.

- Any accommodation requirements in terms of buildings, offices or land.

Summarise these concisely on the action plan but detail them more comprehensively separately.

Partners and Linkages

This section of your action plan needs to describe who, apart from your own department and team, you are going to work with to achieve an objective. This will identify:

- Other organisational departments and what their role will be.

- External organisations, agencies and authorities.

- The terms and conditions of any partnership, joint venture or contract with another organisation. The type of relationship is sufficient here as more detail can be included in a separate but linked document.

- The added value of working in terms of expertise, cost saving or logistical advantage that working with these other organisations will bring.

Development Opportunities

The action plan also needs to set out any future development opportunities in the enterprise so as to create a clear vision of continued progress beyond the immediate plan, should all go well.

In the Dyson case these might be production cost savings that come from moving component manufacture to the Far East, if the initial market reaction is favourable and sales reach a given threshold. Or, it might be the development of different model specifications with perhaps upright and low level light versions of the cleaner being produced.

The purpose of the action plan is to produce a clear and easy to use summary for managers, funders and technicians who have an oversight responsibility for the initiative. To achieve this, it needs to be much tighter than a full business plan and so should stretch over no more than ten pages.

It is best laid out in a table template format with more detail set out on separate but linked documents.

Schedules of Activity and Responsibility

Every operation or project needs a timeline for the duration of its implementation and for this I highly recommend the use of timelines and axis charts. They are highly visual and give a helicopter view of both intention and progression in any operation or project and so tell an immediate story that would otherwise require a long report of many thousands of words.

The most common type of these is the Gantt chart, invented by the American mechanical engineer Henry Gantt between 1910-12. It was used for logistical purposes in the first world war and though now a common tool of project management, in its time it was revolutionary. A Gantt chart enables you to display both concurrent and consecutive activity in a way that identifies the critical paths and I've used them extensively, linking them to my action plan and initiation documents.

They are particularly good at the start of an operation, with other project management tools being used after implementation and to monitor progress.

This is how you construct a Gantt chart:

- On the left hand side is the vertical or Y axis where all the main priority activities can be listed and categorised. As this is an overview, not too many things should be included otherwise the chart will become over-detailed and confusing.

- Below or beside each activity, if appropriate, write the name of the accountable staff member along with their main responsibilities.

- On the horizontal or X axis set out appropriate time periods - the days, weeks of months of the project's planned lifetime.

- From the activities on the Y axis stretch horizontal bars to show their planned starts and finishes. These bars can have different colours to denote priority.

- Each bar can also be partially shaded to display the point reached so far in completion.

- A vertical line on the chart to display the current date.

It should be remembered that this type of chart only shows some timings and activities and that more detailed reporting is needed to manage budgets and the full range of actions under each activity.

Standard Operating Procedures (SOP)

While Gantt charts, action plans and project initiation documents, are appropriate tools for the initial organisation and planning phase of operations, their use in directing and managing day-by-day activity is more limited.

So, to fill that gap another tool is needed, the Standard Operating Procedure or SOP. SOPs essentially tell people how to complete a task by following a set of standard instructions and are a valuable addition to any type of operations department for a number of reasons.

- They provide staff with a consistent reference point that details all the steps that need to be taken to deliver a particular service or create a product in a particular way. This ensures that people 'don't make things up as they go along', which minimises the potential for variance and therefore helps maintain quality standards.

- In the event of emergencies, SOPs give staff a clear set of actions to be taken for any given eventuality. This saves time, as people don't then have to think about what to do next when under pressure. It also prevents confusion so there is greater likelihood of successfully navigating your way through a bad situation. However, a SOP does NOT preclude the need to show initiative if circumstances require a more flexible approach.

- SOPs also avoid the time-consuming need for managers to be constantly directing operations in micro detail. Because subordinate staff are able to get on with the job using a pre-agreed and universal approach they don't have to constantly ask their line managers for directions.

Some quality accreditations, like ISO 9000, demand SOPs as a way to ensure processes are performed in a very consistent manner so end-users benefit from an unwavering level of service or product quality.

I found SOPs to be very useful when overseeing multiple teams across London and have used them to successfully deliver large corporate initiatives concerned with the management of violent crime (Operation Hand-Over, Challenging Wards and Operation Pathways).

I have also used SOPs to explain the phases, stages and steps of individual projects so that hundreds of people that I would not otherwise have been able to direct were able to perform their roles perfectly.

However, unless SOPs are fully understood they will be less than effective. So, they should be written out in a clear plain style of English and collected together in an easily accessible hard copy binder, which all staff can refer to, along with an electronic version.

SOP Structure and Contents

This is the framework I use to set out with maximum clarity the SOPs that I create:

1. A very clear contents index divided into ongoing processes and emergency contingencies.

2. A description of the process or the emergency.

3. The corporate policies that are connected with that process or emergency.

4. The objectives we want to achieve from any process or action.

5. The scope of a process or action and who it affects.

6. Exactly who is responsible and accountable for a process or action, and who has management oversight.

7. The operational steps needed to be taken in each process or emergency.

8. A date when the effectiveness and relevance of the SOP will be reviewed.

Bedding SOPs into a Department

The existence of a SOP does not automatically mean that it will be followed. So, before you can make staff accountable for following it, you need to make sure that it is part of the 'infrastructure' of your department or business by ensuring:

- There is sufficient staff training given in the use of the procedures.

- Emergency SOPs must be practised and tested so that you know with confidence that the actions they contain are relevant and effective.

- That SOPs are used by making compliance with them part of staff appraisals.

Using Resources Effectively

The efficient and effective application of resources to a project or operation is vital to its success and this requires some general considerations to be kept in mind.

Always start your plan assuming the very best outcome in mind. This must not only meet the need but also be to a designated standard, as discussed above. Reverse engineer from this point, setting out an action plan with a detailed description of the entire life of the project or operation. This will enable you to determine costs for:

- Human resources. You will need to allow for ongoing salaries, part-time staff payments and consultancy fees over the period.

- The purchase of equipment and support.

- Materials required to build the product or supply the service.

- Legal and accountancy fees to manage the process

- Insurance against liability, injury and losses for whatever reason.

- Accommodation costs, to include rent or purchase.

- Inflation, if the operation or project is to extend over years then price increases need to be added to all the costs at the RPI rate.

- Monitoring and evaluation expertise.

I am a firm believer that you should pursue the desired outcome without compromise. Over the course of many years I have set up many multi-million pound projects from a standing start with absolutely nothing in the budget. The key has been to develop an exciting vision with an extremely credible plan for achieving it, backed up by a highly effective team of people. I have invariably managed to secure the investment and backing I needed. By preparing a powerful case that outlines the cost benefit gearing ratios and regeneration payback, I have been able to sell concept after concept to my police authority, local government leaders and business backers.

A Case Study – The London West End CCTV and City Centre Management Project 2000-02

In 2000, I was asked by the Westminster police commander and City Council chief executive to join a project team that had been established to develop a new city centre management strategy for Soho, Covent Garden, Leicester Square and Piccadilly. This would exploit the opportunities afforded by a system of thirty-five street cameras using state-of-the-art digital technology.

To do this, I used the knowledge and expertise I'd built up when seconded as chief executive of the Capital Link Partnership to set out the investment case into an exciting vision of co-ordinated street management improvements that would ultimately reduce crime and make the public's experience of the area dramatically better. In this, I must pay homage to the drive and enthusiasm of the late Sir Simon Milton, who as leader of Westminster Council at this time, gave this work his full support.

I began my work with detailed statistical research that took council and police data and combined it with my own previous area survey work on land usage and pedestrian movement pattern, which was based on research commissioned from the excellent Space Syntax centre using advanced computer modelling techniques. From this grew very powerful headline messages I could use to attract investment to cover the new system's running costs:

- The area is less than 5 per cent of the entire Westminster City area but absorbs some 50 per cent of all council and police resources. It also records 50 per cent of all crime there.

- In 1999, over 30 per cent (£13 million) of all council planning and transportation management costs, including licensing, trading standards, health and safety and environmental management were committed to just this one area.

- The area generates over £5 billion, which equates to about 10 per cent of London's gross domestic product.

- There are over 8,000 business addresses in the action area. These include:

  o 5,000 office units

  o 1,200 licensed premises (the highest concentration in Europe)

  o 100 theatres, cinemas and arcades

  o 2,000 retail units

- Every day, 200,000 people commute into the action area to work in these businesses.

To give you an indication of the scale and diversity of criminal activity within Westminster City, this was the area's crime profile in 1999.

- Street crimes – robbery, snatch and pickpocketing – accounted for 19 per cent of all the 5,773 recorded crimes

- Research by Boots the chemist indicates that at least 47 per cent of retail and entertainment personnel were the victim of verbal abuse or assault every year.

- Bag theft represents 50 per cent of all recorded crime in the area with 12,000 incidents per year.

- Drug possession and supply, for which there were 2,000 arrests, represented 8 per cent of all recorded crime in the area.

- In 1998-99 there were 1,500 arrests for begging.

- Public disorder was widespread with some 2,500 incidents of assault – about 10 per cent of all recorded crime in the area – taking place.

- During 1998-99 acts of terrorism in the area consisted of 267 bomb threats with 1 explosion resulting in 3 deaths and 100 seriously injured.

Developing a powerful pitch to potential investors needs to include such facts because they justify and underpin your objectives. So, in this case I took considerable time collecting and then connecting these facts to make clear the improvements the new system would bring about and as a result, the business case began to grow. Together with my project team, I developed the vision further, creating a 'future picture' of pioneering street management that would use the CCTV system to:

- Help in city centre planning and highways control, as the cameras would enable 24/7 profiling data to be collected for design and engineering purposes.

- Pinpoint the congestion points where pedestrians became much more vulnerable to pickpockets and robbery.

- Police the behaviour and effectiveness of door supervisors at hotspot entertainment venues that were subject to violence and disorder.

- Highlight suspicious behaviour by single suspects or gangs and to which police resources could then be directed to disperse or stop and search.

- Co-ordinate the patrol and response patterns of a new police rapid reaction team who could intercept suspects after incidents of serious crime.

- Enable rapid film analysis for evidential purposes through a dedicated office in the new control centre.

- Ensure constant surveying of the action area so as to spot the build up of refuse, obstructions or illegal trading so council environmental street managers might respond more effectively and thereby prevent dangerous situations developing.

- Give the police command and control oversight of public area demonstrations and special events.

- Establish a new radio watch scheme for retail business that would be connected to the control room so staff could better communicate with the police and council.

I also developed a formula for calculating the improvement in land values that would result after implementation. I then brought all these elements together in a single presentation that I delivered over fifteen times at board meetings of various organisations, such as Land Securities, The Crown Estate and British Land. Burford Properties were so impressed by the initiative that they offered space free of charge in the basement of the Trocadero Complex Piccadilly Circus to accommodate a large new CCTV control room.

Eventually I raised £1.6 million to put towards three years' of maintenance and management costs for the system.

This case study helps to demonstrate that by creating a telling vision, that's supported by relevant facts and outcome benefits, your business case becomes irresistible.

Managing a Budget

When funds become available, the budgeting of them needs to be led and managed by someone proficient and competent, such as an appropriately trained staff member, a finance officer or even a paid accountant. It is vital to be transparent in all financial matters if you are to instil a strong perception of integrity among investors, managers and directors.

My former head of department used to seldom share his thoughts or plans as he not only considered all aspects of finance to be solely his remit but also that any openness would incite funding requests. This was of no help at all when I had to deputise for him and was plunged into the political turmoil of top-down organisational budgeting rounds of which I had no awareness, given that this was an area he kept to himself.

Far better that all strand and team leaders should be actively involved in the budget planning process as this adds credibility and transparency to it. Middle managers can then better understand the constraints and opportunities involved in efficient cost control. Everyone should be expected to contribute towards the yearly plan and make any necessary adjustments in their own area of responsibility.

Fundraising does not need to be done by a professional, who will be costly to employ and potentially less effective than someone who can communicate their passion, drive and determination for a project or operation to potential backers and investors.

This is often the chief executive or perhaps the project manager, though ideally they should be left to get on with the task of daily supervision and direction.

Whoever does the fundraising, they must first find the time to identify and then to secure funds. This can be a substantial commitment, and sufficient allowance must be built into the schedule for doing this.

Don't forget to allow for the costs of effective monitoring and evaluation either. You need clear factual evidence of the success achieved by any project or operation as this will greatly help in getting further investment, as being able to show progress from a baseline will add credibility to an enterprise in the eyes of observers. I would suggest that any project or operation has at least ten per cent of its budget set aside for doing this. And if the monitoring and evaluation is to be worthwhile, it should be planned by a competent trained person using effective systems of analysis and data collection, something I will discuss in depth later.

The personal equipment needs of your team are also often forgotten about. But, investing in good communication in the form of phones, broadband and laptop computers can have a number of benefits as:

- You will be able to stay in constant contact with your team wherever they are outside the office 24/7.

- Having access to the massive online research power of the internet can save much money on manual searching.

- Being supplied with good quality equipment has a very motivating effect on staff because they feel valued and trusted.

The Core Budget

There are number of scenarios when it comes to handling core budgets with each requiring a different mindset and strategy:

1. *A central organisational budget used to run a core activity.*

This is normally associated with large corporate organisations where a budget is set for each strand of activity. This covers all fixed and running costs and is agreed a year in advance between the finance committee and the head of department.

- In the service sector the core budget will be heavily determined by human resource requirements for experts, managers and general staff members. As budgetary pressures increase, there will be an inexorable rise in the responsibilities heaped on a static team of people with doing more with less becoming the predominant theme.

- In the manufacturing sector the core budget will be set more by machinery requirements and expertise in maintenance, logistics and quality assurance.

- Generally, in both the service and manufacturing sectors there will be a constant tension between cost control and having to do more with less. The biggest need here is to identify the baseline standards of delivery and isolate exactly what the core objectives are. The biggest threat in my experience will be the layers of additional responsibility that are added over time but without anyone being released from existing roles that are outdated and irrelevant. This is a recipe for disaster as the team members become increasingly demoralised, overstretched and frustrated as they are faced with more and more competing demands on their time.

2. *The new enterprise startup, either private or voluntary sector, whose development is dependent on income generation and borrowed venture capital.*

In some situations, development here will be *entirely* dependent on cash income generation together with borrowed funding, so no steps forward can be made in terms of expansion, marketing and staffing without additional capital. This is the normal scenario facing a small to medium enterprise sector (SME) or a small startup voluntary organisation.

- The pressure here is obviously on the individual founder of the startup. Having gone through this myself, I can vouch for the massive effort and dedication required to just get to the starting line, let alone generate substantial income, as the founder will have to put in a large amount of unpaid time to get the infrastructure set up.

- As the founder or owner must be very focused every day on objectives and priorities in order to tightly control the budget, it is well worth spending several months developing a business plan that details objectives and outcomes precisely so they match your values, skills and aspirations exactly. The business plan then needs to be costed with a very careful assessment made about who needs to do what. So, can you do something yourself or is it an area where you need outside expertise?

- The internet is a massive advantage to such enterprises, especially as much marketing, relationship building and sales can be done free through social media activities. However, for this you will need a website and unless you are an IT expert, my advice is to be very careful about making a false economy by spending vast amounts of time developing a site yourself when buying in expertise would free you up to focus on the bigger picture.

- Set up and planning time needs to be factored into your schedule while you are still in paid employment as this gives you the safety net of a pension or redundancy lump sum while you are laying your enterprise's foundations.

3. *The individual project or operation with no initial budget, and seconded or attached staff from a sponsoring organisation.*

Sometimes an organisation decides that it needs to initiate a particular project or operation that is outside its immediate core activity. Here there is a clear long-term benefit in realising the planned outcome but the risks involved are such that only a seconded staff member is allowed to get things moving. Having been involved in several of these situations myself, I can testify to the sheer exhilaration and anxiety of being given a completely blank sheet of paper to start with.

- In many ways this scenario is the same as for any new enterprise startup, so the initiation phase is still critical in setting the outcome, objectives and plan of action However, the clear advantage here is that your time is paid for and therefore this allows you space to develop the foundations of the enterprise properly.

- The other advantage of this type of seconded startup is that it attracts substantial match funding from other interested parties in terms of staff, funding, equipment, materials and accommodation. Brave leadership shown by one organisation inspires others to join in the effort.

In 1997 as a seconded police sergeant, I initiated the Capital Link Partnership for Piccadilly, Leicester Square and Covent Garden and within two years had generated direct business funding of £100K a year, a further secondee from London Underground and all my accommodation running costs from Westminster Council. This project was paid for through a mixture of direct funding, pro bono work and separate partner strategy development in support of its objectives. Incredible synergy of effort at very low direct cost to the partnership

Setting up an Appropriate Legal Entity

The form your enterprise takes is also of crucial consideration and has a direct bearing on the efficiency and effectiveness of your fundraising and budgetary control. So you need to consider what is the best legal structure for each enterprise so that:

- As a legal entity, recognised in law, it makes best use of the national fiscal framework to ensure it is tax efficient.

- It takes advantage of any fundraising provisions available under UK law.

- It engenders trust and confidence in its integrity by being transparently well ordered and organised.

- It provides basic protection to its employees in terms of health and safety, employment law and liability.

These are the various options such an enterprise can take:

1. A department within a large corporate organisation

- This is a reasonably straightforward option as the department operates under the umbrella structure of the host organisation. In the case of the public sector, this will be the Government Crown where all expenditure comes from taxes. In the case of a private company, it will be either a public limited company or a company limited by share or guarantee.

- The department will be expected to exercise due diligence and comply with all legislation relating to safety, liability, financial conduct, data protection and public information.

- There will be a core budget for running the department with additional funding for special projects being sought from central sources.

- The biggest threat here is runaway expenditure because a department is not tightly controlled by the centre due to too much devolved authority, bad management or, conversely, overly centralised control that strangles the department's effectiveness. I have witnessed both in the police and give examples below.

2. A new enterprise in the private or voluntary sector

There are six main entities for a new enterprise in the private and voluntary sector. These are the sole trader, the limited company by guarantee, the limited company by share, the charity and the community interest company (CIC) and the limited liability partnership (LLP). Some of these are standalone while others combine entities to make maximum use of fiscal and fundraising opportunities.

The Sole Trader

This is an individual who sets up their business under their own name with income to the business assessed by the Inland Revenue Tax Office as part of that person's overall personal liability and allowances.

- The advantage of this is simplicity of set up with the minimum of paperwork needing to be kept and submitted to the Inland Revenue (HMRC).

- The disadvantage is that personal and business income may quickly push you into the higher tax bands. You will also need to register with HMRC as self-employed and give a full tax return each year. Your protection against liabilities and bankruptcy is also more limited.

The Limited Company by Guarantee

Here the business is registered at Companies House and the directors are guaranteed protection from certain forms of financial liability.

- The advantage is that the Directors of the Company are protected from bankruptcy on payment of at least £1. They can also pay themselves a salary and draw expenses from business income.

- This legal entity is often used on its own by not for profit organisations, or combined with charitable status so the organisation can trade and pass the income back into the charity after running costs are covered.

- There must be at least one director and a company secretary.

The Limited Company by Share

This is the normal entity for most private businesses, with stakes in the company divided into shares. This entity is also registered at Companies House and must keep a record of it share owners and submit annual financial accounts to both Companies House and HMRC.

- The main advantages of this arrangement is that tax is paid at a much lower corporation tax rate with the opportunity to offset expenditure for many infrastructure item, such as equipment and training, against tax liability. The directors can also pay themselves out of the company income and determine a dividend that is over and above their personal tax allowance. There is also a high degree of protection against liability.

- The main disadvantage is that more formal returns, professionally prepared and therefore more costly, need to be submitted to Companies House and HMRC each year. A much higher standard of transparency and account keeping is also expected to fulfil legal obligations.

The Charity

Charities in the UK are regulated under various Charity Acts and any not for profit enterprise that provides defined levels of community benefit should consider seeking charitable status from the Charity Commissioners. A charity is run by its trustees who sit on its board and who are voted for by the organisation's members each year.

- The main advantage of a charity is its ability to raise funds tax advantageously through gift aid from business and private individuals. This currently attracts a 28 per cent tax rebate from HMRC over and above the actual contribution made.

- The disadvantage is that the registration process is relatively lengthy and any profits must be ploughed back into the organisation and not just paid out to the trustees. An annual return also has to be submitted to the Charity Commissioners and accounts signed off by a professional accountant. A charity is not allowed to trade.

- Often a limited company by guarantee is combined with a charity to enable trading on one side of the organisation while protecting the fundraising status of the charity on the other. The company is registered first and then charity status is applied for.

The Community Interest Company (CIC)

CICs were established six years ago for those providing a community service but who did not want the regulatory responsibilities of becoming a charity. All profits from such an enterprise have to be ploughed back into the organisation after paying running costs.

- The main advantage of CIC status is that in the eyes of the public it differentiates you from that standard business entity, the limited company

However, there is little else to distinguish a CIC from a limited company by guarantee, except in name. There are some beneficial VAT exemptions but returns to Companies House and HMRC still have to be made each year.

Case Study – The Safer London Foundation

In 2002, I was asked by the Commissioner Sir John Stevens to use my experience and knowledge of setting up charities (the Capital Link Partnership and West End CCTV Project) to create a new charity affiliated to the Met and dedicated to community safety and prevention project work.

Many years of work had already been expended on this and I discovered a file about two feet thick in central records. The last proposal had been to 'piggy back' on an existing charity, using its executive team and infrastructure to avoid separate costs for what would be a heavily scrutinised public sector body. However, the Commissioner and Assistant Commissioner, Tim Godwin, both had many reservations about doing this due to the lost opportunity of branding it with a distinct identity of its own.

I also took the view that a joint venture set up in this way was indeed completely inappropriate for an organisation like Scotland Yard which has such a high global brand identity. We needed an affiliated charity in our own right, dedicated to supporting Met Police objectives for public safety and with a recognised charitable aim.

So, I set up a small working group that included the chief legal officer of the police authority, our sponsorship department, the Commissioner's chief of operations and project officers from my own team.

There began an intense period of research into similar charities affiliated to other police force areas so we could scope out the objectives for our own charity. My team also started to investigate how startup costs could be raised from internal departments and the police authority. A full project initiation document was produced to detail the business case and how we aimed to proceed. I felt that a combination of a limited company by guarantee and a charity listing would allow us to pursue both commercial interests while still maximising the tax advantages of gift aid.

Start-up costs inevitably became a sticking point, taking a staggering three years to resolve, with revised proposals and new presentations flowing in a steady stream to the police authority and management board. Once again, this is where vision, clarity of purpose and dogged tenacity are essential – these initiatives are not for the faint hearted.

To help us, I gained agreement from the Home Office and management board to use the new proceeds of crime act as part of our strategy. This allowed us to recycle seized assets and cash from organised crime through the new charity and return it to the community through the new safer neighbourhood team projects. This had several advantages.

First, it maintained our independence from commercial work and enabled us to use the administrative machine of the charity. It also funded the running costs of the executive team. It was on this basis, that the police authority finally agreed a limited three-year startup finance package of £250,000.

Further efforts were then made to appoint an appropriate board of trustees and to select a chief executive. The board was eventually chaired by a senior partner from KPMG alongside several CEOs from community interest bodies. The commissioner became a trustee and HRH The Prince of Wales enthusiastically gave his patronage.

In June 2005, three years after I began my work, the entire project was launched at KPMG HQ. Up to now (2012), the Safer London Foundation has raised and distributed an average of £1.5 million each year and enjoys full recognition for its success.

3. **Free standing project or operation run by a secondee or attached staff**

These initiatives come in a variety of guises, though generally they involve a partnership or joint venture with one or more agencies. It is important to choose the right legal entity for this type of project in order to add to its legitimacy and status as an enterprise of value and integrity. Possible entities could be:

The formal partnership

This includes an executive and members who manage the enterprise through formal meetings and recorded minutes. While any financial subscriptions must be properly accounted for, this entity is not registered with Companies House or HMRC. Its potential liabilities are much greater if it is mismanaged.

The Limited Company, Community Interest Company or Charity

As described above.

Additional Funding Sources

Inevitably, as objectives and action plans are developed, certain strands of capital and revenue expenditure will need funding, however much voluntary or pro bono time is provided.

There are a number of fundraising options and, in my experience, all require effort which can be hugely time consuming. To minimise such effort, try to follow the principle of killing two birds with one stone by encouraging partners to incorporate project and operational actions into their own mainstream business planning cycle.

Central Organisational Funding

Here the parent corporate organisation provides resources to the enterprise that might include:

- Funding of the secondee's position, in itself a major contribution. Many corporates see this type of attachment as extremely valuable to the development of community relations while also providing a superb self-improvement opportunity for the secondee themselves.

- A staff exchange, which could be of mutual benefit in terms of skills and experience. Scotland Yard used to have an exchange facility with the Royal Hong Kong Police before 1997, with middle ranking officers being swapped at annual intervals. I worked with one outstanding superintendent from Hong Kong at Bow Street Police Station on a major incident when the Provisional IRA (PIRA) exploded a small device in a litterbin on the Strand in 1986. Unfortunately, the superintendent had to return to Hong Kong at very short notice, having been seen by the clubs squad gambling in one of the Chinatown's ubiquitous dens. An untimely and sudden removal for a very talented officer..

- Central funding can often be identified by thinking laterally and applying for monies that come out of the 'community chest' or from other established, but less obvious, funding streams. Between 2002-05, as a project manager, I made the case that assets and cash seized by the police from organised criminals under the Proceeds of Crime Act should be redirected through the Safer London Foundation, the new Scotland Yard charity I'd established, which enabled the Metropolitan Police to channel monies that otherwise wouldn't have been available back to the community through crime prevention programmes.

- Central organisation resourcing can also be provided in the form of provision in kind. Between 1997 and 2002, my Capital Link Partnership was accommodated in Westminster City Hall at no cost. All heat, lighting, telephone and tax liabilities were absorbed by the council as part of their contribution to the effort. The cost saving to me was enormous and ran into thousands of pounds each year, making the project much more viable.

Government Funding

This is a very thorny area and one in which I have seen all manner of issues over the last fifteen years. In the public sector, activity is essentially funded by the central and local government tax system. For instance, policing is largely supported through a precept component in the council tax with additional funding for special projects and security operations generally made up by central government.

The general movement since 1997 towards joint community partnerships has also involved the police in multi-agency work. But while I applaud this as a principle, I have significant reservations about what has happened in reality.

Multi-agency prevention and regeneration projects require dedicated funding and what I saw first hand was central government using this to extend its reach into local operational policing through the back door. Special regeneration monies were often made available to the police on the understanding that there would be compliance with central deployment instructions. These were often formulated by civil servants in regional government offices far removed from the operational front line and who based all their work on official research sources.

Often funds were being provided in response to a current burning concern, which often gave a strong political imperative to the monies.

So, what became of concern to me was the gradual political control these funding streams posed to operational decision making in clear constitutional breach of the independence of the police. This pattern was insidious due to its implicit nature.

For example, between 2002-03, I was asked by the then Commissioner, Sir John Stevens, to set up a pilot small business crime initiative for Brick Lane in Tower Hamlets, East London. Attached to the organisation, London First, which represents many 'corporates' across London and promotes the economic and security interests of the region, I worked with my main partner BT, the Tower Hamlets council and local business groups, to trial a number of connected projects on improving business and street security.

With a partnership board and working group set up, the Government Office for London (GOL) became increasingly interested, as the trial complemented their work on combating the vulnerability of ethnic minority groups across London. Accordingly, a large sum of funding was offered towards the action plan and its associated evaluation.

I had already employed a respected small business researcher, to develop a monitoring and evaluation plan but while still waiting for the actual transfer of GOL monies, I received a number of phone calls from a senior civil servant. He asked me to use their preferred consultant to conduct the research. I explained that an appointment had been made after a careful tender process and that the board had already made their decision so I was not in a position to countermand this as I was working in a partnership role.

After this came a further phone call from the head of department directly threatening me and making it clear that if I did not switch to the new consultant my position at Scotland Yard would be threatened and my chief superintendent would be contacted.

Naturally, I was astonished. This was the first time this had happened to me. I made enquiries and found that this same official had bullied other officers and partnerships.

Ultimately, the funding offer was withdrawn and 50 per cent of the entire project became untenable. This was an extreme personal example but I discovered that this tactic was not uncommon and represented a growing trend of political manipulation; a very ugly development indeed.

Trust and Charitable Sources

Trust and charities in the UK make up a multi-billion pound social enterprise sector with an astonishing range of literally thousands of small to large charities employing a vast workforce and providing a multitude of services to vulnerable and deprived people.

Many of them provide grant assistance to community projects and any operations manager looking to make approaches to them should bear the following in mind:

- The Charity Commissioners maintains a comprehensive database about the aims, grants provided and contact details of the organisations accredited by them.

- Different charities often work in concert with each other on operational projects by pooling expertise, resources and funding. Though creating such arrangements isn't always easy in reality given the strong competition between them for funds. However, they can work successfully together when the individual executive teams get on well and trust each other.

- The Social Directory Organisation, based in Kings Cross, provides an excellent brokerage service that will put you in contact with an appropriate charity as well as providing voluntary sector training, very good employment services for those looking to go into the voluntary sector and useful books and information.

Private Benefactors

Wealthy individual investors are also a worthwhile source of funding and there are publications that list rich private benefactors and the interests they like to support.

When seeking funding from these benefactors, I make the following comments and recommendations:

- Approaching such individuals is often best done through a third party who is well known to them and who can champion your cause.

- Obtaining funds from benefactors takes time and requires relationship building to cement understanding and trust in what you are doing. Some will want to be involved in shaping strategy by being on the board, while others will want to remain 'hands off' and at a distance from the project

- Good research is needed to identify the best fit between their interests and your needs.

Business Investment and Sponsorship

This is another difficult area but an important one. Business clearly has an interest in providing resources and support to local regeneration projects as this adds to its own credibility and can improve the operating environment in which they are involved. Sometimes the advantages of investment are not always clear to an individual business and so the case for its support has to be carefully researched and presented, as investing companies will want to know what the return will be on their money.

In my experience there are two main types of business investment.

Sponsorship

Here a business gives money in return for advertising, lobbying access or product channelling. For instance, in the Metropolitan Police, a very large sponsorship office oversees any TV or media use of the police's corporate logos on uniforms or on cars in dramas, which is paid for under license.

The scale of sponsorship funding available will depend on what extra value the business believes it will add to its sales, profits or reputation.

General Investment

A company may resource a public community project by providing staff or through direct funding. This can take many forms but invariably investors will always need a clear business case for such investment with objectives and potential returns clearly set out. To research and prepare this requires a substantial amount of time but once such funding streams are secured they can provide a stable and secure source of resources.

Between 1997-2002, I had set up a charitable limited company, the Capital Link Partnership, to work with other organisations and businesses to create the case for one of the UK's first business improvement districts, based on the New York Times Square model. Our intention was to initiate a range of environmental and safety improvements that would be paid for from a business tax rate surcharge.

This has worked well with clear benefits from the regeneration work as it not only attracts a higher quality tenant but the relative value of their holdings also increases due to increased safety and amenity value of the area.

Obviously, this structural investment is attractive to business and there are now proposals to extend the surcharge to land owners as well as the tenants.

Venture Capital

Today there are many sources of private and public banking venture capital available for public, private and voluntary sector use. The main ones are:

Seed Enterprise Investment Scheme (EIS)

This new government scheme was introduced in April 2012 to encourage investment in small startup companies. The scheme allows investors to put £100,000 in a single tax year into several small unlisted companies as long as:

- They cannot control the company and have no more than a 30 per cent stake in the business.

- The company is be UK-based, unlisted and with no more than 25 employees.

- The company must have been trading for NO more than two years.

- The company must have assets of less than £200,000.

- The shares are either categorised as A class with voting rights, or B shares with no voting rights.

- The scheme is for companies in the financial or property sectors, though there may be exceptions.

In return, investors will be entitled to up to 50 per cent tax relief in the year of investment and generally a full capital gains tax exemption when they sell their shares.

Crowd Funding

Crowd funding uses the internet to attract money from masses of individuals to directly finance a single venture, project or business startup.

Such 'peer to peer' lending is increasingly popular with numerous websites offering excellent interest rates that are far superior to the banks. The only drawback is that there is currently a lack of insurance underwriting if there is a default, though this rarely happens in reality.

As a funding method, it is really taking off given the current lack of liquidity in the banking sector stemming from the 2008 financial credit crisis.

It should be encouraged as it cuts out the middle men who have made vast fortunes from lending to us and encourages true entrepreneurship. Bank to the Future is a prime example of this, run currently by Simon Dixon

End-user Funding

In certain situations, the end-users of your service or product may even be happy to contribute to the development and running costs if they see value and a potential payback.

For example, when I was project manager of the London West End CCTV initiative, we secured £1.2 million of central government funding for the capital purchase of a thirty-two all weather digital camera network to monitor key streets affected by crime and public safety issues. To cover the system's annual running cost I developed a funding strategy that saw retailers and licensed premises in the area having direct radio contact with the control room for which they paid for the upkeep of the CCTV.

Although businesses were already paying business rate tax, they made this additional contribution, because the return on investment was clear and distinct giving them a means of communicating directly with patrolling police and council enforcement officers. This meant emergency and proactive intelligence sharing about suspicious behaviour could happen faster and so help prevent crime and costly disruption to business.

The same principle could be adopted by other sectors in different scenarios. For example, in the 1990s customers of the Pizza Express chain were asked to contribute towards charitable activity in the area through a surcharge added to their bill. They were happy to do so because the value was carefully explained in marketing materials. This added to the status of the chain as a responsible local retailer with high community interest credentials. The surcharge was modest but the cumulative effect was nevertheless substantial, raising millions of pounds.

Human Resources

People are usually your most expensive and valuable commodity, particularly in a service-oriented organisation. They also present the greatest challenges in terms of performance management with many supervisory implications. In my opinion there are a few guiding principles you need to observe, some of which I discuss in greater detail in the next section on team development:

1. Which areas of your activity need core permanent staff to service them? To decide this, consider the following factors:

    • What areas of commercial and business sensitivity will generally need staff with an extended tenure? These positions require loyalty and discretion from individuals who have a long-term interest in the organisation's success.

    • What areas of production and service need ongoing specialist expertise that would be very expensive to constantly outsource? It is often better and more cost-effective to have a permanent staff member performing these functions.

- What are the core areas in the enterprise? These should be managed by permanent staff supported perhaps by outsourced assistance. Devolving core functions to an outside organisation is an abnegation of accountability, in my view, that ultimately undermines end-user confidence as no one clearly knows who is responsible for what. If core functions are outsourced the end-user needs to clearly understand that a consortium or partnership is delivering the product or service.

- What legal obligations do you have in areas such as data protection, health and safety, public information disclosure and finance? When individuals need to be accountable for meeting regulatory standards they should be permanent staff.

Currently in the UK, there is a huge debate about outsourcing enforcement and investigative powers to the private security industry. The argument goes that they can provide the service in a more cost-effective way than a public body that is under enormous budgetary pressure and with finite resources. Surrey and the West Midlands police have already started this process, though the commissioner of London is resisting such pressures. But arresting and denying people their freedom is such a core and fundamental responsibility that it should only be done by warranted officers of the Crown. Otherwise, what is the point of having a police force at all?

2. The role and responsibility of each member of core permanent staff must be crystal clear as to where the buck stops in terms of accountability for performance. There is no room whatsoever for vagueness in this, so job specifications must be carefully prepared along with a clear contract of employment to ensure there is no ambiguity.

3. Surrounding the core staff should be concentric circles of appropriate and effective contractors who can be hired and fired

quickly in case of weak performance and without pinning the organisation down in lengthy employment litigation.

4. All staff must be highly flexible so they can take over another role in an emergency or at times of increased demand. In my experience, there is no room for dogged intransigence here, so even better qualified staff should be ready to do more menial tasks at certain times. This is not a slur on their status but a sign of the interoperability required in a modern operating context.

On a recent visit to Shenzhen in China, I experienced this first hand when I saw qualified professionals doing cleaning jobs when their expertise wasn't needed at that moment. There was no stigma in this changing of roles and it created an incredible sense of community cohesion as a result. With no welfare benefit system in mainland China, families have to be self-supporting at times of illness or other emergencies so there is no room to be precious.

5. Hours of work are also an important factor to consider as certain roles may be best done part-time or at particular times of the day or night. Shift working does not have to be confined to the emergency services and in manufacturing and many other sectors shift-based teams are an essential element. It can also be time and cost efficient as travelling outside normal office hours is often much easier.

6. Place of work is also an important factor for a modern operations team with home working now highly effective thanks to broadband and Skype, which means making conference calls and communicating is simple and fast. As long as the outcome and work objectives are clear, the greater flexibility this offers can lead to increased time efficiency.

7. True leadership comes in many forms, not just in the image many people have of Lord Cardigan leading the charge of the Light Brigade in the Crimean War. Leadership can also be about individuals in a team taking responsibility for their work area and showing initiative, drive and commitment to doing the tasks in hand. Leadership then is not about sitting back and letting a superior give all the directions or waiting for someone to rally the troops. So

the department head must show their real worth by selecting and developing the very best strand and team leaders, then setting them first class objectives and releasing them to get on with their job.

Policing is a good example of this. At its best, individual constables are empowered to make life and death decisions using enormous individual discretion to choose the best course of action when out on the street. Tactically, day-by-day, this does not involve the chief superintendent or even the team inspector sitting on their shoulder.

Apart from using paid staffing, there are also many other ways to supplement the team with key human resources:

Secondments and Attachments

I discussed these earlier but it's worth re-emphasising just how much added value and understanding those on secondment or attachment can create between two departments or organisations. They are also an excellent way of encouraging self-development in managers which is why KPMG, Price Waterhouse Coopers and the Metropolitan Police all have extensive secondment facilities.

Internships

These are a welcome arrival as they give postgraduate and undergraduate students the opportunity to work in organisations where they can test out newfound skills and expertise in a real time operating environment.

In 2006 I identified two students on courses at the Criminology Department of Sam Houston University, Texas. One was a retired homicide detective, the other much younger. They assisted me with research into the effects of serious and organised crime on London's minority ethnic groups and how we could better build their resilience to it. Getting professional paid researchers would have cost me a fortune and I was not in a position to do this, but I was able to organise a three-month internship at Scotland Yard together with accommodation in Belgravia for them.

My only caveat about internships is that you need to give the same amount of selection time to them as you would to a paid position if you are to ensure compatibility and appropriate levels of skill. My two interns had a complete personality clash and I spent much time resolving conflicts between them and supervising their work. The age and experience level between them was too great and this caused some of the problems.

Volunteers

Volunteers can make a very useful contribution and the Metropolitan Police uses them extensively in the form of special constables, who are trained and warranted police officers to the Crown but give their time on a voluntary basis, and the cadet force.

Scotland Yard is currently moving towards a position where you have to be a special constable if you want be considered for full-time paid positions in the regular force, a way of testing the individual and ensuring that they are a good fit with the organisation's values and standards.

My only qualification about using volunteers is that their attendance must be well organised otherwise operational planning is very difficult and causes major disruption if they fail to show up. I remember one Lord Mayor's show in the 80s when there were large gaps in the crowd control lines because Specials failed to attend for various reasons. This is totally unacceptable, but through clearly agreed rotas should be avoidable.

Materials

The last element of resourcing is the materials that are needed to produce or support the product or service. Here considerations about quality are just as crucial as they are when outcome planning.

In my policing career, the biggest material requirement I had was for data and information that could be distilled into intelligence and then classified under different categories. This was the life-blood of policing.

The raw information I collected from informants, neighbourhood residents and my own observations was key to fitting together the jigsaw of crime patterns of who was doing what. We had a saying that: 'The intelligence you get out of the analytical process is only as good as the quality of data you put in'.

Sadly, over the course of many years I witnessed a general decline in data inputting which adversely affected the analytical standards, and often led to misinformation or only a partial picture of what was going on. This came about through ever-expanding bureaucratic requirements that created time pressures.

Joint Ventures and Partnerships

Joint ventures and partnerships were a major component of the latter stages of my police career and I am now totally convinced that modern operations management needs to embrace them to a much greater extent than it has in the past. This is because, with more and more specialisms developing, one organisation cannot hope to fulfil all the needs with limited staff operating under a tight budget. The big corporates may have been able to do this in the past but in the face of a global internet communications revolution, it is my contention that end-users will now seek better prices and greater value for money from niche providers, something that will serve the smaller SME sector extremely well.

As ever it's 'horses for courses' so it is also my contention that these smaller enterprises will need to come together more often through collaborative ventures and partnerships that use each other's strengths to achieve the best outcome. This is much more than simple outsourcing and requires a much deeper level of understanding and ownership of the process among the different partners involved.

Many challenges are presented by this type of working.

1. Selecting a partner organisation is as important as selecting your own staff. A high degree of fit between your areas of common interest, work culture and objectives is crucial for successful

collaboration. Determining this requires careful research into the following areas:

- What is the strategic plan of the other organisation over the next three years and do these strategic aims match with yours?

- What are the specific objectives of each strand of its business?

- What is the planning cycle of the other organisation for finances, patterns of demand and executive appointments, over a twelve month period?

- What is their decision making process and who has the ultimate authority for directing operations?

- What types of team do they use? Are these hierarchical and generalist or flat and specialist?

- What is their work culture? Creative, individualistic or a conservative hierarchy, for instance?

- What strengths and opportunities can you exploit by working together?

- Are there key individuals who can bridge between the organisations and champion joint work in their respective camps?

- What is their rate of staff turnover? High levels may indicate poor management and low staff morale.

- Exactly what are your areas of common interest?

- What are their quality standards for materials, operations, staff and outcome design?

2. You need to identify the main cost benefits of working together by determining what work should be done by whom so to best use the relative strengths of staff and resources in each organisation.

3. You must also develop a joint plan of action that clearly identifies which department and individuals are accountable for delivery performance. Many partnerships fail because the rhetoric that

surrounds their intentions is not backed by appropriate action and delivery in the agreed areas. True partnership goes far beyond just friendly relations and involves hard resource backed action, not just having a pint together in the pub.

Case Study – 'Operation Pathways' to Combat Street Gang Violence, London Region, 2007-10

In 2007, London lost twenty-seven young people under eighteen to stabbings and shootings that were generally connected to a 'respect' or territorial gang issue.

The situation had been deteriorating gradually over the previous ten years, with the roots of this in my opinion, and those of many social researchers, stemming from a wholesale social breakdown in family cohesion and discipline, exacerbated by wide scale community apathy. In many areas of London, and not just the most deprived, young people had lost their sense of belonging and purpose due to an unrelenting tide of selfish materialism and dysfunctional family life. This had created an army of young lost souls living a feral existence on the streets. Gang life replaced family life for many as an entire street culture began to flourish, based on a twisted set of ethics about personal honour, strength and territory.

This meant that just looking at someone's girlfriend, stepping on the wrong toes at a party or being knocked into on the street often resulted in extreme retributive violence being exercised by the entire gang of the person supposedly slighted. The senselessness of this violence was of such growing concern to community groups that eventually the then Prime Minister, Tony Blair, became involved, hosting a series of summits at Downing Street to discuss a high level response.

It was at this time that I joined forces with Dr Gloria Laycock, who headed the new Jill Dando Foundation at University College London. We were working together on a training initiative to enhance the theoretical knowledge of my project managers and analysts in crime preventative sciences. As part of that training, we invited Professor David Kennedy, one-time director of the Boston Ceasefire Gang Programme, to the UK to present his findings.

His words were so well received, that he was then invited to address a large audience of police practitioners and senior officers at Scotland Yard. Out of this was born 'Operation Pathways', London's response to the threatening phenomenon of gang tribalism. The fundamental basis of our approach was to enforce the collective principle of joint accountability between gang members for single acts of serious violence by one of their members. The US programme used a three-pronged response:

- A 'Call In' of the entire gang to a location, such as City Hall, a court room or other large public centre. Here the community then had the opportunity to explain in explicit terms to the gang that their behaviour would not be tolerated and that any further violence would trigger harsh punitive action against all the members.

- The gang members would then be offered help to exit their lifestyle through training, coaching and job placement, *if* they stopped their violence.

- If there was further violence, then the consequences would be immediate and harsh and involve the entire gang being arrested and charged with joint involvement under federal law rather than state legislation. This attracted much longer prison sentences.

While there are many differences in the context of gang behaviour between the two countries we thought that by developing the US model we could act decisively to regain control where possible.

Several pilot areas were established in the London Boroughs of Lewisham, Southwark, Lambeth, Greenwich and Croydon, where gangs were of major concern

I was made responsible for the consequences strand, together with a senior representative from the London Criminal Justice Board and a project manager from my own team. I then developed a five-phase approach with separate systems and methods that were all co-ordinated under a united programme operations board in each pilot area.

Phase 1 was Risk Assessment. I set up risk assessment panels that collated intelligence from several agencies including the police, the probation service and the Youth Justice Board. This information was then used to compile gang membership lists and grade a person's propensity for violence as high, medium or low.

Phase 2 was Case File Preparation. Here I established a process of multi-agency case file preparation on each gang member. This detailed their outstanding warrants, civil order violations and what I called 'lever point' influences in their lives, such as a high value car, a property, a girlfriend or mother. If enforcement was needed, then these lever points could be used to exert maximum pressure on the individual through seizure, loss of liberty or the influence of others.

Phase 3 was the 'Call In'. Just as in America, after declaring an active operation in a pilot area and announcing through the media and advertising, after any further incidents would come the Call In, organised by the local police commander. At this, community representatives would be invited in to talk about their anger and fear while surgeons from the local hospital would speak about the consequences of knife and gunshot wounds. Finally, the local consequences strand leader would set out the enforcement actions that would be taken in the event of a further attack so everyone in the gang was in no doubt about their joint accountability.

Phase 4 involved Consequence Operations. This was a co-ordinated multi-agency strike by police, the local council and bailiff officials who would raid individual gang members' addresses using the previously compiled case files to give them leverage.

Phase 5 was Ongoing Offender Management. For those times when gang members went back into the criminal justice system, I developed a method of including them in Multi Agency Public Protection Arrangements (MAPPA), so there could be ongoing management of them by the probation and youth offender teams. This had never been done before and it was a cost-cutting innovation that brought an existing solution to a new problem. It also enabled offenders to be placed on the national computerised index of dangerous offenders so they could be monitored and managed across local authority boundaries.

What I was determined to do was put into practice all the learning from my previous operations about offender management and to build on the strengths of the UK criminal justice system and various central offender management programmes.

4. Develop a written statement of understanding and undertaking signed by the Chairman and CEO of both organisations that sets out:

- The duration of the partnership.
- The aims and objectives of the partnership.
- The added value that will come from working together.
- The quality standards to be set in the relationship and outputs.
- The income streams that will come back to each organisation.
- Accountability and responsibility levels for shared delivery.

5. Make it clear to end-users who is involved in the partnership and who is responsible for what. Evidence of such working together effectively is invariably welcomed and instils confidence in the

customer base that a responsible and thoughtful management process is in train.

6. Leadership is again crucial and the right individual must be selected to chair a joint partnership executive team. This could be someone independent of both organisations, or an appropriate person from one or other. Whoever they are, there is a need for them to be diplomatic but extremely focused on outcome delivery with an ability to get the very best out of the team or strand leaders.

Case Study – The Capital Link Partnership Central London, 1996-99

In 1996 I was selected to project manage the city centre working group of the Westminster Safer Cities Partnership. This partnership, together with several others across the country, had been set up by the recently elected Labour government to trial new methods of tackling crime and disorder at a neighbourhood level.

The rationale behind this was that to prevent crime you need a holistic approach that involves executive action from local health, education, environment and policing departments in a joint co-ordinated strategy. This work was the forerunner of the local partnerships necessary under the Crime and Disorder Act of 1997, and required local partners to work together year by year to ensure that crime and safety issues that affected their communities became part of their mainstream corporate planning process.

Out of my particular working group, we developed a new concept that focused on the main pedestrian corridor connecting Piccadilly Circus to Leicester Square and Covent Garden. This 800 metre stretch, the length of a Eurostar train, is used by over 60 million people each year, amounting to the entire UK population, and as such it presents particular challenges in terms of congestion, crime, safety and cleaning.

It struck me and the working group that this corridor typified many other key arterial pedestrian routes in London and other major cities and that we could conduct some valuable pilot work to test out how to make the entire user experience more pleasant and safer.

As a project manager on secondment from Scotland Yard, I was in a leadership position but very conscious that the project had to have a clear identity if it was to excite the imagination of residents, businesses and tourist groups alike so that they became properly engaged with the work and felt a sense of ownership about its development. To achieve this, I:

- Created a charitable company by guarantee to give the enterprise legitimacy, credibility and financial efficiency.

- Established a partnership board of key trustees from Westminster Council, the local Metropolitan Police, London Tourist Board, London Transport and landowners.

- Organised a membership group of main stakeholders from business, the residents and other key users of the connecting route who could vote on proposals coming forward.

- Set up working groups for the three main thematic areas that had revealed themselves through baseline research – spatial design and management, management in crime hotspots and the development of a more responsive community justice approach to offenders.

- Established a full explanatory and promotional marketing plan using 3D mapping, leaflets and media events to highlight what was being done.

Effective leadership would always be crucial to our success given the number of interconnected forums. But identifying and then securing the right person for what would be a voluntary post was a major undertaking and one I took extremely seriously.

To do this I enlisted the help of my old friend and mentor, Grace Cook. Grace had previously chaired the Covent Garden Trust and Police Consultative Group after retiring from a career in publishing. I remember with fondness meeting this eighty-year-old doyenne of the area in the new Sainsbury's Wing restaurant of the National Gallery overlooking Trafalgar Square. Over the course of several meetings, we pondered many potential candidates based on their availability, credibility, chairmanship skills and drive. Eventually we honed our lists down and then I spent many hours pursuing, persuading and eventually securing some extraordinary talent. Eventually:

The Rt Hon Sir John Wheeler JP DL – former Northern Ireland Minister and MP for North Westminster became Chairman of the overall Partnership Board.

Councillor Tim Joiner – Westminster Council Education Committee Chair was appointed Deputy Chairman of the Partnership Board.

Commander Paddy Tomkins – Westminster Police Crime Investigation Commander became Chair of the Risk Management Working Group.

Judge Gerald Butler QC – former Resident Judge at Southwark Crown Court was made Chair of the Community Justice Working Group.

Dickon Robinson – Director of the Peabody Trust, former member of Lord Rogers' Urban Task Force in 1996 and Covent Garden resident, became Chair of the Spatial Design & Management Working Group

This effort to get the best people led me, along with Sir John Wheeler, a Privy Councillor to the Queen, to HRH Prince Charles and the door of St James's Palace on St George's Day, 1999.

Prince Charles has long had a particular interest in the urban environment and has set up his very own architectural foundation. Our objective in meeting him was to get his support to become patron of the charity and to help identify a suitable chair for the spatial design group.

So in what was a somewhat surreal experience, we were ushered into his private apartments in St James's Palace by his resplendent butler, where we met His Royal Highness and his private secretary, Mark Bolland.

Having been given tea in the best china cups and saucers, I was directed to a huge sofa and asked to give my presentation on the Capital Link Concept.

I sat down only to find myself sinking into the depths of the overly soft cushions to a point where it seemed that only my upper body was showing. Undeterred, and with Sir John on my left for moral support, I set up the folding desktop presentation case I'd brought with me. Then with Earl Grey balanced precariously in my left hand, I doggedly began to turn over the slides with my right, taking a sip of tea as and when I felt I could do so without tipping the contents onto the royal Axminster. It was like fighting your way out of a swamp, with the added complication of trying to keep eye contact with HRH.

I think my message in all this is that when a situation calls for voluntary effort to support the partnership's work, selling an exciting vision can be extremely motivating and is something to which busy people will positively respond if they feel it's worthwhile. Remember, I was only a sergeant at this time so the engagement of the great and the good was based solely on the logic and opportunity that such a pilot offered. My passion and belief in the concept was far more important than my rank. This is a salutary lesson to all, as it shows what can be achieved.

Monitoring and Review

However good your planning is, it is essential to put in place an equally effective monitoring and review process as this helps ensure that the outcome originally designed stays focused, obstacles overcome and momentum built. If this is done properly, it will also provide a basis for final evaluation later. Monitoring and review is equally applicable for projects and ongoing operations, although the agenda for each will have a different emphasis.

Progress Reviews

These meetings need to be programmed into the implementation period at regular intervals. The strand leaders who are accountable for delivery and performance should be present at all, with more peripheral project officers invited only as required. These reviews should be tightly managed and strand leaders given the opportunity to be honest and candid, otherwise they are only going to hide developing problems. I'll use one of my operations as an example of the process.

Between July 2007 and February 2008, my department was leading Operation Hand-Over, the aim of which was to combat the illegal supply and criminal use of imitation guns across London. Previous research and police operations had shown that there was a growing use of highly realistic looking automatic rifles, machine guns and handguns in street robberies, and for gang intimidation and personal protection.

The penalties for having these fake firearms on the street were far less severe than for viable weapons and yet the quality of the imitations' finish made them undistinguishable from the real thing. More worryingly, many of them could also be converted to fire live ammunition.

To give an idea of the scale of the problem, intelligence suggested that about 10,000 such guns, purporting to be toys, were arriving each month from the Far East through Felixstowe container port.

I was tasked by the commander of the Violent Crime Directorate (VCD) to develop a London-wide response to the problem. This corporate operation involved two Scotland Yard departments – Territorial Policing and Specialist Crime – working together with outside partners such as HMRC and local authority trading standard officers. The plan had several phases and stages of research, analysis, problem solving, tactical options and implementation, as well as a full monitoring and evaluation process, which was undertaken by the Jill Dando Foundation at University College London.

The entire operation was to culminate in a joint operation throughout January and February 2008 involving port seizures, neighbourhood retail checks, internet supplier raids and a London-wide amnesty during which these weapons could be handed over at police stations.

Frequency and Duration

The frequency of review meetings depends on a number of factors including the complexity of the project or operation and the risks and deadlines associated with it. So the greater the complexity, risk or immediacy, the more frequent should be the meetings. This may therefore necessitate a daily, weekly or monthly schedule, though care be should be taken not to spend unnecessary time on meetings.

I used to chair a ninety-minute meeting of my strand leaders every Friday morning at the St Ermin's hotel with my department inspector responsible for port and local enforcement action, together with a chief inspector from VCD responsible for the London-wide amnesty operation, all present.

During the final three months of the operation, the head of the Metropolitan Police marketing department, who was responsible for media communication and advertising about the operation, also attended. Holding these meetings on a Friday was very helpful as it enabled both a review of the week's activity and an opportunity to look forward and into the following week.

In this case, the frequency and duration of review was determined by the fast moving nature of the work, its intricacy and the high reputational risks attached to a corporate initiative involving guns and violent crime. With no more than four people at these meetings there was time for the strand leaders to give a progress report and to set out their concerns to me in a relatively short space of time.

Purpose and Agenda

As the project manager, these review meetings were very important to me as they gave me an opportunity to get a real sense of progress and to probe my strand leaders with searching questions. Just as importantly, it also gave me a chance to encourage and support them when the going got tough. All in all, I became quite deft at interpreting body language and eliciting issues and problems from each of them after hearing their reports. Tone, cadence and pauses together with body position, can all indicate stress levels, something I would not have learned from written reports or phone conversations alone.

Our agenda for these meetings broadly followed the following framework:

- An overview of the strategic considerations affecting the operation and its progress to date. This would include an outline of any major threats or opportunities identified by ongoing environmental scanning. As the project manager, this is when I would remind those present about the overall aims and quality standards expected from the initiative.

- Each strand or team leader would then outline their progress since the last meeting using a Gantt chart activity list and timeline as a document reference point. Their review would cover the following points:

  o Progress against the plan's milestones with a percentage completion rate.

  o Any constraints or obstacles that were disrupting progress and an update about how these were being tackled, or whether central project management support was needed.

o A report on the quality standards of the main outputs produced so as to gauge the level of compliance with the original requirement.

o Use of the allocated budget and a report on any major variance from this because of unforeseen problems or issues.

o Priority activities for the coming week and any resource needs stemming from them.

- I would then summarise the main points made and go back over the major constraints and obstacles that had been highlighted to determine whether the situation was under control or if special measures were necessary such as setting up problem solving sessions or getting higher level authority to direct resources, make decisions or provide support from other departments.

Obviously personal pride comes into play during this type of meeting, so officers are sometimes reluctant to admit to the problems they were encountering or the mistakes they might have made. However, by showing leadership and being honest myself, I was largely able to overcome this as an issue. If I did detect any worrying body language in others, I would always follow up with a one-to-one meeting to discuss the situation further. Likewise, when I was dissatisfied with the quality standard of outputs, I would call the team leader aside to discuss the situation. Eventually, I was able to engender a very high level of trust and mutual support between us all even though the personnel came from different departments.

I also encouraged strand leaders to keep a daily journal of their main activities and the problems they were facing. Experience has taught me that this type of detail is quickly forgotten when you have a hectic schedule and that this is valuable evidence for future project evaluation and self-development. Such journals are therefore pure gold dust.

Progression Charting

Paperwork is the bane of a manager's life but still essential for effective monitoring and accountability, though it must be balanced by the need to push forward and make things happen at the sharp end. So my aim was always to keep bureaucracy to a minimum and confined to:

- A detailed Gantt chart charting progress and completion levels.
- A cash flow chart showing income and expenditure against the planned limits.
- A special strand leaders' report template that summarised any major variance in quality standards and problems encountered.
- A project manager's template that acted as a report to the project director (chief superintendent) showing monthly progress along with risks, resource needs and problem solving measures.

Problem-solving and Adjustments

The key point to bear in mind here is that prevention is always far better than cure, which means that with meticulous planning it should be possible to identify and allow for any major risks or needs in advance. The trouble starts when senior management or the fast moving dynamics of a situation force the pace making for a 'quick and dirty' response that just leads to much time being spent later correcting mistakes or dealing with unintended consequences. This can be very costly in terms of money and human resources.

Any project or operation will encounter problems, however well planned it is. But these should be relatively manageable unless there is a crisis or sudden emergency, as discussed earlier. In any event, special contingency planning sessions should be factored into the planning schedule at which possible emergency or 'what if' scenarios can be discussed with your team leaders.

Of course, any well-planned project or operation will inevitably experience some need for adjustment as reality meets theory, with circumstances on the ground changing, once perfectly logical assumptions are now found wanting.

We experienced this in Operation Hand-Over when commissioning armoured skip bins into which we thought members of the public could deposit weapons anonymously and with no possible risk from the firearm discharging.

Our research had shown that these bins had been used successfully by the military in Iraq. So, our original plan was to position them away from police stations, beside supermarkets for instance, securing them to the ground so they could not be stolen.

However, the manufacturer's claims were found to be somewhat inaccurate as it was still possible to retrieve weapons from within the bins, and therefore the risks to health and safety were thought to be too high for their use in a civilian environment. We then fell back on the idea of using a deposit process at police stations, with firearms officers then being called in to declare that each weapon brought in was safe.

In planning an operation or project like this, the main problem areas you will encounter most often fall into the following major categories:

People Problems

As always, people present the biggest problem because of their complexity and tendency to change behaviour in different situations. So no matter, how skilled or motivated they are, in a crisis or under pressure they will still display traits that are counterproductive. These could show themselves through domestic problems, depression, selfishness, anger management issues or lack of tact and diplomacy in dealing with others.

Your response as an operations manager is then crucial in keeping a happy and high-performing team, something I will discuss in greater detail in the next section. However, it is possible to manage the people problem in a number of ways.

- First, use very careful selection and appointment procedures to assess a person's skills, values and personality in the round. There must be a clear fit with the team to ensure balance and compatibility.

- Adopt 'horses for courses' selection with team members chosen to best meet jobs and roles – there is no point putting a square peg in a round hole. However, this does not absolve a manager from the responsibility of introducing new experiences and self-development opportunities to their staff to take them from their comfort zone into their stretch zone.

- Value and encourage ideas and contributions so there is a process of continuous improvement.

- Have zero tolerance of selfish posturing and self-promotion that goes against the team effort to meet objectives. The team is the main component and the individual just plays one role in achieving the desired outcomes.

- Undertake careful and supportive performance appraisals of individuals so as to address any issues, weak competencies and to encourage self-development through training and new experiences.

- Meticulously plan and organise each staff member so they are completely clear as to their role and responsibilities for delivering performance. Hold them to account for this.

Equipment Problems

The old saying 'you get what you pay for' still largely holds true so purchasing high quality equipment and maintaining it correctly is rarely a misjudged investment as its durability will save you from considerable problems in sorting out breakdowns later.

Quality equipment not only gives your team a sense of worth and value but also leads them to unconsciously treat equipment with greater respect. Providing a good laptop, broadband and smartphone can be very motivating.

Supplier Problems

Good suppliers of materials and equipment are essential to an operation's success, with continuity, quality and service all critical elements in this. So the same amount of care needs to be given to supplier selection as it does to staff selection and fundamental to this are those individuals who manage the supply process.

Today, more than ever, key people seem to keep some organisations going in the face of a more general decline in standards. So, when negotiating a supply contract, the person you deal with and trust needs to be named and a period of tenure put positioning place for them. I am not saying this is the ideal as a contract should be consistently honoured whoever is in charge, however reality suggests otherwise with investment companies following a fund manager and not the fund, and retail bank customers looking for support only from certain staff at their branch. I would long ago have left RBS if it had not been for the support of my private banking manager, who effectively became a firefighter for me sorting out maladministration on my account by different departments.

Power Politics

As discussed earlier, much thought needs to be put into how the process of implementation can be smoothly rolled out in the face of internal and external opposition. Most projects and operations will need senior champions on board to protect your back and flanks from unwarranted interference and obstruction.

Process Constraints

This is another major area of difficulty as issues that could not have been foreseen in an exemplary planning exercise often come to light when capacity, capability and quality are exposed to the harsh reality of implementation. For example, however well accredited or skilled a process or person, the demands of the situation may just overwhelm them to the point of weakness. Even suppliers with ISO 9000 accredited standards can fail badly which is why the running of the UK Border Agency and the G4S Olympics debacle has highlighted structural and management deficiencies.

The best response to this in my experience is to use the process mapping tool discussed earlier. This describes what's going on currently and then helps to identify re-routing opportunities so that the problematic part of the process can be isolated or reconfigured using a new supplier, method or system.

The 'Challenging Wards' initiative was a major operation I undertook between 2006 and 2007. It was established by the Violent Crime Directorate to develop and test a new business model for the management of violent crime at a neighbourhood and council ward level.

Given the thousands of reported crimes including assaults, gun crime, domestic violence and sex crime, we'd found that we couldn't see the 'wood for the trees'.

Research clearly showed that most violent crimes were being perpetrated by a relatively small number of offenders in hotspot locations and on particular vulnerable victim groups. Using Pareto's Law – 80 per cent of your results come from just 20 per cent of your effort – I decide that policing resources needed to be redirected more effectively to control the risks without trying to dash everywhere at once and to little effect.

So, I set up pilot sites in eight locations throughout London with a co-ordinator for each area. Then, using a structured four-phase process, I set out a sequence of crime profiling and analysis, problem solving, local resource auditing and tactical planning. The purpose of this was to get a truly objective helicopter view of what was going on and where resources could be applied more efficiently.

There were two areas I was most concerned with during this process, and which had bedevilled previous initiatives. The first was trying to take short cuts to speed up the process, and the second was an inability to share good practice from across London because of the sheer scale and density of policing bureaucracy.

To tackle both issues, I set up a quality and advisory panel. This consisted of experts in analysis, risk management, tactical planning and problem-solving, to whom the co-ordinators could submit their phase and stage reports regularly for review and comment. These reports highlighted any obstacles they were facing and gave the panel the opportunity to then relay suggestions and advice while also giving me a report on quality standard deficiencies. The entire process was very robust and comprehensive and led to a highly relevant and proportionate tactical response. Consequently, all eight locations experienced falls in recorded crime ranging from fifteen to twenty per cent as compared to neighbouring wards and the London area as a whole.

Evaluation and Constant Improvement

As the success of any operation or project is determined by measuring a range of qualitative and quantitative factors, monitoring and evaluation have to be an integral component. However, on many occasions it is only included as an afterthought when there is a mad scramble to find post-event evidence for investors, supporters and senior management. If this is to be avoided, monitoring and evaluation techniques should be planned at the outset of any project or operation. So while on secondment to the national Safer Cities initiative in 1996, I put aside ten per cent of the entire budget for this.

Evaluation is important because it helps determine:

- Satisfaction levels of end-users before and after the new service or product is introduced.
- Sales turnover of a service or product together with profit margins.
- Increased efficiency and effectiveness of the business in the area of operation.
- Any displacement effect, either detrimental or positive, the new product or service may have on other business areas.
- The relative costs of the new service or operation as compared to the return it brings.

- Any further improvements that need introducing to make the new product or service even more efficient and effective.

- Any further problems in the service or production process that need to be addressed.

- Any future opportunities or threats to the project or operation that should be planned for.

Evaluation is basically an analysis of the movement over time of the factors listed above and is therefore an ongoing process.

One further key consideration is who is going to do the monitoring and evaluation. There are two schools of thought on this. One side of the argument says that this should be done by a completely independent and objective assessor, while the other side opts for an internal integrated approach.

In my experience there are a number of factors to weigh up if you are to make the best decision.

Cost

Getting an outside agency to undertake the monitoring and evaluation can add greatly to the credibility of the entire initiative as backers will have a high level of trust in the transparency of the findings. However, this can come at a high cost so a judgment call needs to be made as to the best balance between limiting potential reputational risk against the higher costs of doing so.

Integrity of Process

If the techniques used for evaluation are fallible and weak then these will be exposed by the closer examination of independent observers. Therefore, if the process of monitoring and evaluation is to be conducted internally, a framework should be developed by someone who knows what they are doing and is qualified and competent in these matters. Often a separate department should be responsible for this, giving the dual benefit of cost efficiency and objectiveness. Alternatively, a partnership or joint venture agreement could be established, with an independent organisation providing evaluation services on an ongoing basis and at a largely discounted rate.

False Accounting

With new initiatives, a hell of a lot is at stake for the credibility of both individuals and organisations. If the work culture is confused and operating standards weak, then any monitoring and evaluation process is open to compromise and manipulation. Even in cases where outside bodies are legally responsible for this process, the entire function can become vulnerable. Just consider for a moment the massive financial scandals that have been uncovered in recent years involving respected names such as KPMG and Price Waterhouse Coopers and which have involved the negligent auditing of accounts in several global companies.

Here the entire process was compromised by the highly lucrative consultancy contracts that sat alongside the auditing role. These put auditors under enormous pressure to paint a rosy picture of the client company or put at risk these high value revenue streams. Not surprisingly, even independent assessment won't always work under such conditions.

Baseline Positioning

Right at the outset and before any project or operation begins, research is needed to determine the current situation both statistically and qualitatively. This is fundamental in enabling progress to be monitored and evaluated properly. Don't skimp on this in the interests of 'just getting on with things'. Further investment and development will depend on you being able to show evidence of success that will justify your work. The baseline statistics you are looking for could include:

- Current sale levels of the product or service.
- The costs of the issue that the operation is going to address.
- The demographic and economic profile of the end-users of the product or service.

- The geographical profile of an area in terms of property, land usage and population density.

- Similar assessments of surrounding geographical areas, or the region as a whole, for comparison.

- The scope and type of problem or need to be addressed.

- The current behaviour trends of end-users towards the existing product or service provided.

- The current behaviour trends of end-users generally, without the proposed initiative.

- The dynamics of interaction between end-users and others around them.

As every operation or project has a budget, the next key consideration is which of these statistical components are you going to evaluate and how you are going to collect data about them for analysis on an ongoing basis?

This means that careful thought must be given to the relevance and value of any evaluation process. Simplicity, as ever, is very desirable and the outcomes and objectives we discussed earlier should be central to the decision making process.

As a first step, list the outcomes and objectives you have developed for the operation and, beside each of them, detail:

- What is needed to evidence activity in this area and for what purpose will this be required?

- What existing data sources could be used without additional cost, such as census information from the local authority?

- How could you automate your data collection requirements using the search fields of your existing computer systems? Field and key word selection could be vital in determining useful data sets and mean there may be no need to set up a special data collection process. Remember though, that the quality of data out will depend on the quality of data in.

- Is there a need to survey the end-users and executive staff before, during and after implementation for their observations on the process and outcomes? This could be done through online surveys, personal interviews or postal questionnaires. However, response rates will vary dramatically unless there is a strong incentive or vested interest in taking part.

Impact Assessment

A full impact evaluation, based on the monitoring data collected earlier, should be done during or at the conclusion of operational phases. So as to get a comprehensive understanding of the data, I used to divide the evaluation into quantitative and qualitative elements.

Qualitative assessment covers such elements as changed behaviours, feelings, satisfaction levels and perceived success, which is revealed by asking questions such as:

- Since the start of the project or operation, what has improved and in what way?
- Has the problem or need been addressed and to what degree?
- What has changed since the start of the project or operation in terms of behaviour of the end-user and those around them?
- What have been the management lessons learned from the implementation process?
- What needs doing next to take advantage of any further opportunities or to address emerging threats?

Quantitative assessment looks at the statistical factors that describe the outcome and process including:

- Increased or decreased levels of activity that are the result of the operation.
- The quality standards of outputs produced by the process.
- The costs associated with implementation as compared to the returns achieved.
- Comparative statistics from the areas immediately

surrounding and further afield where the operation or project has not been running.

Case Study – Operation Baseline with Professor Nick Tilley and SCD3 PhD Intern Students at Scotland Yard 2006-07

In 2006 I was Deputy Head of the Specialist Crime Directorates Serious Crime Reduction Team at Scotland Yard when the then Assistant Commissioner, Tarique Ghaffur, commissioned our unit to examine the hypothesis that 'victims of distinct communities are disproportionately affected by serious crime and yet less police resources may be proportionately allocated to deal with these offences.'

The stimulus for this was intelligence that indicated there was a heavy under-reporting by London's distinct communities of some very serious crimes for a variety of reasons, including language difficulties, fear of retribution, the victim's own illegal immigration status and distrust of the police based on their home country experiences.

London's distinct communities now speak a total of over 260 different languages, giving an indication of the vast ethnic diversity that is still growing.

Due to the scale of this undertaking, I estimated that the time and resources available to my unit were insufficient to cope and so I asked the two criminology students, mentioned earlier, to conduct research under the supervision of the renowned UK criminologist, Professor Nick Tilley of Nottingham Trent University. Together we set about establishing a methodology to examine the most problematic crimes – gang murders, blackmail, rape and commercial robbery – defined by four work streams that were:

1. A full examination of London demographics in partnership

---

with the GLA census analysis unit at City Hall.

2. An analysis of ten years' of recorded crimes in the categories above.

3. A six-week collection of live case statistics drawn from active investigations.

4. The interviewing of key community practitioners from the biggest distinct communities to qualitatively assess the impact of serious crime on their communities.

This methodology established a measurement criteria that relied principally on the Metropolitan Police computerised Crime Reporting System (CRIS), which all departments used to record initial details, the investigation and results of a case. This system also enabled comprehensive analysis of crime patterns. Progress was monitored weekly and an inter-department joint venture agreement was established with the department of information, who managed the CRIS system.

The final evaluation was in many ways unsurprising, but it did identify some alarming issues.

- While the census office information was very comprehensive, there was clear evidence that many residents had not responded to the survey or were not on the voters register at all.

- The census office definitions of ethnicity were quite different from those used by the police and clearly reform was needed to ensure that mutually agreed definitions were used so as to enable more meaningful analysis of the statistics and any correlations between them.

- There was clear evidence that the major distinct communities of London were disproportionally affected by serious crime, but this could only be gauged in the broadest of terms as the quality of victim information recorded on the CRIS was insufficient to allow for deeper analysis.

- There was a substantial and very alarming absence of ethnicity data recorded on the system with many inconsistencies even when it was.

- There was a lack of training, supervision and quality assurance in the use and application of the CRIS system that was crippling the organisation's ability to properly evaluate the impact of serious crime on distinct communities.

For these very reasons, many observers considered this research to be a failure, but I took a completely different view that the monitoring and evaluation methods used had thrown up fundamental weaknesses in, and threats to, our databases that needed addressing. Such issues were set out in detail and then forwarded to the senior ACPO officer responsible and the director of the department of information for action.

Quality Checks

As part of the monitoring process and final evaluation, quality standards must be closely examined. This should to be done with reference to the original quality settings determined during the planning stages. Remember, you want a quality that is fit for purpose and no more, otherwise the costs of implementation will escalate disproportionately. So, monitoring and evaluation needs to assess:

- The quality of the materials supplied to the operation within the inbound phase of the value chain.

- The skills, competence levels and numbers of staff engaged in the operation.

- The efficiency and effectiveness of the management systems that is being applied to the process. Achieving accreditation for British and international quality assurance standards such as ISO 9000 while admirable, must never become a 'tick box' exercise, where the real quality of end-user experience is compromised in favour of a process-driven enterprise, something I have witnessed on far too many occasions. However, used well, such accreditations can improve consistency of delivery.

- The effectiveness of the product or service in meeting customer need and expectations.

- The durability of the service or product in terms of its usable length of life.

End-user Feedback

Ultimately, it is the end-user who determines the relative success of a project or operation whether this is in the public, private or the voluntary sector.

For instance, on occasions my friends and relatives were the victims of crime and so I received first hand reports about the relative strengths, and the level of care and professionalism of the attending police. There was often a wide variance in their experiences, ranging from the outstanding to the negligent.

As a supervisor, I was only too well aware of the need for care and consistency towards crime victims in the face of relentless demand and how many factors such as training, supervision, leadership, personality, how busy the day was and professional knowledge, go into creating a good response.

Feedback is fundamental to the evaluation process and this needs to be collected using a variety of appropriate methods that include:

- Telephone or internet spot checks which ask the end-user about their experience.

- Personal interviewing of end-users to get a complete and detailed description of their experience, including both the good and bad points.

- Participation in postal or internet surveys by end-users in exchange for prizes.

- Suggestion boxes, positioned in easily accessible sites, where anonymous comments can be posted about the service received or product bought.

- Focus groups at which paid end-users can discuss the relative merits and faults of a product or service. These groups should be facilitated by a trained professional who can elicit information and enable the group to properly debate the issues.

- Observation using video, photographs or even CCTV coverage over a 24/7 period, of the service or product actually in use. This may detect behavioural changes between day and night that could provide a very valuable means of evaluation. For example, I used CCTV and video footage to observe the vulnerability of pedestrians to pickpocketing and robbery in central London. As a result, design changes were made to barriers, signage and road junctions, which altered behaviour patterns for the better and led to an easing of troublesome congestion points.

Continuous Improvement

The information provided by end-user feedback provides an excellent source of information on how to constantly improve the efficiency and effectiveness of any product or service. And this quest for constant improvement is a way of thinking that should be built into the DNA of you and your team, as your survival and success will be directly linked to this attitude.

But for constant improvement to occur, two fundamentals must be considered. These are first, changing circumstances and second, the need to sustain competitive advantage over your rivals.

Case Study – Crime Prevention Furniture Design with Partners Central St Martin's School of Fashion and Design, the Capital Link Partnership and Whitbread Pubs 1998-99

During my secondment to the Westminster Safer Cities Programme in 1998, I established an entirely new charitable limited company called Capital Link. And under this partnership umbrella sat The Spatial Design and Management Working Group, which was grappling with the age-old problem of personal theft in pubs, bars and restaurants within the West End area of central London. The taking of handbags, briefcases and holdalls from beside sitting and standing customers was running at an unprecedented scale and amounted to at least one third of *all* recorded crime (3,000 cases a year in just our area of interest alone).

The thefts involved organised gangs of smartly dressed men and women who used distraction techniques to steal bags and cases, the contents of which were then gone through in a back alley or toilets. Valuables were taken and anything else dumped in builders' skips, on waste ground or just out on the street. The devastation from this type of crime is considerable as it not only causes immediate shock but also much inconvenience later as door and car keys, laptops and work papers have to be replaced. So, the trauma was considerable for all the victims with great damage done to the area's reputation. I also had a personal interest in stopping this type of crime, given that DC Jim Morrison, a close colleague, had been murdered by a bag thief he was trying to arrest in 1990 in the same area.

While many ideas, such as the 'Chelsea' table clip or improving cloakroom facilities, had already been tried, it struck me that what we needed was an even greater range of design options, and where better to get them from than the Central Saint Martins College of Fashion and Design? The college was located in the area and attracted undergraduate and postgraduate students from around the world, all eager to earn the college's prestigious qualifications in textiles, industrial and graphic design. What's more, as the students were also regular customers of the area's pubs and clubs they had a vested interest in solving the problem so using them made perfect sense.

My suggestion of a joint venture with the college was met with great enthusiasm and there began a lasting relationship that eventually developed into a full research and development centre called 'Design against Crime'. This ultimately resulted in another venture with the UK Design Council. The added benefit of this joint venture was that our new links with international designers and manufacturers gave us a clear opportunity of mainstreaming the best innovations.

The following are just some of the principal development stages we went through to tackle the problem of bag theft:

1. I gave a fully illustrated briefing to selected students from the graphics and industrial design courses about the scale of the problem and the methods used by the criminals to execute their crimes. This involved demonstrations, statistical analysis and visuals about the spatial considerations in hotspot locations.

2. Storyboards and concepts were then worked up by the students. These were exhibited later in the school's main exhibition halls together with other Capital Link projects and area profile information gathered using police helicopter footage of pinch points and hotspot crime locations. Local residents, businesses, police crime prevention officers and stakeholders were invited along and their feedback canvassed on the pros and cons of each design.

3. A feasibility matrix was then created to assess the best design options and a short list of preferred projects drawn up. This included tabletop warning cards, public

information films that could be played in bars and chair and table designs that incorporated an anti-theft insert into their frame on which personal items could be hung.

4. I invited a number of venue operators to the exhibition, one of which, the Whitbread Pubs Group PLC, showed a keen interest in trialling prototypes in their Leicester Square Hogshead venue.

5. An assortment of measures were further developed for this location, including additional staff training, revised crime reporting system, the collection of qualitative feedback and intelligence, and changes to furniture design to accommodate the new security measures.

6. The programme was introduced for one year and then evaluated by the police quality assurance unit at Charing Cross police station. Satisfyingly, the theft of personal property plunged dramatically by 70 per cent during the trial.

The success of such work is testament to the opportunity afforded by systematic problem solving and exemplary design. I was truly inspired by this project and so were Whitbread who were surprised and delighted by the competitive advantage these measures gave them by boosting their reputation for security, customer care and staff safety.

Section 3

Developing Your Team

Introduction

Your team needs to be treated like a second family.

It consists of different personalities and people at different levels of maturity, experience and skill. Just like any family it goes through periods of difficulty with bouts of tension and conflict. But its strength lies in the mutual support it gives in caring for each other and enabling development through shared learning, experience and discipline.

Some observers may disagree with this opinion and suggest a much more clinical performance-orientated approach where people just get on with the job in hand and nothing more. My career of front line policing and management experience has clearly shown me that this attitude does not foster the kind of cohesion and supportive atmosphere that is so crucial for high performance achievement.

Take the British military as a classic example.

Through the ages and even to this day, the esprit de corps, camaraderie and working for each other has been our armed forces' paramount philosophy and something that has done much to help create its well-deserved world-wide reputation for excellence.

On the big screen, Steven Spielberg and Tom Hanks exemplified this in their outstanding portrayal of C Company 101st Airborne Division in the World War II tv drama 'Band of Brothers', which starred Damien Lewis. This film was a testament to how a closely knit team with the right leadership, can keep going and eventually succeed in the face of great adversity.

On the VIP Close Protection course I took shortly after leaving the police, I had the pleasure of working with soldiers, some of whom were Special Forces. I was truly astounded at the way this group of complete strangers quickly got to know each other and bonded. Without posturing or squabbling we applied ourselves day and night to the various exercises we were set, dividing up the responsibilities and tasks with startling speed. This was all done with humour, compassion and total selflessness. It reminded me of my earlier days in the police when team effort was held in the highest esteem, something that now has changed to the obvious detriment of the service.

In this section I reveal what I believe to be the crucial elements of creating a fantastic team, which moves gradually from just a group of people doing things together to the creation of a truly homogenous unit with great synergy and high levels of performance. When this point arrives, it's a real pleasure and an honour going into work each day to complete a worthwhile task alongside colleagues who are so committed and supportive.

Choosing the Right Type of Team

Types of Team Work

Each situation dictates the type of team required to deal with it and the methods that must be used. So as a manager this means that you have to select the right people with the right skills and aptitudes to do what's needed.

Given modern ways of working, this may necessitate people having to change their roles and methods frequently. For example, from day to day, staff must be prepared to contribute to different teams or even be temporarily drafted to them away from their normal work. This is definitely not a case of one size fits all.

What's important to emphasise though is that it is likely that all these different functions will have to be fulfilled by a single group of people who feel that they belong together, possess an underlying sense of ownership of and responsibility towards what needs to be done.

Functional Team Roles

A modern operations team must be adaptable. So, while individuals within it may have particular specialisms and skills that are their core signature, they will still be expected to contribute as circumstances dictate. Such flexibility and adaptability is a crucial key to success in fast changing situations when you could find yourself having to switch between different types of team, such as:

The Operations Team

Here, consistency and constancy of effort and quality is fundamental. A manufacturing production line is a classic example of this, where what is produced cannot be allowed to differ from what is expected. Such consistency of output is also applicable to the public sector, including the emergency services. After all, end-users don't want to be faced with great variations of professionalism and effectiveness every time they call for the police or an ambulance.

While there is a difference in complexity between producing a loaf of bread and dealing with a multi-issue domestic assault involving real people, there are common themes between them in terms of prompt delivery of service, interest in and care for the end-user and the professional knowledge required to ensure problems are dealt with directly and effectively.

Some of the main functional elements required when heading up an operations team are:

- Ensuring the outstanding training of personnel in all necessary key skills, for example, quality control, customer care, general management, supplies and logistics.

- Assessing if staff have reached the required competence through appraisal, examination and observation.

- Observing if end-users are being properly served by regular quality spot checks on staff and outputs.

- Establishing highly effective automated and manual process systems to achieve the best efficiency of output.

- Instilling a philosophy of constant improvement that encourages suggestions, innovation and problem-solving as a way to ratchet up the effectiveness of the operations team.

The Multi-disciplinary Team

To give a greater degree of flexibility, roles sometimes need to be interchangeable which means that individual staff members should be expected to perform tasks beyond their core skill areas. For example, in my policing career when I was on an emergency response team, my mix of supervisory management roles included control room duties in computerised dispatch, incident control and quality control. Alongside this, I was also trained as a search manager, a prisoner custody officer and a tactical advisor for raids and special operations, so that from one day to the next I could be assigned different roles according to the need. Being able to function to best advantage in a multi-disciplinary team requires the ability:

- To mentally refocus on different sets of responsibilities and then to choose and use an appropriate skill set.

- To be highly flexible, valuing variety and constant challenge. You cannot be set in your ways.

The Problem-solving Team

From time to time, staff will be expected to contribute to a special problem-solving exercise that uses their acquired experience and skills to develop a response to a specific issue or need. Mostly this will be slow time work that necessitates an analytical, creative, perceptive mindset and highly collaborative approach to working with other internal and external agencies. The main requirements here are:

- The ability to pick apart a problem or issue in a systematic and thorough manner so as to identify its causal factors.

- A creative approach to developing new responses to a situation, but which are still appropriate and realistic.

- The ability to work with others in an open-minded and collaborative fashion.

The Specialist Project or Operational Team

Sometimes the technical demands of a situation are such that the skills of specialists need to be drawn together in a team, each member concentrating on their own core skill, though with a full understanding of all the others' roles. For example, a special project or operations team might be created to develop a civil engineering initiative, such as a new bridge, or to respond to an armed hostage situation, as is the case with a police Special Weapons Operations Team (SWOT). Here you will need:

- Exemplary planning and organisation skills from the team leader.

- Intimate knowledge, awareness and empathy between team members, so they can move and think as an integrated unit.

- Exemplary technical knowledge and competence from each team member in their area of expertise.

One of the best examples I can give to illustrate this type of work comes from the Toronto Emergency Task Force in Canada, to which I was attached for a series of night duties in 1995.

The Task Force provides 24/7 coverage to the Toronto region, responding to all specialist emergencies such as the discovery of explosive devices, armed sieges, hostage situations and set piece pre-planned operations. The entire command operated from a single base with its own integrated infrastructure of vehicles, equipment and communications. Each team had specialists trained in tactical command and control, sniping, explosives, radio and technical surveillance measures, negotiation and building-entry techniques. All worked, trained and lived together which ensured that the levels of camaraderie and effectiveness increased exponentially.

Unlike the Metropolitan Police, which calls in separate departments to an incident, the Toronto teams were seamless units. So while each team member was a specialist, not a generalist with constantly interchangeable roles, they nevertheless worked as a homogenous team with breathtaking efficiency and a complete understanding and awareness between them. Everything that they needed in terms of equipment and expertise was also there on one armoured truck ensuring no wasted time. They even enjoyed the benefit of a unified administrative system.

I reported my findings to Scotland Yard on my return and sought to encourage a similar approach. Not surprisingly, I came up against some very dogged asset control power politics in senior echelons. To many it seemed, there was a clear advantage to themselves in separating out the specialist commands rather than taking a more holistic approach that was obviously better for all.

Team Dynamics

Just what goes into making a great team?

I have reflected long and hard on this and the clearest analogy I can find is that it is like preparing a gourmet meal, and although this is something of a cliché, there are many similarities between the two.

First, quality ingredients are needed that complement each other in flavour and texture. Then those ingredients have to be organised and mixed by a chef who has a clear vision of the outcome they are aiming for. Once the ingredients are mixed and heat applied to them, the mixture takes on a natural momentum as quality materials and the expertise combine. In this there is a high degree of artistic intuition, as no top chef follows a recipe but instead feels their way forward based on experience, skill and intuition. This is where science meets art.

Let's consider this idea from the perspective of the team.

The Leader and Manager

I use the words 'leadership' and 'management' with care, as I equate a leader with someone who has a high degree of intuition, while a manager is proficient in the use of management tools and methods. So one injects the artistry and the other the scientific method, and both need to be present in an outstanding operations manager.

But these qualities don't appear overnight. They have to be developed through experience, training and nurturing to ensure the quiet self-confidence necessary to assert yourself as required. So, while my confidence was non-existent at the start of my management career, through brutal exposure to tough situations I grew to trust myself and my judgment. I displayed this not in a loud arrogant way but through clear rational thinking backed by meticulous planning and organisation.

Your role then, as leader, is to organise and galvanise your team into action around a common purpose using proven management methods and a high degree of intuitive direction and guidance.

Individual Team Members

These are the main ingredients of a team and, believe me, if you get this right you can do incredible things with very limited resources. Each individual will come to you with their unique 'signature' that's made up of:

- Their competence in key skills. This will be evidenced by their academic and professional qualifications, but more particularly by their actual real-time delivery in these areas.

- Their personality traits that encompass factors such as their sense of humour, how positive they are by nature and personal qualities like tenacity, patience and tolerance. These are key in putting together a team because they are the oil between the cogs without which you won't have cohesion, momentum, or eventually any team at all.

- Their willingness to accept the need for change, development and constant improvement. This is vital because without these qualities, performance of both individual and team will be stunted at best and at worst destroyed because of a lack of flexibility.

How Individuals Must Complement Each Other

Meredith Belbin in his research for the Henley Management School, pointed out how people with different skills, personality and aptitudes blend much better than a group of Alpha driven leaders – the surest and fastest route to conflict and catastrophe. So, when selecting who works with whom on a particular functional role, the key thing is to base your decision on how well people complement or contrast with each other.

Leadership 'Tone'

In bringing together a team, the first point to consider here is the influence the leader has in setting the 'tone' for the entire team:

- The leader will look to influence the behaviour of individuals in the team so that characteristics that complement the leader's are amplified, while those that annoy them are suppressed. Progression and survival within the team will be dependent on this ability. If the leader sets a good example this will accelerate team performance while the opposite is also true.

- The expectations of the leader as to the behaviour and performance of team members should be explicit and clear, something I discussed earlier.

- The leader must develop a very motivating vision of purpose for the team, one which has clear objectives and outcomes.

Technical Competence

Depending on the role of the team, thought should be given to the technical abilities of team members:

- In some instances, the entire team needs to have a basic competence in particular fields of expertise to allow for interchangeability and flexibility. In my latter role reducing serious and organised crime, my team was expected to be able to do basic research, problem solving, analysis and project management.

- Are the technical demands of the role such that dedicated specialists are required for key positions who will then work with each other on a common task?

Personality

There is a strange chemistry that sometimes enables opposites to get on extremely well with each other whilst at other times this can be disastrous as values, beliefs and personality traits all come into play in a strange high-octane mix that can explode. A person's sense of humour in particular can have a startling effect on those around them, putting others at ease, making for enjoyable company and creating a 'resonance of understanding' among the team.

There is no easy answer as to why this does or doesn't happen, so it is vital for team leaders to closely observe those under their supervision for signs of positive or negative interaction. Sometimes conflict can be a good thing by creating an edge to competitive rivalry that heightens performance, however on other occasions it can simply make someone withdraw and become less effective. Some of the first class psychometric tests now available can help determine the best candidates to put together for any given role.

Aptitude for Change

One difficult team member who dislikes change can slowly destroy team performance and morale. Being set in their ways and never entering into their stretch zone can act like a dragging anchor on performance. Selection processes need to identify these individuals at the outset, while existing team members with this attitude are carefully coached and developed so as to instill in them greater flexibility.

What Outcome Do You Want?

Just what are you trying to achieve is a fundamental question for any operations manager.

If your purpose is worthwhile and has clarity, this can be a very motivating factor for the entire team, as they will feel that their efforts are worthwhile and that they are contributing an essential piece to the jigsaw. This is something that I discussed earlier in the *Making Things Happen* section, but it's worth reiterating here as this is an essential component of effective team working.

By keeping the team focused on the big picture and the final outcome, especially when the going is tough, or work is menial and boring, you will be able to keep your staff concentrated and still applying the effort that's needed for success. So the leader needs to keep spelling this out at progress and review meetings, by illustrating how each element of the work fits into the success of the final outcome.

How to Mix Individuals to Achieve this Aim

However good they are, if the individuals in your team are not mixed properly and carefully, the results will always be patchy and inconsistent.

This is where the balance between individual, team and task maintenance issues is so important, something that John Adair, the leadership guru, articulates so well. If the focus of effort is too biased towards one of these elements, the entire ship will become lopsided and unsafe.

During the later stages of my career, I worked in a team that pioneered many extraordinary projects to reduce serious and organised crime in Scotland Yard's Specialist Crime Directorate. We worked flat out, sometimes 12-14 hours a day and weekends included, as the number of teenage deaths from gang, gun and knife crime spiked and the pressures to come up with new strategic and tactical approaches increased. As part of that work, I spent many months visiting America's Pacific Coast to gain experience and to engage with key researchers and practitioners, such as Professor David Kennedy, director of the pioneering Boston Ceasefire Program.

During this period, it is fair to say that our office became ever more task-oriented, with the needs of the individual or team becoming secondary to 'doing things'. What I became aware of in myself and others was that there was very little recognition of our efforts, time for any training became almost impossible and there was almost a pedantic attitude to the quality of our outputs.

Our purpose may have been fine and motivating, but there was such pressure on us to deliver a plethora of projects that work became very demoralising. To combat this I embarked on a series of initiatives to help build individual and team development. This included a new professional training course on serious crime prevention led by Professor Nick Tilley and Dr Gloria Laycock of University College London; the creation of thematic discussion forums for the team; intensifying the quality of staff appraisals; and various recommendations for revising individual training courses.

As leader and manager getting the balance right requires some very determined and focused planning in order to:

- Constantly assess the priorities you are faced with so that you can make best use of your available resources.

- Resist the pressure from above to take on new work beyond your capacity. After all, it will be you who is judged on the quality of your outputs and outcomes achieved, nothing else.

- Nurture, encourage and develop individual team members through effective appraisal techniques and appropriate training. I discuss this in greater detail later.

- Create room to breathe for the team so that you can socialise together and have open discussions during which you let off steam or contribute a different perspective. This all helps bonding and understanding.

Gender and Cultural Considerations

In so many instances today the issue of gender and culture has had a bad press with numerous stories of prejudice and tensions caused by misunderstanding or insensitivity. I have always tried as a manager to keep focused on the overall performance of a team while still giving high regard to personal circumstances and encouraging the development of potential regardless of culture or gender. I have always found that by displaying common courtesies at work or socially, gender or cultural issues rarely come into the equation. Rather, differences in attitudes and skills actually provide a great opportunity for increasing the adaptability and performance of any team. Therefore, these differences should be valued and treasured particularly with many teams these days being brought together from around the world to work on a specific purpose, project or task.

I have worked on many different teams containing a mixture of gender and ethnicities. Moreover, I have also often been managed directly by female or other senior officers of different ethnicities or cultures. I have been able to observe their many different strengths and qualities."

Women and Men

Needless to say, women and men are starkly different from each other in nature. However, both need the other's strengths to be effective so while the points below are generalisations, I have largely found them to apply.

- Men tend to be extremely good strategists and see the big picture. They can objectively analyse a situation and identify the main links, weaknesses and opportunities for development.

- Women tend to be extremely good tacticians and work very well with detail making sure things are finished and done properly.

- Men enjoy working with women because they are different and often there is a sexual frisson between them that can be very positive, unless the relationship steps over a professional threshold and becomes too personal.

- Women tend to be more sensitive and diplomatic in their interactions with others at meetings and in the office.

- Men tend to be extremely good at prioritising things and taking decisive action when needed.

Cultural Differences

I have worked alongside many officers and civilian staff of various ethnic, religious and cultural backgrounds. I have also worked alongside gay staff who have been courageous, loyal, funny and completely selfless.

I remember an occasion when one of my close colleagues, a gay sergeant at Notting Hill, who had a prolific record of arrests, apprehended a violent man and called for a police van. With none available and the sergeant determined to bring the offender into custody rather than releasing him back onto the street, he handcuffed him hand and foot and bundled him into the boot of his saloon car. Arriving at the back yard of the police station he walked to the rear of his car, from where there were muffled shouts and screams, and trying to avoid being seen, opened the boot. Unfortunately, just at this moment the chief inspector operations came out of his office and watched the entire scene unfold.

This assortment of backgrounds, values and beliefs I think is a testament to how different people can work effectively together. It's not without its problems though and in managing a diverse team you need to be aware of certain factors such as:

- Asian staff members who may be much more reticent about coming forward in public meetings or group discussions with their suggestions or challenges. Often it is best to canvass their opinion separately before the meeting and when on their own.

- Criticism of staff from certain cultures is sometimes considered insulting and an affront to their honour. So, while development issues connected to performance must *not* be ignored, they should be treated in a sensitive way.

- Women in leadership roles may be viewed critically in some instances by Asian staff due to the traditional decision making role of men in their culture. However, this attitude is changing fast because of the increasing integration of the genders in professional workplaces across the world.

- Private and domestic situations may also need careful handling to avoid resentment and distress. I remember a delightful Indian civilian colleague at Scotland Yard who married a very young bride from his home village and brought her back to London to live. One morning she phoned him in a complete state of distress because of the heavy rain that was falling on the conservatory roof and creating a din, something she had never experienced before. Her husband had to go home to reassure her and explain that this was a common English phenomenon.

While both gender and cultural differences give depth and strength to a team, at the end of the day, staff are there to do a good job and so should be selected and appraised on this basis. If the selection methods I discuss later are applied carefully, then you will develop a balanced team of different skills, aptitudes and personalities whatever their gender or cultural background. The key is to develop selection criteria that are appropriate to the roles and objectives the staff are going to perform and pursue.

Joint Ventures and Partnerships

Another aspect of modern teamwork is joining forces with people from other agencies or organisations to get a job done. This presents a completely different set of challenges as team members may not be under your line management and there could be a complete contrast of work cultures.

In 2007, while project managing the London Pathways initiative to counter gang violence, I experienced this first hand when working alongside representatives from the prison and probation services who had starkly different work cultures from what I was used to. So while probation service representatives were driven by the ideology of rehabilitation, those on the prison side of things were guided by the need for good order inside jail to stop rioting. From the police's perspective the wider protection of the public from danger was the prime focus.

Of course, all had a part to play in this holistic approach that used their respective powers, resources and expertise but it required a great deal of tact and a thorough mapping out of common areas of interest and respective constraints. This meant I had to immerse myself in the other agencies' agendas before I could effectively chair any meetings. The benefit of this effort, although time consuming, was astounding, but it did need a particularly inclusive and flexible leadership attitude that is often missing.

I have lost count of the number of initiatives in which the police representative bounded into the room wanting to take control but without any understanding of anyone else's perspective. Inevitably on these occasions, there was almost always a complete breakdown of relations within the team and therefore loss of effectiveness. However, by taking the time and trouble to understand the other side you will gain trust and respect. Quite rightly, Steven Covey emphasises this as one of his guiding principles of high performing people.

The last aspect of this way of team working concerns accountability and responsibility, something I discussed in 'Making it Happen'. If joint initiatives aren't to become just talking shops with no action or delivery there need to be clear terms of reference and a joint venture agreement with roles and responsibility for all the work defined.

Mixing and Matching Individuals to the Team

Managing What You Start With

Unless you are very fortunate, you will inherit an existing group of people from whoever you take over from. This can be daunting, frustrating and challenging as members of the old team are often set in their ways, for better or worse, and may very well be difficult characters who are either underperforming or disrupting others through their behaviour.

Remember, people are complicated and as the most expensive and valuable of resources, it requires much time and effort to shape them into the fighting unit that you want. But however long is needed, you must take the time to do this, otherwise you can do more harm than good by bounding around like a bull in a china shop. There will be egos, relationships, sensitivities, personal troubles and behaviour traits in abundance, sufficient to fill any exotic menagerie, and all have to be managed.

To 'house train' a team, I would recommend the following approach even though it can take anything up to two years to achieve the transformation needed.

1. Obtain a very full briefing from your predecessor about the team's portfolio of work and more particularly, a complete run down on each individual regarding their:

   o Personality and behaviour traits.

   o Competency levels.

   o Current performance levels.

   o Their ability to work with others.

   o Any office relationships either of conflict or allegiance.

   o Personal difficulties.

2. Before doing anything, think carefully about your leadership style because you will need to determine how you are going to behave and interact with the team. This was discussed in the section on *You as an Individual Manager*.

3. Treat the briefing from your predecessor with a degree of caution. Forewarned may be forearmed, *but* do not make pre-judgments based on what you have been told as this may be inaccurate or coloured by personal prejudices and beliefs. Concentrate instead on thinking about the work portfolio and the team members and then consider your options for consolidation and dealing with difficult individuals. Remember, just because people are difficult does not necessarily mean that they are underperforming. Sometimes quite the opposite is the case. If you had Apple's former CEO and icon Steve Jobs in your team how long would he have lasted with his difficult behaviour? But by getting rid of such people, you may be killing the golden goose. Just bear this in mind, and plan for different scenarios.

4. As a leader and manager, I have found it best to set the tone and your broad expectations for your staff from day one. In a fast paced department with high risk situations, stuff just happens all the time and if you leave several weeks or months to slip by without declaring what sort of ship you intend to run and the basic behaviours that you expect, there could be consequences.

I do not mean however, that you should throw your weight around by changing everything and posturing – that would be disastrous. But staff will want to know who you are and what you stand for. If the team know where the lines are, if there are any clear breaches then they cannot pretend they did not know what they could and couldn't do because you had let things drift for a while.

So make a short clear positional statement upfront that defines and describes:

o Who you are and your previous experience and specialisms.

o What term of address you expect in formal meetings and socially.

o The importance of the department to the organisation's future.

o The basic behaviour standards of dress, language and courtesy to others that you expect daily in the office and at meetings.

o Your lack of tolerance for any displays of posturing, bullying, selfishness or other inappropriate behaviours.

o Some of the broad performance objectives you want to develop or sustain.

o Your accessibility when it comes to receiving suggestions, complaints or talking about personal difficulties.

o Your wish to observe working practices and get to know staff for a suitable period before considering any changes.

5. Observe everyone closely and keep a journal of all your observations and comments over the course of several months:

- Meet each team member on their own and after viewing their record of achievement and appraisals so as to get to know them. Then you can assess:

  o What's given them satisfaction in their work?

  o What achievements are they proud of and why?

  o What are their aspirations and objectives?

  o What areas do they want to develop in themselves?

  o What are the opportunities and threats facing the department from their perspective?

  o Watch the interaction of both staff and team leaders for signs of:

    » Tension and conflict.

    » Overfamiliarity.

    » Close alliances.

    » Effective collaboration.

    » Courtesy and selflessness.

    » Inappropriate behaviour such as bullying, sexism or racism.

  o Seek to discover the competency levels of each person in terms of their technical abilities and softer skills such as planning, negotiating, team work communication and leadership qualities.

  o Make an assessment of the current staff appraisal system's efficiency and effectiveness. Use the methods discussed later under *Team engagement and performance.*

6. Conduct Belbin, DISC and Myers Briggs psychometric tests of your staff to identify the skills, personalities and aptitudes present in the current team. Collate your results into a matrix using the techniques previously explained in the *You as an individual manager* section.

7. Write up your observations into a full team development report that covers the following areas:

- Individual competence levels of staff members in both hard and soft skill areas. (See below for more information)

- Individual personality and aptitude traits.

- Positive and negative interaction levels between staff members.

- The balance of technical and soft skills on the team and whether this is sufficient to meet the main department objectives in terms of time, quality and cost.

- The balance between individual, team and task orientated priorities.

- The need for individual and team training in specialist or broad areas of importance. Consider introducing a training needs assessment and indicate who you think could supply this.

- Opportunities for the staff appraisal system to be improved.

- A time-lined action plan with the scheduled phases and stages needed to implement change.

- A calculation of the main costs required to implement any changes.

8. Get the backing of your line manager by presenting your findings and a recommended plan of action.

9. Brief your team carefully about your findings and the phased action plan to bring about any improvements. In particular, your team supervisors and leaders need to be very clear about the staff appraisal system that you now expect them to use, as this will form the bedrock from which you assess rewards, recognitions, development needs and sanctions. This will probably need a separate training day with your HR officer for this.

10. Implement the action plan in phases and stages.

11. Using the appraisal system, start to identify staff of potential for progression, specialist development or official recognition. Likewise, underperforming staff need to be managed effectively through coaching, training and encouragement. In some cases, proceedings will have to be taken to sanction or remove staff if they are not willing or able to effect change in themselves. This must be based on the hard evidence that comes from an objective appraisal system not on personal prejudice. There is a big difference.

Inevitably, you are going to have to manage some very difficult characters that you have inherited. My golden rule in such situations is 'Don't pass the monkey on'. By this I mean it is your duty and role to deal with these situations and not to pass the buck with a quick transfer to another unit or department, who then may have to deal with the same factors but which, by then, may well have become even more deep seated, as a result of your negligence. Apply the same incisive problem solving techniques you used for business issues to the person in question.

And what makes them difficult?

Is it their inappropriate behaviour, conflict with certain individuals, selfishness or a personal agenda that is causing the problem? What are their strengths and how can these be amplified while minimising their weaknesses?

In some situations their underperformance has to be faced full on, without skirting around the core issues. This needs courage and assertiveness.

I was faced by just such a situation whilst overseeing the appraisal report of an officer under my command. He had been awarded an outstanding overall grade but I considered that there was insufficient evidence to justify this. I asked for this to be collected and the report re submitted. When this was unforthcoming the grade was reduced one notch. Several weeks later myself and all the line managers became subject of employment tribunal proceedings for racism and victimisation at the central London Tribunal Court in London. I will come back to this case later as its implications were so important

Personality and Technical Fit

Each team member comes with what I call a range of soft and hard skills - hard skills are technical and professional skills in specific fields of expertise such as engineering, accountancy or general management, while soft skills relate to personality traits and aptitudes such as tenacity, diplomacy or creativity.

Blending the attributes of one with those of another is both an art and science. If done well it creates synergy with the whole becoming greater than the sum of the parts. Matching people together requires careful thought, understanding and awareness, so, take your time over this because it can save you a whole bundle of trouble by helping to avoid conflict and disruption later.

Team Profiling

There are two types of psychometric profiling technique that I really commend to you:

- The first of these – the Belbin Test – looks at an individual's aptitude for teamwork and the role they can best perform within it using their soft and hard skills.

- The DISC test, which I discussed earlier under *You as an individual Manager*, complements this through a closer examination of the individual's personality traits in both relaxed and pressurised circumstances.

Belbin's Team Role Profile

In 1969, Dr Meredith Belbin undertook research for the Henley Business School on what characteristics made an effective and high performing team. Dr Belbin came to this work as a highly respected academic and industrialist having been the co-founder of the Industrial Training Research Unit, which was set up by the Manpower Services Commission.

Over the course of seven years, he completed detailed research using a ready source of material – high potential business managers attending the ten-week leadership course. He and his associate researchers, Bill Hartson a mathematician, Jeanne Fisher an anthropologist and Roger Mottram an occupational psychologist, developed three tests based on data compiled from the teams as they passed through the three annual courses. This information enabled them to draw conclusions about the contribution different types of individuals made to each team.

Their findings identified and defined nine specific roles within a team, and more importantly, demonstrated that successful teams were based on a mix of these types rather than the proliferation of just one. In other words, successful teams needed to be balanced and co-operative in nature.

The resulting personal and team profiling products and publications have now been accepted worldwide as a validated method of appraising and developing high performing teams.

The nine roles identified were:

Team Role	Contribution	Possible Team Roles
Plant	Creative, imaginative, free-thinking. Generates ideas and solves difficult problems	Active member of a problem solving team particularly in the option generation stage. An original and creative thinker
Resource Investigator	Outgoing, enthusiastic, communicative. Explores opportunities and develops contacts	Goes out and forages/ networks for information, equipment, finance, personnel and accommodation
Co-ordinator	Mature, confident, identifies talent. Clarifies goals. Delegates effectively	Chairman of team or work strand leader
Shaper	Challenging, dynamic, thrives on pressure. Has the drive and courage to overcome obstacles	Excellent team worker
Monitor Evaluator	Sober, strategic and discerning. Sees all options and judges accurately	Critically assesses the options and processes for strengths and weaknesses
Team worker	Co-operative, perceptive and diplomatic. Listens and averts friction	Good basic teamworker who can also mediate and be effective in conflict resolution
Implementer	Practical, reliable, efficient. Turns ideas into actions and organises work that needs to be done	Excellent operations executive
Completer Finisher	Painstaking, conscientious, anxious. Searches out errors. Polishes and perfects	Makes sure quality standards met and is a good finisher who ensures all details covered
Specialist	Single-minded, self-starting, dedicated. Provides knowledge and skills in rare supply	Specialist expert in narrow topic field

I have used this profiling technique extensively in my own police management role and to assess my own team contribution so I can vouch for its relevance and usefulness.

The skill here is in ensuring that the right types of personality are in a project team. This is not always easy to do as you have to work with what you are given, which means there is often an over emphasis on skill and experience rather than personality traits.

However, by adopting Dr Belbin's findings to your selection methods you will be well on the way to creating a high performing team. You can find out more at the Belbin Resource website (http://www.belbin.com/rte.asp?id=3) where there are many free and purchasable products.

Both the Belbin and DISC tests have a real value not just from a team management point of view, but also from the perspective of individual staff members, as it will help them discover their own strengths and aptitudes. This is crucial for their self-development and progression planning.

When you introduce these tests, explain carefully to the team why you are doing so, that way they won't feel like guinea pigs in a glorified experiment. And you can bring them online either as standalone tests or as part of the appraisal system.

Selection for Success

Selecting for success is one of the most important functions of your management career, so I'll discuss it at some length.

By gathering around you the right people with the right attitudes and skills, your task as a manager becomes considerably easier and team performance will take off. So, you skimp on doing this at your peril.

I have witnessed countless occasions when use of a weak selection procedure has resulted in a totally inappropriate person being appointed. This can have disastrous consequences that are then very difficult to correct.

Modern selection methods may be scrupulously fair, but in my experience they often miss crucial points of consideration and so can become just tick box exercises. I have been on the wrong end of this myself many times.

There are two primary situations when selection becomes critical. The first is when appointing a totally new person to a vacant position in your team, and second in the selection of a suitable team member for a specific task or project. Both require similar methods, although the first is far more important as this is a long-term position with clear contractual implications.

I have outlined some of the main considerations below and indicated, where appropriate, different degrees of emphasis.

Roles and Job Description

Obviously, these need to be given careful thought. I have seen many occasions in the police when the job description has not been given proper consideration which has then led to disputes and difficulties in the delegation of jobs or in completing appraisals because the baseline role was never properly defined in the first place. The factors in creating an appropriate role or job description include:

- **Departmental Priorities**. What is the department's main purpose and how will the role or job support this? This should be very much about both the current and future position. In a dynamic environment the candidate must be made aware of the need for continuous adaption and improvement.

- **Areas of Accountability**. What exactly will the candidate be responsible for? This will need some explanation as misunderstandings can lead to many inappropriate applications from unsuitable candidates. Which staff members will the person be responsible for supervising, and in which work areas will the person be held to account for their performance? It should also be made clear if this is to be a highly specialised role or a more generalist position needing a high degree of interchangeability between functions.

- **Personal Task Responsibilities.** What are the specific tasks the appointee will be responsible for, such as staff appraisals, and to what standard will they be expected to work? Activities that are deemed too important to be delegated, should be described here.

- **Length of Tenure/Contract.** What will be the expected tenure of the position before the person can apply for another vacancy? Knowing this helps prevent major disruption caused by a highly transient staff base.

- **Accountable to whom?** To whom will the appointee report to about their personal and team performance, and what will be their position? This person will also be responsible for their welfare, development and appraisals.

- **Salary and Pay Scales.** An indication should be given about the pay levels. This could be within a range and dependent on the candidate's experience and credentials and is something that will need negotiation.

- **Place of Work.** Where will the person be based and what will be the level of administrative support available to them? This also needs to make clear the need for travel to satellite sites and for other work purposes as necessary.

- **Credentials Required.** The main qualifications and attributes required to do the job should be outlined. There may be a professional requirement for specific qualifications or accreditation of competency that will form a minimum acceptable benchmark for the position.

- **Selection Process Requirements.** I think it is also reasonable to make it clear that you will require the person to undergo a selection process that might involve an interview, a presentation exercise or psychometric testing using any of the methods described earlier. It should be explained that these tests are necessary because you need someone with particular technical skills, personality and aptitude to fit in with the team.

- **References and Referees**. Though this is a most important area for consideration, it is one that is all too often omitted or neglected. In many ways, this is your insurance policy as it is the referees who are being asked to vouch for the competence and character of a candidate. If they cover up in the interests of moving a difficult person on then they are the ones who can be challenged in the future if glaring behaviour traits or incompetence are revealed. This should be made very clear to them when you are researching the candidate and that they must give a candid opinion of the individual. Obtain a mixture of references so you get different perspectives from line managers, end-users and work colleagues.

The Job Specification

The purpose of a job specification is to set out in more detail the qualities and skills you are looking for in anyone who is going to carry out the role. It will explain the skills, personality and aptitude needed in anyone who is to be effective in the position. They should be used not just for new appointments but task allocations as well.

The job specification can also be a very helpful piece of management evidence as you keep it in your decision log, along with the job description, and produce it during appraisals or at moments of accountability. This will help demonstrate your thought processes and the care you have taken about decisions.

A job specification should always go with the job description, and can be as detailed or as concise as necessary to fit the purpose.

Skills and Competency

These need to be defined for both the hard and soft skill areas, as discussed earlier. They may include professional qualifications that are a prerequisite for the position or other appropriate competencies in areas such as communication, strategic awareness, planning and organisation. I strongly recommend that you refer to national guidelines on this that are produced by organisations such as the

Chartered Institute of Personnel and Development. They have a list of the positive traits required for numerous roles, that can act as indicators of competency and can be used as criteria for selection.

Personality Traits

These are the personal qualities that you are seeking in a candidate and can cover areas such as the need for tact and diplomacy, tenacity, confidentiality and having a positive and creative outlook. Using psychometric tests you can identify if the candidate:

- Is task or people orientated.
- Will perform well as part of a team.
- Has sufficient drive and determination
- Has the skills needed to influence others.
- Has the necessary attention to detail
- Possesses values and beliefs in life that will be compatible with the team.

Be honest about what characteristics are actually required and don't just create a catch-all list. For example, the role might be highly specialist and so necessitate great determination and fast decisive decision making. If the person is only expected to get the job done effectively, then tact and diplomacy may not be priority traits.

Remember, at appraisal time these documents can be used to judge performance.

Adaptability

For me, the main consideration in this area is the candidate's ability to adapt to changing circumstances. This is something that can vary enormously between people with some finding change very unsettling. However, your department's survival depends on this quality and all staff should be encouraged to seek out ways of improving themselves and the services and products they deliver. Psychometric tests will help determine the degree of adaptability in candidates.

Advertising and Searching for Candidates

Recruitment has changed dramatically over the last few years thanks to the internet, with HR departments now increasingly using executive search engines and the social media to hunt for suitable candidates. Below are some things you should consider when using these different recruitment vehicles.

Setting Out Application Requirements and Job Information

- Make sure you describe the application process clearly so that it details:

    o The timeline and milestones for the selection process.

    o The job description and specification.

    o A template application form that describes skill, personality and aptitude requirements and gives the candidate the opportunity to explain how they meet these by offering up supporting evidence.

    o The need for a short summary CV to be attached.

    o The need for a covering letter of introduction which explains why the candidate is interested in the position.

Internal Advertising

- Getting the best candidates often means encouraging existing employees in the department or other internal departments to come forward. They are familiar with the work culture and are in an ideal position to meet the requirements.

- Ask your own staff to come up with suggestions based on their knowledge and awareness of potential candidates. In effect, they then become headhunters for you and so will appreciate the trust you are placing in them.

- The HR manager needs to be briefed on the position and should be asked to act as a headhunter.

- Approach any staff that are recommended to you and canvass their interest, highlighting their possible fit to the position without making any promises as the selection process has to be open and competitive.

- Advertise on the internal staff notice board, computer network or staff journals and newsletters.

Internet Advertising

- Brief the HR manager about the role and get them to search various executive recruitment sites for suitable candidates using appropriate keywords for the skills, personality and aptitude profile you need.

Traditional Newspaper and Journal Advertising

- Because it is so well known to job seekers, The Guardian continues to be a major placement platform for executive positions, although the costs of placing an advert here are high.

Headhunting Agencies

- There are many such agencies but they are expensive and often, if your own HR manager and staff are headhunting, unnecessary.

Job Fairs and Exhibitions

- In my experience, these are an excellent way of promoting your business as well as recruiting high quality candidates so they serve a dual purpose very cost-effectively. Earl's Court and the Islington Business Conference Centre in London frequently have job and careers exhibitions of international significance, so by hiring stand space you acquire a small window on the world.

Sifting Applicants Down to a Shortlist

There may be a large number of potential candidates for a position and you will have to narrow these down using basic selection criteria. All candidates need to realise that the quality of their application form is also judged. For me, the following is the easiest way I know to build an appropriate shortlist.

Assess the Quality of Application

- Basic spelling, grammar and literacy levels must be adequate. There is simply no excuse for not getting this right. However, experience shows that many do not give this the attention it deserves, but if they can't be bothered why should you, particularly if the position requires good communication skills?

- Does the candidate answer the actual questions on the application or do they just waffle and skirt round the required information?

- Does the candidate meet the minimum requirements in terms of professional experience and qualifications?

- Has the candidate answered all the questions on the application?

All of the above factors can be used as a means to automatically sift out those who do not meet a minimum standard.

Assess the Degree of Fit

- Under the categories of skill, personality and aptitude, compile a very specific list of the essential qualities you are looking for. This then needs to be overlaid onto the application form as a template, so marks out of ten can be awarded against each category for the degree of fit.

- Add the marks for each category together to give a total for each candidate.

- Decide on a threshold mark for shortlisting candidates. So as to be manageable, the shortlist for a managerial role should normally come down to about five people

Thoroughly Research the Shortlist

Once you have a shortlist, the serious behind the scenes work really begins. I take the view that background and reference checks should be made on shortlisted candidates *before* anyone is invited for interview as your enquiries may further reduce the list so making it even more manageable.

Others take a different view and conduct the checks after announcing the preferred candidate and, if these are unsatisfactory, just appoint the next in line.

People applying for posts do so for a variety of reasons, many of which are not valid. However, this can often be extremely difficult to determine if a candidate is extremely literate and well able to express their experience and technical skills on paper and at an interview. So the only way to really uncover undesirable behaviour traits is through thorough research in much the same way you would if you were buying a property. After all, you don't just accept what an estate agent is telling you in their advert. Instead, you visit the house and the area, speak to neighbours and conduct local checks for crime or disputes.

Background checks on personnel should be a part of your managerial role. This means that you should:

- Speak at length to the referees and references about a candidate's performance and character. Ask them what they think is the motivation for the application as this can often be revealing.

  I remember on one occasion an officer who was appointed to my department on the basis of exemplary technical qualifications and front line operational experience, all of which had completely overawed the selection panel. However, if they had dug a little deeper they would have discovered that his true motive for moving was to give himself more time to pursue an external professional course.

- Do a Google search of the candidate's online public presence, as well as any materials they have posted on LinkedIn, Facebook or Twitter. This can be alarmingly revealing about the true character and behaviour of the candidate.

- Read staff appraisal reports on the candidate covering the previous three years.

Selection Procedures

Clear Criteria and Score Card

In my experience, this is where things can go seriously wrong. Modern selection panels use a marking grid for each part of the process. This is fine and in the interests of fairness does offer a yardstick that can be held up against each candidate.

However, if too much emphasis is placed on the actual assessment, those who are truly the best could be overlooked as nerves can play a big part on the day with even the finest communicators becoming tongue-twisted and not coming across in their normal way. Now I am the last person to say that such pressurised situations are not a good test of a candidate's calmness under fire, but sometimes the desire for a position can be so strong that it distorts a person's normal demeanor to such a degree that the process doesn't reveal their true strengths and abilities.

My contention is that the previous stages of sifting and background research on the shortlist must try to elicit the candidate's normal performance in different circumstances. This should be recognised at the outset of the assessment and opportunities afforded for them to display and present evidence of their abilities through structured questioning and exercises. Their performance on the day can then add to or subtract from this starting mark.

DISC and Belbin Tests

These have already been covered and I strongly recommend their use as a way of evaluating personalities and aptitudes to see if they'll fit with your team. These tests are tried and tested over many years and very easy to conduct with minimal expense and time.

The Interview

The interview is at the core of any selection process and should provide an opportunity for the candidate to:

- Display their verbal communication skills under pressure.

- Demonstrate their thought processes and rationale by answering searching questions about the role and their suitability for it based on their skills, personality and aptitude.

- Bring forward evidence that demonstrates that they possess the competencies required to perform the role.

This is also an opportunity for the selection panel to test the candidate's motives for applying for the position and to see if they are ready, appropriately motivated and able.

As an aside to this, make sure you have the right candidates in the room for the right interview. I remember one hilarious situation in 2001 when I was a project manager on the new West End CCTV initiative. The selection process was in full swing for the post of control room manager at the Trocadero Complex in Piccadilly Circus. One candidate, having answered questions about CCTV for ten minutes, suddenly declared that he thought there was too much emphasis being place on this type of surveillance just to see how clean the streets were. It then turned out he should have been at an interview just down the corridor for a completely different department.

The Presentation or Scenario

Sometimes it's appropriate to include a scenario or to request a presentation on a topic that's related to the advertised role. This gives the candidate the opportunity to show how they would approach a current and relevant situation using their problem solving and communication skills. This is something I discussed earlier in *You as an Individual Manager.*

The Contract of Employment or Terms of Reference

The final appointment must be accompanied by a contract of employment or clear terms of reference if it is an internal assignment. The job description, if it has been written properly, will constitute the main body of the contract as it should already cover all the key points. Please bear in mind that this document will be an important future point of reference for all parties about expectations, support, pay and conditions and future performance evaluation.

The Probationary Period and Appraisal

I have always found it useful to include an appropriate probationary period in the contract during which the performance of the individual can be judged and any glaring gaps in skill, personality or aptitude addressed or the appointee dismissed. Modern contracts often have a rolling month or three month clause in them that allows notice to be given for poor performance or inappropriate behaviour but a clear probationary period is often much more appropriate and transparent to all parties.

Team Engagement and Performance

Developing Real Engagement

I truly believe that the relationship between task, individual and team is crucial in developing an atmosphere of real engagement and performance. However, in so many cases over the years I have seen the total breakdown of this dynamic, with one or more of the elements becoming dysfunctional, causing a complete imbalance, that quickly leads to deteriorating morale, increased stress, conflict and indiscipline.

Managers must keep a very close eye on the time and resources they invest in each element to ensure that the effort and attention paid to each remains in balance. So often today, the sheer pressure to deliver, means that most managers zero in on the tasks, gradually neglecting the individual and team.

This is a natural tendency as the other two elements are complicated and time consuming because they involve people, and people are complicated at the best of times. The payback though of keeping them in your sights is huge, as you will prevent costly and disruptive situations in the future as the individuals and team will feel valued, well trained and ready to deliver real performance.

I believe this holds true across operations management in all sectors, whether public, private or voluntary. Even in manufacturing, where there is a high degree of automation, people are still key in terms of overseeing design, quality control, maintenance and logistics.

The Individual

There are obvious and well-researched factors as to what motivates and drives a person to turn up for work each day. These include:

- A need to pay the mortgage and other life essentials in order to keep a roof over their head and food in their belly.

- A desire for additional luxuries in their life and to raise their standard of living through job progression and pay increases.

- Wanting to feel part of something worthwhile and to which they are contributing.

- A need to feel appreciated, with their efforts and abilities recognised.

- A yearning to feel part of a team where they are valued and can find support.

- A need for social contact with other people every day so as to enrich themselves through laughter, shared experience and discussion.

- A requirement to develop and improve their own skills and abilities in the workplace and give themselves new experiences.

Managers often forget these different motivations, but by recognising and using them in a positive and joined up way they can give the astute manager many lever points to develop their team into being more effective and productive. How do you use these lever points in a co-ordinated way?

1. You need to know each team member thoroughly. In the same way that you analysed what made yourself tick in *You as an Individual Manager* you also have to immerse yourself in your staff, getting to know them intimately and as quickly as possible. This needs

an investment of time but the benefits are worth it as you will be able to identify the motivations that really drive them. You will also be able to uncover any personal difficulties that may affect their work as well as particular behaviour traits. This does not mean that you have to become over familiar with them or get drunk together, but just talking and asking them searching questions about their aims and ambitions. Everyone likes to talk about themselves and if this questioning is done away from the workplace in a relaxed environment then your efforts are likely to be recognised as showing a positive interest.

2. In the same way that you undertook a baseline evaluation of actual operations under *Making Things Happen*, you need to do the same with each member of your staff at the outset of your relationship so you can determine:

    •   Their competence to carry out their role and tasks.

    •   The standard of their working relations with other members of the team and management.

    •   Their level of performance and engagement in meeting personal and departmental objectives.

    •   The degree of motivation and momentum that they bring to their work.

3. Then for each of the bullet points above, decide what needs doing to move individuals upwards from their current baseline position. So:

    •   What further training and experience do they need to become more competent?

    •   How could they benefit from individual coaching or mentoring to help them overcome limiting beliefs and to give them renewed focus or to overcome personal difficulties?

    •   Do they need to be working alongside other team members who would better complement their personality and qualities?

    •   Do some of their behaviour traits need controlling or changing?

- Do they deserve more recognition through commendation or performance awards, or even just a few positive and encouraging words from a line manager?

I remember spending several days in 2007 preparing a set of London guidelines for the control of violent offending in hotspot neighbourhoods affected by gun and knife crime. This involved many long 12-14 hour days collating all the best practice from previous operations and projects into a set of universal tools and methods for analysis and tactical planning. I recall sending this to my line manager who gave it a pedantic critique with lots of negative comment. This was not done with any malice, it was just his normal way of looking at things. I then sent it to the commander of the Violent Crime Directorate who sent a message back thanking me for its clarity, structure and relevance. The document was later distributed to all thirty-two London Boroughs as good practice, and became a piece of work for which I received a performance award. If I had not had complete belief in my own abilities I would have ditched the document after my manager's first comments and it would never have seen the light of day.

My contention is that through the use of a comprehensive staff appraisal system, all these lever factors can be managed in a concerted and effective way that is both systematic and highly personalised. There is more on this in the staff appraisal section below.

The Task

I've discussed this subject in great depth in *Making Things Happen*, but here are some key points worth reiterating:

1. If the outcomes and underpinning objectives are well researched and designed, the clarity of purpose is clear to everyone and so a team is far more likely to take ownership and pride in its work. This leads to greater dedication and applied effort so that

even menial tasks are done better because the team recognises how these small elements fit into the bigger picture. However, outcomes and objectives require constant explanation and re-emphasis by the manager.

2.   Select staff for tasks carefully and on the basis of 'horses for courses'. Define what needs to be done first and then the type of person with the skills, personality and aptitude needed to do it.

3.   Ensure there is balance between capacity and capability in the staff members available to carry out tasks. The team needs to be stretched and challenged but not to the extent where resentment and stress goes up and the quality of the work goes down. The manager will have to exert active and vigilant supervision of the tasking and co-ordination process to ensure a proper balance is maintained. This may require a high degree of assertiveness to resist top-down pressure for fast and dirty delivery. It is here that true leaders show themselves, as this may be an unpopular stance to take, but if you carefully explain your position and priorities, you will eventually earn the respect of your senior managers and staff.

4.   Exemplary planning and organisational skills are constantly called for if you are to deliver consistent levels of performance so that jobs are finished to budget, brief and deadline. This skill needs to be ingrained and developed in all your staff however junior they are.

The Team

Getting a fusion of effort, awareness and momentum in your team is the Holy Grail of all operations management. The ultimate goal is a synergy where the performance overall is much greater than the sum of all the separate parts alone. This takes time to achieve but, once reached, creates an optimum level of performance that is self-fulfilling with a palpable buzz every time you go to work that comes from the sense of belonging, status and achievement that permeates everywhere.

I have experienced task, team and individual being in perfect harmony only twice in my thirty-three year police career, and based on these occasions I would say there are a number of dynamics at work in such high performance teams.

1. The leader and manager have set the tone and standard clearly for the team by everyday examples and through their expectations of others. If this is done in a fair and professional way with a keen eye on the balance between task, team and individual needs, such leadership can take many forms and styles with equal effectiveness.

2. There is an atmosphere of friendly support and care for one another that's engendered by respect and loyalty towards others in the team. This ultimately becomes the esprit de corps that is so coveted by the military. By working and socialising together this will develop over time, as long as negative behaviour is managed and controlled effectively.

I remember with great fondness my time on B Bravo Team at Notting Hill Police between 1990 and1992. This was a uniformed emergency response team of thirty officers with one inspector, five sergeants and twenty-four constables. We had a 24/7 remit of responsibility that was shared between other teams who worked in eight-hour shifts. All the elements I have discussed in this section were there in abundance and it was just like having a second family to me.

We worked for each other, covering each other's backs at times of danger and working tirelessly to control and police the streets around Ladbroke Grove and All Saints Road. We had the highest crime arrest and clear up rate of any team and were renowned for being close-knit, both operationally and socially.

Unfortunately, in 1992 the entire Metropolitan Police moved away from this type of response team to a multi-disciplinary community sector structure with separate teams for each council ward and neighbourhood. The esprit de corps was immediately shattered and a period of much more fragmented policing began, albeit with the intention to deliver a more local approach.

On the very first day of this new arrangement, officers from different teams were patrolling the streets and I remember a call from one asking for support to deal with a disturbance involving violent suspects. I went but found no other officers accepting the call even though I passed several on the way, a situation that would have been inexcusable and almost impossible on my previous team. It was an omen of the far more parochial attitude that would be taken towards our new responsibilities.

3. There is a good mixture of personalities on the team with many characters who are interesting, funny and individual in their own right. Laughter and fun should be an integral part of your work, as long as this is not derisory or undermining of anyone else.

I recall my good friend and colleague nicknamed 'Gunner' at Paddington Green in 1979. He was a real character, quiet but highly professional and fearless. He would patrol the Lisson Green estate moving slowly from doorway to doorway watching and waiting for trouble.

Having been trained as a firearms officer he also had a very thorough knowledge of firearms and associated deployment tactics. This could mean that in between his normal uniform patrol duties, he might be sent on protection jobs and raids where his skills could be used. I remember one vivid incident when he was assigned a long tour of residential protection duties at Yasser Arafat's London Home in Maida Vale. Yasser was the Palestine Liberation Organisation's head for many years and often came to London to lobby and liaise with the UK Government about Palestinian affairs.

Gunner was posted to the ground floor corridor by the communal front door of the block of flats where Yasser lived. One night duty, Gunner had an accidental misfire on his police issue .38 revolver. Legend has it that the bullet passed through the front door and ricocheted off a tree overlooking the Little Venice canal, before narrowly missing a poodle being given a late night walk by its affluent owner. After an investigation and a refresher course, Gunner was reinstated to firearms duties and the dog reputedly recovered from its trauma after specialist pooch counselling.

4. There is a sufficient mix of experience and skill on the team not only to carry out its responsibilities but also to allow guidance and development of its more junior members.

5. By matching individuals to the task and other colleagues carefully, you will improve performance so even the quiet members develop and display their true value.

On my All Saints Road team at Notting Hill, I had the most driven and enthusiastic female officer I could wish for. Somewhat shy but a consummate professional, I nicknamed her 'Road Runner' after the TV cartoon character because she was always the first officer to leave the back of our unit police van when suspects were spotted on the street taking up the pursuit through the narrow alleyways off Ladbroke Grove.

She was a tenacious bloodhound; relentless and extremely fit. On night duty I allowed her to wear her running shoes and her effectiveness in the chase increased by 50 per cent. I truly loved that officer and constantly worried about her safety as she was normally way ahead of her male colleagues. The care she took over evidence collection and presentation was equally admirable. The Metropolitan Police is still full of these characters and the public should be truly proud they have such fearless guardians working on their behalf.

6. Everyone is actively encouraged to contribute to a culture of constant improvement by making suggestions about process, tactics and design. This should be done in a constructive positive way with team members given room to develop their proposals and to show leadership and ownership. This does not in any way need to be seen as threatening to the manager as long as it is clear that they are the ones who hold the ultimate decision making authority about what is or isn't pursued. A good manager will justify his decision making rationale and that is all that is required.

Selfless Participation

Whilst recognising individual needs and aspirations within a team, the overwhelming requirement from all is a selfless contribution to the overall effort. This is something that must be constantly reinforced by managers through example and expectation. The team is there to do a job of work and this can only be done effectively through joint effort and applied skills. The disproportionate demands for attention that come from the needs of a few members of staff who shout the loudest, must be firmly resisted.

To me such selfless participation means:

- Every staff member is aware and understands that they are there above all else to do a good job of work. Personal aspirations and grievances will be dealt with in parallel to this effort but not to its exclusion. This needs to be explained explicitly and professionally through the staff appraisal system.

- There is absolutely no room for individual officers, however senior, posturing and seeking self-promotion through the media or internal processes. Everything must be done in the name of the team and on behalf of the end-users. Any other behaviour that does not contribute to this is totally unacceptable.

Between 2005-08 Scotland Yard was riven by such posturing and self-promotion and, most alarmingly, often from some of the most senior officers. This was particularly hypocritical, as at that time the service charter of values had a focus on the need for selfless work and the ideal of 'together we will make London a safer place'. This was being rammed down everyone's throats through workshops and compliance statements.

To junior ranks this was laughable as it was self evident that many senior ACPO officers were doing quite the opposite by the widespread use of private media briefings to air some grievance, emphasise personal achievement, gain competitive advantage for a promotion or merely to grind a personal axe. This disunity was having a dramatic destabilising effect on the credibility and authority of the commissioner. In my opinion, it was accentuated by the increasing devolvement of power to the borough commanders, who in effect became thirty-two local chief constables vying with each other for public recognition and status.

There is just no room whatsoever for these types of antics in an effective operational organisation such as the police who have a clear responsibility to reduce crime. This can only be delivered through well-motivated and trained individuals working together under a united and co-ordinated front. Policing is not there to serve individual officers' ambitions.

Working for each other to get the job done, also fosters co-operation, trust and loyalty and by investing enough time to train, develop and manage the individuals in a team, this spirit of collaboration is far more likely to come about between them as their individual values are recognised.

Horatio Nelson and Ernest Shackleton both knew this, which is why Nelson spent inordinate amounts of time training the gun and sail party teams in drills, outside their normal allotted time. He did this to such an extent that each small team knew its role intimately alongside that of others so that their movements became fast and seamless as they all worked to a well understood common purpose under Nelson's instruction.

In fact on Trafalgar Day, Nelson was criticised for raising a flag signal that read 'England expects every man to do his duty', when his men actually wanted to feel they were going into battle for Nelson himself. Unfortunately, Nelson had run out of the necessary flags.

Recognising and Managing Stress

Not only has a manager to be responsible for their own state of mental and physical wellbeing, but also for the wellbeing of their team members. However, day-to-day policing is so busy and full of decision making demands that you can quickly lose sight of this. In a team that is close and supportive, there is a strong element of self-maintenance among its members but it is still easy to miss the signs of stress particularly in less united teams.

While going out and getting drunk with your colleagues may be a way of relaxing and letting off steam, it is no substitute for supportive action when work or personal issues are weighing heavily on a person's mind. What's more, drunken escapades can also lead to major disciplinary situations. I cannot count the number of times valued colleagues have then gone on to drink-drive or been involved in fights and disturbances while under the influence. This can have catastrophic consequences with even the loss of their own life or, at best, a criminal record and dismissal.

I recall a situation in 1984 when I was the early shift section sergeant at Bow Street police station in Covent Garden, London. This police area is the home of the original Bow Street Runners and the early British policing in the 1800s. It covers Leicester Square, Covent Garden with some of London's most iconic landmark sites alongside the River Thames.

At 7.30am we received a call from the Thames Police Marine Unit to attend Waterloo Bridge where they had fished out from the water a twenty-five year old male who appeared to have attempted suicide. The river at this point is particularly treacherous as there is a strong tidal cross current running at different depths and which surges at certain times of the day. No policeman would attempt a personal rescue at these times so police boats are always used.

When we got this young man back to the station, wrapped him up and treated him for hypothermia, I began to talk to him as we waited for an ambulance. He was tall and athletic, seemingly in the prime of his life but it transpired that he was a serving police officer from Hounslow in West London. His girlfriend had left him and this had had a devastating effect as he was very close to her.

After suffering months of desperation he had finally decided to end his life. Unfortunately, given that he was a champion swimmer he had chosen the least appropriate way of killing himself. Swimming was so much a part of his DNA that he just kept bobbing up to the surface. Unfortunately, because he was so obviously depressed he couldn't see the funny side of this.

After treatment, he was sent to the police welfare service for counselling but the whole episode demonstrated how the signs of stress can lie hidden with devastating consequences. So when it comes to team management I make the following recommendations:

- Use the staff appraisal system as a way of checking on welfare issues that might stem from work as well as personal problems. The appraisal system is *not* there as a bureaucratic necessity, as many seem to see it, but as a means to regularly review performance, development and the welfare of team members. Although there may be one or two formal reporting points in the year, ongoing checks should be made in order to talk about things and collect performance evidence. These offer ideal opportunities to enquire about any problems that may be affecting an individual's performance.

- You and your team leaders *must* be vigilant every day as to what you see and hear about your staff such as:

  o Signs of behaviour that are out of the ordinary like outbursts of anger, being withdrawn or overly excitable.

  o Anecdotal stories of excess drinking and drunkenness.

  o Comments by friends and colleagues about another's circumstances that they haven't themselves shared with you.

  o Repeatedly being late for work.

  o Frequent absences from work with various sicknesses or welfare requests.

- Get out and socialise with your team. This is essential and in no way should undermine your authority if you are careful about the propriety of your behaviour. This is the best way of finding out what is happening within your group and what they are feeling. A couple of pints of beer in a social context allows people to open up and may give you vital information that you wouldn't otherwise uncover. You can then follow this up separately and on an individual basis.

- In clear welfare cases, you should prepare a confidential action plan with the individual so as to help them deal with the causes of the problem, with referrals to suitable professional practitioners as necessary. In cases of depression, you can use the treatment advice contained under the earlier section on *You as an Individual Manage'*. Helping someone take control of their situation is a fundamental part of being a manager and if you skirt around this you are not ready for the role.

- In cases where the person is unwilling to take action themselves, be prepared to make a compulsory referral to your organisation's welfare service. This will also protect you if the person then later does harm to themselves or others as you will have shared responsibility for risk management.

- Allow them time off work to attend welfare appointments or to deal with their given situation, as long as this is part of an agreed action plan.

- Every day possible, get alongside staff who are undergoing difficulties and give them your encouragement, advice and even just a shot of morale-boosting humour. Try to make them see the funny side of a situation rather than always taking the grim view.

- Make sure team members who are in personal difficulties are always invited out to team social events and not forgotten, just because they are currently withdrawn and difficult to get along with.

In 1990 I went through an episode of severe depression after losing my former colleague DC Jim Morrison, and then having to deal with a traumatic child murder as well as the day-to-day pressures of policing the high crime area of Notting Hill. I was literally paralysed in thought and movement and off sick at home for five weeks.

As my sense of desperation and isolation deepened, it led to severe tensions with my wife. Even today after twenty-two years, it still brings tears to my eyes when I think of the care and consideration shown to me by my junior officers. They invited me to various Christmas functions whilst I was still off sick and although I didn't want to go, they encouraged me back into the fold, making me laugh about situations they had dealt with.

Eventually, I returned to the team and I can still feel the warmth and camaraderie I was given when I did. On my very first night back we had to deal with an enormous pub fight that entailed closing the premises down and declaring a crime scene and I will always remember the way my team protected me.

This all came flooding back to me recently when I was watching an episode of 'Everyone Loves Raymond', the American TV sitcom. The storyline revolves around a New York Family that includes two brothers, Ray who is a sports writer and Robert, a NYPD police sergeant.

On Robert's first day back from a long period of sick leave, the result of being gored by a runaway bull, he encounters a group of young thugs; while he falters, his partner Judy steps in. She lays out one of the youths on the floor and then asks Robert whether he wants to wait in the squad car. This was a remarkable and telling portrayal of what often happens to police officers and how a good team will always rally around.

Managing Conflict

We now come to another difficult area and one which you will often have to face, so just buckle up and listen, because inevitably you are going to have to manage a variety of challenging characters on your team. The art here is in turning any negative behaviour into a more constructive and positive contribution towards overall performance and team balance.

Strong Characters

What I mean by a strong character is someone who is very assertive about what they want and how things should be done. This does not necessarily mean that they are poor performer, often quite the contrary. However, they do tend to pose problems for a manager. Some of the following characteristics may present themselves:

- They can be very demanding in terms of your attention. Often this means frequent requests for additional resources or personal development training.

- They tend to be very self-opinionated in meetings taking an inordinate amount of time to present their views and proposals.

- From time to time they may even have the temerity to challenge or question your management decisions, something that can be annoying and unsettling.

- They submerge the needs of other team members beneath their larger than life presence by speaking loudly or seeking attention.

- They can have an inordinate amount of influence over weaker characters who may look up to them. This can either be a positive or negative factor depending on the nature of their behaviour.

- They tend to have a very strong view on how things should be done and don't always listen to advice or directions from managers.

- Their behaviour can sometimes become very negative. Without proper control this can lead to disciplinary action, and at this point they become dangerous.

I had to manage just such an officer on one of my teams. He was extraordinarily industrious in his work, completing several extremely innovative crime reduction initiatives. These were officially commended and I often graded his work as outstanding.

He was always asking for new terms of work in the office using a compressed hours schedule and often pursued personal objectives that were outside the department's priorities. So, I found myself spending more and more time supervising him and having to sit on his shoulder day-by-day to ensure he was following his allotted tasks. He was a very assertive character who was used to working on his own and did not like being challenged.

The whole period culminated in a serious disciplinary situation on the 7th July 2005, the day of the London terrorist bombings. There was a general recall of team members to Scotland Yard to be reassigned emergency duties. This particular officer could not be raised on the phone and when we eventually got through to him discovered that he was in Paris. He had deemed that he was entitled to leave due to the amount of overtime he had been putting into his projects and which were now ahead of schedule. He was effectively absent without leave. He was ordered back and disciplinary proceedings began. It's true, he had been putting in a lot of overtime but, assuming the right to award himself a day off without asking for permission was indicative of his general mindset.

Another example occurred between 2008 and 2009 when I was responsible for overseeing the activity of a managing consultant who had been appointed to establish and develop a new independent organisation for conflict resolution in gangs and life threatening disputes. He was bright eyed, keen and astute. However, he was badly let down by a complete lack of tact or diplomacy. In dealing with various partner organisations across the region he exhibited a take it or leave it attitude that accepted no compromises. While in one way I really liked and admired this focused and determined attitude, his bullish and rude manner in meetings quickly isolated him and so he gained little support or agreement.

I remember having to spend dozens of hours trailing behind him on a damage limitation exercise, smoothing ruffled feathers and cajoling key people back into position. I would also spend a lot of time with him explaining the circumstances of the multi-tier executive structure of London. He was an ideal project manager but disastrous in public relations.

In 1984, I also recall being on duty at Ollerton Colliery, Nottinghamshire during the coal miners' dispute. This was a particularly difficult and sensitive time as we were providing assistance to the local police by keeping demonstrating miners apart from their colleagues who had chosen to continue working. These were long sixteen-hour days of gruelling duty, preventing violence and disorder on the picket lines. My team was policing a large group of striking miners at the colliery entrance with ten of us and a hundred of them, most of whom were over thirty, six feet tall, as strong as oxen with steel-capped boots.

One of my team was an exuberant young officer who tended to be rather full of himself. He shouted at one striker who kept lurching forward into the road with clenched fists shouting "Scab, scab, scab" every time a work bus pulled into the entrance, "If you do that again my son you're nicked."

In the half light of the dawn I remember seeing this miner extend his huge arms and quite literally pick my officer off the ground by his lapels and, putting his face close to his, utter the immortal words: "I'm not your son. I'm old enough to be your dad and I'll squash yer if you say that again."

Being completely outnumbered by these gladiators, I decided that the best option was to direct the officer away to other duties so as not to escalate the situation. Words of strong advice were then given to him about the need to engage brain before speaking like this in the future.

I have the following recommendations for managing such characters:

1. Take your time sizing up this type of character. Assess what is negative and positive about their behaviours, but don't be prejudiced just because they may have questioned your decisions. Observe their behaviour in different environments, in the office, during meetings and at social events. How closely aligned are they to the department objectives and what is the quality of their work? Make diary entries that can be used during their one-to-one staff appraisals.

2. Make sure you conduct a DISC and Belbin test on all staff members during the application process or when you take up position and inherit a team. This will give early indicators of the types of characters you have on board, including those with strong opinions

3. After a suitable period, initiate a staff appraisal with the individual, even if it is not officially due. Do this in a relaxed non-confrontational manner away from the office and during which you can set out your observations on their behaviour. Begin to match their positive behaviours to team and task requirements while challenging and changing others that interfere with performance and always explain the reasons.

4. If possible, assign a coach or mentor to the individual who can help explore their behaviours with them and help them develop more positive objectives and make any necessary behavioural changes.

5. After the initial appraisal, continue to observe them closely, noting any attempts they make to modify negative behaviours. Arrange frequent follow-up meetings with them to review progress. Always make it quite clear when a staff member is falling short of what is expected or the targets that have been agreed with them for improvement. Show courage in this and mark any areas of behavioural competency that are of concern. A strong character rarely withers in the face of this and will probably be determined to come back stronger and better. This means they may challenge your opinions and you must be ready to assert yourself forcefully using the collected evidence of your observations. You owe it to them, yourself and subsequent managers to deal with the situation and not to just 'pass the monkey on'.

6. Encourage the positive aspects of their behaviour and when possible give them a leadership role that allows them to shape and deliver specific projects to a deadline.

7. Team them up with another strong team member who will not be frightened of challenging them when needed. In certain circumstances, even get them to assist you directly so you can advise, coach and supervise them day-to-day, thereby keeping them close to you until you can trust them to work effectively on their own.

Troubled Characters

Troubled characters are those who are non-confrontational and normally quiet and reserved but who, on closer observation, lack any drive or commitment to the team or task. In them, you may observe the following traits:

- They may say something to your face but then do and say something entirely different behind your back.

- They may go missing from the office, be constantly late, take extended periods of sick leave or have ad hoc holidays.

- They may be completely lacking in self-confidence and appear non-committal, furtive or withdrawn.

- They may pursue their own personal objectives and priorities in variance to assigned ones, but unlike the strong character they will attempt to disguise this sometimes in covert ways.

Great care needs to be taken over the handling of such people as there may be some serious underlying reasons for their current weakness, such as depression, a nervous disorder or a complete and temporary breakdown in self-confidence caused by work or personal issues. Their abnormal behaviour may be only temporary, if they are managed properly, so, with these characters you will need to:

1. Make sure you take careful notes about their behaviour traits that concern you. Particularly look for evidence of good performance and character, as these can be used as positive examples in the appraisal process.

2. If their behaviour is causing concern, conduct a DISC and Belbin test before it is due.

3. Sit down with them and ask many structured searching questions about their motives, any difficulties they may be having at the moment and their aspirations for the future. This will give you a complete and clear picture of where they are currently at. A confrontational challenging approach can be disastrous in these circumstances as issues need to be slowly and sensitively drawn out. Make sure their appraisal focuses on their strong areas and you offer plenty of development opportunities.

4. Assign a coach or mentor to them to help bolster their self-confidence and belief in their own abilities.

5. Make sure they are paired only with team members who are diplomatic and quietly confident in their work as this will help nurture them back to a stronger position. Sometimes this may mean working directly with them yourself so you can keep a close eye on their progress.

6. Despite concerted action and effort their behaviour may not change. This must be faced and dealt with by challenge, sanction or compulsory referral to professional support such as counselling. Again, you owe it to them, yourself and following line managers to do this.

I dealt with one such case in 2003 just after arriving at a new department in Scotland Yard. The existing team were preparing for a multi-agency conference that was to be led by the assistant commissioner, Tarique Ghaffur, on managing, reducing and preventing gun and gang crime.

In my first week I met one of the team's female detective constables during a working group session on the conference but the day after she went on sick leave and, while I never saw her again, the legacy of the problems she left behind hung over me for a further four years.

Responsibility for her case passed to me as well as her immediate line manager. On the face of it there seemed to be a case of stress and depression, caused by a previous discrimination claim that had arisen while she was serving on another unit. As the months and then years rolled by with the officer still on pay, increasingly strenuous efforts were made to help her overcome any issues and return to work, but all to no avail.

She refused all visits to her home, declined any welfare support and insisted on being retired with an ill health pension. Her attitude was brazen and aggressive.

As a result, I was involved in literally hundreds of hours of work arranging medical examinations by the chief medical officer and when it transpired that there was nothing essentially wrong with her, my time was then taken up with performance and disciplinary proceedings.

Finally, after climbing this bureaucratic mountain that involved countless statements and a succession of internal performance boards, she was finally dismissed from the service in 2007.

Dangerous Characters

Though they are rare, from time to time you may unfortunately have to deal with dangerous characters among your staff. They are dangerous because in a premeditated way they try to destabilise you or your department for different retributive reasons. Sometimes they do this on their own, sometimes by inciting others. These are the traits I've observed in such people:

- On some occasions they will do their utmost to undermine your authority by either retributive legal action or by trying to smear your character

- They have a grievance about a perceived injustice involving selection, promotion, a disciplinary issue or even an appraisal grade.

- On some occasions they will do their utmost to undermine your authority by trying to smear your character, rally dissent behind your back or even carry out acts of sabotage and criminal damage to your work or personal property

- Over time they may collect without authorisation work papers and documents from the office so as to find 'incriminating evidence' that will enable them to make a personal litigation claim for monetary compensation

- They may also photograph the office or work areas and voice record conversations in a covert way with a view to litigation

I had to contend with two such instances in the course of my career, both of which caused me considerable stress and anxiety and affected my work and personal health. One emanated from a dislike of my management style by junior officers and the other followed a grade readjustment on a staff appraisal. The first, which I've discussed previously happened in the early stages of my career, while the second, described here, occurred later in my service.

The latter involved a close colleague who was on my team. He had gone through very turbulent times himself some years earlier, having been accused of sending malicious mail from his internal police computer. He had fought a protracted series of actions to clear his name finally being re instated from suspension after a full employment tribunal hearing.

However, he obviously felt aggrieved, so his immediate line managers and myself made strenuous efforts over several years to give him welfare support, coaching and retraining. We became, or so I thought, quite good friends but that changed when I was promoted and became his staff appraisal countersigning officer responsible for reviewing the performance evidence collected by his immediate line manager.

This had awarded him an overall grade of outstanding. However, on reviewing the appraisal it became quite clear there was insufficient evidence to justify such a high grade and I asked the officer and his supervisor to collate further supporting materials if the grade was to stand.

Nothing was forthcoming and the grade was lowered to a more appropriate level. I then made significant efforts to explain what type of evidence was needed and how this should be set out to his best advantage.

He complained to the head of department and then several weeks later, I and the other line managers, received notice that he was issuing proceedings against us for racist and victimising behaviour towards him.

We were all frankly astounded that he should make such a personal and unjustified claim on the basis of one lower grade level when so much time had been spent supporting him over the years.

To refute the claim, there followed months of statement taking and evidence collection from records and emails. The case came before the central employment tribunal with barristers representing both sides, his paid for by the Police Federation staff association.

Over the course of two weeks we underwent hostile, aggressive cross examination about our treatment of him. In my own case, this involved two complete days in the witness seat with personal allegations being made against my integrity and professionalism.

All the allegations were quashed by the court, but not before what must have been a bill of nearly £250,000 had been run up at the taxpayer's expense.

What's more, during the course of the hearing, exhibits were produced that clearly showed the officer had been trying to collect what he perceived to be incriminating evidence for several years, photographing notice boards and copying materials in a covert way, all well before this particular incident. At no point, at the relevant times, had he made any complaint to his line managers.

To deal with staff who present indicative signs of similar behaviour, I make the following recommendations

1. Be scrupulously fair to all your staff and, when possible, explain your decisions carefully so they fully understand the rationale behind your thinking. Remember, you are not there to be a friend to them, but a respected manager who supports, guides and is in control. This will lead you inevitably into personal confrontations about declined promotions and other staff issues. However, you must show them that you are doing what is needed to improve their performance through personal support and training.

2. Make sure you keep a record of all such conversations, actions and decisions and I strongly recommend using email as this will create a timed and dated communication trail. In the above case, my bacon was saved because I was able to present an email stream that detailed the guidance and support I'd offered to the officer concerned and in complete contrast to his claims. So while

emails can be a bind, for a good manager in these instances, they are an insurance policy and a blessing. That means you must never delete or clean the hard drive of your PC. You should also periodically save the emails you send and receive to CD for storage and then keep these for least three years. The sent box of your server is the most important as it holds both the original emails and any replies you have given.

3. Use the appraisal system discussed below to your advantage by being thorough in your collection of observed evidence. This can keep a difficult staff member focused on their work objectives and performance.

4. You will have to be very firm, assertive and clear about what you require from these characters. This is not always easy for managers to do when they themselves may be under incredible stress from other issues at the same time. This can result in a tendency to put the lid back on a particular can of worms, so as to avoid the inevitable aggro that will come from challenging some people in the way that's needed. Therefore it's best to pick a time and place to do this that's of your choosing when you have all the necessary facts at hand and a clear action plan in your head to cover all eventualities.

5. Accept that in certain cases, disciplinary action will be necessary. If this is on the horizon, make sure you brief your line managers about the circumstances and the possible options for dealing with the situation before you make your move. You will need their support, understanding and resolve as in extreme circumstances they may also have to divert themselves from core work for substantial periods to handle the crisis.

6. Discuss the case, possible courses of action and their consequences with your HR manager or someone who has an expertise in employment issues. In some high profile cases, there may be a corporate tendency to avoid confrontation for fear of the resulting negative publicity. Ultimately this will be a mistake as dangerous behaviour is likely to not only get worse but also lead to a complete destabilisation of your department as morale plummets and discontent rises among staff who are indirectly affected by the disruption.

Individual Development and Appraisal

I can honestly say that in my entire career there was only one line manager who truly took his staff appraisal responsibilities towards me seriously. By that I mean he had an ongoing interest in my performance, development and wellbeing by investing time to help me exploit my potential.

His tenure of responsibility ended after just six months when he fell into conflict with the department head. For the rest of the time I felt as though I was being treated purely as a resource. Consequently, my appraisals often felt as though they were being done by someone who considered them to be an inconvenient necessity.

Does that sound familiar to you?

This was a major factor in my final retirement decision after what I considered to be the disgraceful handling of my Superintendent's application by my directorate, despite presenting hard performance evidence that spanned many years

The Interface between Development and Performance

To become a high performing operations department there has to be a point of balance where individual, team and task meet. The staff appraisal system is one of your main tools for achieving this. It also offers one of the main pivot points where work objectives, individual skills and development can be matched and actioned in a process of continuous improvement for your staff as much as for your products and services.

A first class appraisal system should be based around a competency framework that lets you consider in a structured way an individual's combination of skill, knowledge and behaviour in specific areas such as planning, strategy, customer focus, leadership or managing change.

Having used just such an assessment approach successfully for some ten years, I was frankly astounded that in 2011 Scotland Yard dropped it in favour of a much looser and unstructured process.

This was done to reduce the paperwork burden for line managers, though I contend that it will just exacerbate the situation and lead to a confused and vague way of evaluating staff. It is yet one more manifestation of muddled thinking that allows for even more inconsistent and abnegation in managerial behaviour. It also skews the focus increasingly onto the task rather than the investment that's needed in the team and individuals. This I believe will result in a decline in standards of behaviour and performance.

In contrast, a good competency-based appraisal system provides the following opportunities:

- It can inspire and motivate an individual by highlighting their strengths and exploring how these can be used to best effect in pursuing the department's objectives. It also allows that person to display their true value and have this properly evidenced.

- It enables the appraiser and subject to look back both on the preceding period and forward to the next with a view to building on strengths and developing weaker areas.

- The appraisal system can be used as the key source of evidence for promotion or selection procedures. If this is done properly the moment at which an individual is ready to progress will become self-evident.

- In cases of poor performance or behaviour it also provides a key source of specific evidence as to what has happened and the attempts that have or are being made to correct or develop the individual.

- It allows the manager to match jobs and projects to the most appropriate staff members based on skills, personality and aptitude. As these will change over time, the appraisal in effect becomes a living document that lets managers monitor an individual's progress.

- A good appraisal system is able to monitor not only *what* the staff member is doing but also *how* they are doing it. This combination of skill, knowledge and behaviour then becomes a competency. This is crucial information, as some individuals who are very good at getting things done might also upset so many people in the process that they become counter-productive to the team's overall performance. I talked about this earlier in the section on strong characters.

Structured Appraisals

Job and Role Descriptions

As discussed earlier, there should be a clear job description for every role or position in your department. Such descriptions need not be complicated and so can normally fit on one sheet of paper.

They should list the main activities that a person is expected to carry out and be accountable for. For instance, in the police there are dozens of roles in both uniform and detective work that involve a range of particular activities that include public order, community policing, emergency response, marine river policing, mounted horse policing or different investigative roles.

Many personnel institutes and professional bodies keep electronic indices of key roles and can provide you with easily accessible competency requirements for each role.

What Competencies Are Needed for the Role?

If a role is to be performed effectively, certain competencies must be present. Remember, a job description is about *what* you do, whereas competency is about *how* you carry out your role, which means having the right combination of skill, knowledge and behaviours.

For example, a milkman needs to be competent in planning so as to organise his round. He might also need communication skills to be able to interact well with his customers but will not have to have strategic or leadership competencies for his everyday work.

Once again, you can find the competencies needed for particular jobs and roles on the websites of professional bodies who hold comprehensive databases.

The Main Competencies of Operations Management

In the case of operations management, I consider the following competency areas to be crucial:

- Planning and organising abilities.

- Verbal and written communication skills.

- Strategic awareness.

- Problem-solving capabilities.

- An aptitude for team work.

- Leadership skills.

- The ability to manage change.

- Customer-focused thinking and awareness.

- A willingness to accept personal responsibility.

These skills and behaviours will drive and underpin your effectiveness as a manager and leader enabling you to perform at your very best. These will take time to develop because there's no magic pill that you can take to acquire them overnight. As Steven Covey, the famous personal development guru says: 'You have to pay the price' in terms of the sustained effort necessary to gain the experience and skill needed. However, by applying yourself to all these areas and developing the right combination you will eventually reach optimum performance levels together with supreme self-confidence in your own competence and abilities.

Positive Competency Indicators

Every competency is made up of different behaviours, each of which can be assessed as either positive or negative and can be scored as *competency indicators* on a sliding scale.

For example, when it comes to planning and organisation, some of the listed positive behaviours might include:

- The ability to carefully plan by setting suitable milestones.
- To be able to appropriately delegate work to staff based on their skills and experience.
- To ensure that staff are thoroughly briefed, so they are clear about what is expected of them.
- Being able to regularly review progress and make suitable adjustments necessary to ensure continued smooth progress.
- To make certain that a plan is executed to budget by using a suitable financial planning system and tools.
- To make sure that all necessary resources are available in a timely and effective manner.

In a similar vein, there are also negative indicators for each planning and organising behaviour that might be:

- Having an unclear plan with only vague and non-specific milestones.
- Failing to delegate work, or delegating it to inappropriate staff.
- Not questioning staff so as to ensure they are clear about their role and the tasks assigned to them.
- Insufficient review of progress so problems and blockages to progress are not identified soon enough, if at all.
- Insufficient financial control of projects and operations resulting in large budgetary overruns.
- Resources arriving late, leading to delays and increased costs.

As a manager of any major project or operation, you should observe your team leaders for signs of these traits, noting in their appraisal journal specific occasions when you see either positive or negative indicators.

As an individual's level of competence increases, positive indicators will be seen with growing regularity until a point is reached when they are all displayed consistently in every situation. This is optimum performance.

A Staff Appraisal Structure and System

Every staff member should have an appraisal report form. This is a living document so it is not just opened at specified reporting times but stays open throughout the year with the line manager *and* the staff member able to make entries about activity, behaviours and achievements at any time.

I call this a journal rather than a report because that is what it should be, an open and honest document that describes not just obvious success stories, but also the difficulties faced by a staff member and how they have been overcome. In this way the journal will provide evidence of instances of tenacity, problem-solving and taking personal responsibility as well as achievement.

The Appraisal Form's Structure

The Metropolitan Police appraisal form was called the Personal Development Review (PDR) form and frankly I liked it, although to many of my colleagues it was just another bureaucratic system that had to be tolerated. The form was divided into:

Personal Details and Reporting Period

- The staff member's name, position and role.
- The period of reporting.

Work Objectives

- SMART work-based objectives established at the beginning of the reporting period and concisely set out. This was the place where you as line manager would agree work targets in support of the department's overall objectives.

- These objectives could be amended or added to during the course of the year by mutual agreement and with the reasons for doing so being noted down.

- Beside each objective, the progress towards it was recorded.

Personal Development Objectives

- SMART personal development objectives were set out here based on what was needed for that individual to carry out their role and to become more effective.

- These objectives could include private courses of academic or professional study, training courses to help them acquire particular experience or expertise, such as public speaking.

- This section was developed through discussions between the line manager and the staff member and gave an opportunity to agree a development plan that was relevant and appropriate to their needs and role. This meant that frivolous and expensive training was avoided and so the line manager could better budget for approved courses.

- These objectives could also be adjusted or added to during the year by mutual agreement, again the reasons for doing so had to be noted down.

Areas of Role Responsibility

- This was the section in which the main areas of responsibility were listed based on the role description.

- Beside each area of responsibility, the staff member could record *what* they had done during the reporting period.

- This section provided evidence of the range and depth of an individual's activities and so demonstrated their experience and levels of success.

- Staff members were actively encouraged to keep this section up to date themselves, rather than leaving it to the end of the reporting period by which time many relevant things might have been forgotten.

Competency Behaviours

- This was the section in which all the requisite competencies expected of a position or role were listed. In the case of an operations manager the behaviours listed above would be set out.

- This section was entirely focused on *how* individuals performed the various activities and roles laid down in the previous section. The purpose of this was to allow the staff member and line manager the opportunity to record both positive and negative indicators of the competency, as was explained earlier.

- Both the staff member and line manager were actively encouraged to include entries in this section every week, so instances of behaviour, good and bad, were not forgotten.

- Beside each competency was a column where the line manager could grade that competency on a scale of 1-5 based on the evidence collected throughout the year.

Line Manager's Overall Comments

- This was the point at which the line manager had an opportunity to summarise progress during the year in terms of:

  o How an individual had completed their tasks and contributed towards the work objectives of the department.

  o Improvement of an individual's competencies.

  o Any notable achievements or successes.

  o Any remedial action needed to address poor performance or behaviours.

Such comments have to be balanced and, where possible, supportive so that they give the staff member a real boost and help move them forwards even when remedial action is required.

Overall Grading

- This was an aggregate score based on all areas of the appraisal. In the Met, this was done on a scale of 1-5, ranging from Outstanding through to Immediate Action Required because of serious under-performance.

Such grading should be a true and balanced reflection of the year's work, though all too often I saw inflated grades being awarded to placate difficult staff and to avoid confrontation.

Staff Member's Comments

- Here a staff member had the opportunity to note their own comments about the reporting period in question and to highlight the challenges and achievements. This was not intended to be a place for comment about the line manager's grading, though if there were strong objections about anything that had been written, these could be included here.

- The staff member was expected to then sign off to signify that they had received the report, not necessarily that they agreed with it.

The Countersigning Staff Member

- This section was completed by the next line manager up who had to sign to confirm that the report had been completed in accordance with instructions and to comment on the suitability of the grading given and the evidence provided for it.

If quality standards were to be maintained this was not something to be undertaken lightly, otherwise it might become just a rubber stamp exercise. That is why I challenged one of the first reports submitted to me for countersigning.

What Should be Included on the Form

If crucial pieces of information were not to be forgotten and lost, I would encourage both the staff member and their line manager to include absolutely everything on the appraisal form in the appropriate sections and to do this week by week. This meant that the form became a major information capture point. Any irrelevant material could be removed at the end of the reporting period, from the final, edited report.

When to Complete the Report and How Often

- If you are following a similar system to this, then every year a new report form should be opened with work and development objectives agreed with the staff member.

- For easy entry and monitoring, the report should be held electronically on a shared folder accessible by the staff member and manager alike.

- It's important to note however, that it is the line manager's responsibility to maintain the appraisal and if there are entries that cannot be agreed by the parties then in these cases it is the line manager's prerogative to insist on inclusion.

- At the Met there were two formal reporting points, mid-term and at the end of the year when the report had to be updated and submitted

Ongoing Review and Development

For me, the appraisal form was a living document that I used to take out whenever I was reviewing the work portfolio and performance of staff, so much so that it became a signature element of my management style. However, it did keep us focused on the goals we had set and gave me an opportunity to discuss any challenges they were facing and how these could be overcome.

Conclusion – All Pull Together

Each leg of this three pillared approach to operations management: you as an individual; how to make things happen and; developing your team – has a role to play in helping you become successful in your career. However, an outstanding manager knows that they must bring all three elements together in the right proportions, if they are to achieve optimum performance. This is something that requires experience, skill and above all an intuitive grasp of how to plan for each day's new challenges.

So, this last section seeks to bring together the main points from each section with two types of manager in mind.

The first of these is relatively junior, newly promoted and never having headed up their own team before. The second type of manager is more experienced, perhaps even a director who is seeking to accelerate their department's performance.

Whichever category you fall into, I would emphasise the need for you to set aside time for some deep thinking about the actions you are going to take. There is so much pressure on us all these days just to 'get on and do' that the *how* often gets forgotten. This leads to a lot of wasted time going down numerous dead ends or producing poor quality work.

If you are to avoid this, then you must get into the habit of forward planning each year, each month, each week and each day in a systematic way with periods of your diary struck through for 'Thinking SMART'. This will enable you to obtain an objectiveness that comes from having a 'helicopter view'. This is essential when prioritising, designing and organising work. Without this, you will quickly descend into a spiral of firefighting, stress and wasted effort.

You as an Individual Manager

You are the manager and leader and as such you are the one who sets the entire tone and standard expected from your team. The art and science of doing this well is in knowing when to step in and to lead from the front, and when to step back and allow others the chance to push forward. It is also about meticulous planning in everything that you do and in motivating your team to continued selfless effort. This requires skill, high standards of behaviour and great intuition.

1. Before doing anything you must understand yourself completely and utterly – to know the values and beliefs that you hold for living and operating in this world. This requires a high degree of self-awareness and analysis where there is no room whatsoever for denial or kidding yourself as to what kind of person you are.

2. What sort of leadership style will you have? This is driven by your personality and aptitude. For instance, are you people or task-oriented and to what degree? Complete the full range of psychometric tests I have recommended, including DISC, Myers Briggs, Business Leadership Profile and the Belbin team tests. Get these tests fully analysed by computer and then manually interpreted by qualified practitioners if you require a deeper interpretation for yourself. You need to see yourself in reality and not just get a reflection of what you want to see.

3. With this information, you are then well equipped to do some profound thinking about how you are going to conduct yourself in the workplace. Again, be true to yourself and don't try to be someone you are not. There are many different styles of leadership, many of them equally effective if based on sound principles of behaviour.

4. A major priority is *always* to look after your physical and mental wellbeing above all else. Without regard for this, your effectiveness will quickly evaporate and you will no longer be able to manage others. This will entail a consistent regime of good fitness, diet, sleep and relaxation. It also may mean taking regular breaks to recharge your batteries and deal with any causes of stress and depression before they fester and grow.

5. Every time you go into work, prepare your mind for the day ahead. You have to be positive and determined so that you see each challenge as just a problem to be solved and not as a conspiracy sent by the gods to bring about your downfall. The problems will come thick and fast, but that's just life. The grass is never greener on the other side, I can tell you. Take a calm pragmatic view and work through each issue systematically. Try and see the funny or positive side of every situation because laughing about yourself and life is immensely therapeutic. So, don't take yourself too seriously and don't beat yourself up. Stuff just happens and that's the way things are. As long as you have taken every effort to plan and do the best you can, you can do no more.

6. Always look for opportunities to expand your experience and skills through training or by volunteering to do things that are out of your comfort zone. This is the only way you will develop properly.

7. Take a long hard look at the standards you expect of yourself and others. Then once you have established these, stick with them without unnecessary slippage or compromise. You will be greatly respected for this by others and more importantly by yourself.

8. Take time to think about how to position yourself in your department for maximum leverage. This isn't about self-promotion but to make your operations more effective by presenting yourself, your team and its work in a way that will make you appear more credible and worthy of respect in the eyes of others. Pursue the five steps to becoming a 'Key Person of Influence'.

Making Things Happen

There is clearly a big difference between just doing things and making things happen and work successfully. This requires a mixture of skills, knowledge and awareness of a completely different order with unparalleled levels of drive and clarity of purpose. Keep in mind the main elements of consistently achieving a desired outcome:

1. Your internal and environmental awareness has to be first rate. This means constantly scanning for opportunities and threats from the outside world and being aware of the relative strengths and weaknesses of your department and others so you can either exploit or counter them.

2. You need to totally immerse yourself in the needs or issues of your end-users whether you offer services or products. As the dynamics of this can change quickly, you will also need a high degree of adaptability and willingness to change.

3. Invest sufficient time in the design of new services and products so that they meet end-user needs, but do so by concentrating on the desired outcome and not by giving all your focus to the process. By making this conscious effort to keep clarity of outcome at the forefront of your mind, you will continue to be relevant and effective in meeting changing customer needs through continuous improvement.

4. Set only the required quality standard in materials, process and outputs needed to meet the purpose. If you don't do this then you will waste resources by working to a higher specification than is required.

5. Take a systematic and broad perspective towards problem solving. To better know how an issue can be overcome, involve all relevant viewpoints so you gain a comprehensive insight into what's going on and why.

6. All planning and organisation that you do must be exemplary. By thinking through potential developments and eventualities you will have a much higher chance of success and prevent most major causes of disruption and failure from happening.

7. Constant improvement has to be in the DNA of both yourself and your staff. Never be satisfied and always strive to improve the efficiency and effectiveness of your services, products and team. By doing this you will retain competitive advantage, credibility and the respect of your end-users.

Developing Your Team

Your team should be like a second family to you and as such is at its best and strongest when there is a mutually supportive atmosphere with each member pulling their weight and carrying out their responsibilities as best they possibly can. This requires a high degree of shared experience, guidance and encouragement between members if the team is to grow properly.

To achieve this takes time and involves an investment of effort to shape, galvanise and organise a group of individuals into a united and effective 'fighting force'. Without this effort being made, a disjointed and unhappy team results, one that performs in a patchy and inconsistent way.

Ultimately, the team needs to be an extension of what is best in you, reflecting your standards, drive and quest for constant improvement. Once this point is reached, the team will take on a momentum of its own, pushing forward relentlessly towards optimum performance.

To make this happen, you need to keep in mind some key elements:

1. In the same way you came to understand yourself, you must do the same for your team. What and who have you inherited? What gaps are there in terms of skill, personality and aptitude? You can only assess this properly by profiling your staff using the techniques recommended such as DISC and Belbin psychometric testing. This will give you a baseline from which you can then match people to jobs.

2. What types of team or staff pairings do you need to perform certain functions like problem solving, project management and ongoing operations? Out of your staff, who would best be teamed together to ensure compatibility of skills, personality and aptitude? With the higher degree of understanding that comes from profiling your staff and from your own observations of them you will be better able to do this.

3. There needs to be very clear terms of reference for each delegated task and clear role descriptions for each position. Without these, accountability and boundaries of responsibility will always remain vague, and vagueness breeds confusion, and confusion leads to poor performance.

4. The quality and effectiveness of your staff selection procedures both internally and for external appointments will determine the future shape of your team so these need to be given very careful attention. Don't just rely on the written word or people's qualifications. There must be a fit of personality and aptitude as well, but to determine this requires careful investigation to ensure that the true nature of any prospective member of staff is revealed.

5. You will need a range of different characters on your team to give it depth and breadth, as it's this diversity that will encourage the development of that all important esprit de corps, where trust, loyalty and respect are engendered. Remember, it is a selfless regard for each other that binds a team together so that those within it become united and inseparable. You can only bring this about by selecting the right range of personalities as well as skills.

6. Inevitably, you will have to contend with some very difficult characters who present a challenge to your authority and who through their behaviour will be disruptive. By being prepared and determined, you can modify their behaviour so they blend into the team with positive results.

7. If you are to create a high performance team, then an effective staff appraisal system needs to be one of its cornerstones. This will allow you to monitor and understand your team better while also motivating and guiding them to performance that is increasingly focused on achieving your department's work objectives. It is therefore essential that all managers on your team must be trained and accountable for the effective use of the appraisal system.

Balancing and Bringing Together the Needs of Individual, Team and Task

The interface between individual, task and team is crucial in bringing about the sustained development and growth needed to create a high performing team. This is all too often neglected in the maelstrom of day-to-day operational demands. Get the balance wrong and the ship will list and very soon you are heading for the rocks.

If you make the individual the focus then you breed selfishness and posturing; concentrate overly on the team and you risk developing an aimless herd mentality; become too task-oriented and stress, frustration and in-fighting will result.

However, by motivating and developing the individual they will become more selfless and committed. By engendering a spirit of camaraderie, individuals will co-operate and support each other so that everyone gives of their best. Lastly, defining and designing work goals in such a way that they are perceived as inspiring and worthwhile will give the team a real sense of purpose. These elements will then begin to work in harmony and so become mutually supporting and reinforcing.

Continuous Improvement

The other key aspect to a high performance team is its willingness to change in the interests of constant improvement. Unfortunately, many teams chug along very much in their comfort zone, churning out average work which ultimately leads to their demise in a fast changing world where a high degree of flexibility and adaptability is required. Just note the issues revealed at Nokia Mobile Communications recently, where a failure to recognise the impact of smartphone technology on their customer base has locked them into an outmoded platform for which the market is rapidly declining. It will now take years to change direction to meet end-user needs.

As long as the foundations of individual and team strength are established, new roles and tasks can be taken on with energy and enthusiasm, no matter how challenging they may be. Even now, every day, I am constantly learning something new which hones my perspective, methods and aims.

Motivation, Momentum and Synergy

Just what is at the heart of being an outstanding operations manager, who oversees a high performance team producing incredible results?

We have all seen those who just turn up to their job, do it adequately enough, then leave at the end of the day having gone through the motions but without any real spark, or taking ownership over what they produce. Such people are not programmed to excel. As a new manager or an ambitious director, getting them beyond this point is a major challenge but the first thing you must do is motivate them.

Motivation

For me, the starting point for any achievement is your motive for moving forward. If you base these purely on personal ambition, increased status or income then your chances of real success are severely reduced. If you are to make a real difference to your end-users, then you must have *a genuine interest in the quality of your work* and to take pride in its delivery.

In the last ten years of my service at Scotland Yard it was apparent that this was not always the case. Naked personal ambition was driving some senior officers to succumb to political expediency for fear of making hard, but frequently much needed, decisions, that might put them in the wrong light. So much so that in many instances the core of our purpose was completely forgotten in the interests of asset control politics and the quest for personal advantage.

As a result, the benefits of team effort were lost as other officers and staff saw what was happening and became demoralised by the hypocrisy of their superiors. It gives me absolutely no satisfaction to say this, given that there were and still are many professional and selfless people trying to do a great job for the people of London and under the most adverse conditions.

Of course, such situations are not unique to Scotland Yard and I am sure they are present in many organisations throughout the public, private and voluntary sectors.

So remember what I said earlier. You are the pivot point around which change for the better will occur. If you are motivated by the right reasons, others will sense and recognise this in you easily, because, believe me, the signs are unmistakable. Your staff will then take the lead from you and be much more willing to apply the additional effort needed. This means that, when you apply for promotion, make sure your mindset is good and truly focused on making a greater contribution to achieve better outcomes, not just on putting a new Mercedes in the garage.

Momentum

Building momentum is another crucial dynamic. This is all about moving people and things from a standing start and into ever faster motion through progressive organised action. This is much like a snowball rolling down a steep hill. As it gains pace it gathers more snow to it, increasing its mass and adding further to its speed.

Creating this momentum in your team requires two things. First, that your staff have both the skills and motivation needed, and second that you organise them properly for the work to be done.

You have to be genuinely interested in your people if you are to achieve this, and that doesn't just mean being a good socialiser. It also means supporting, developing and controlling your staff effectively in the ways discussed throughout this book. To do this the goals, purpose and value of their work needs to have been made clear. In other words you must design objectives in the best way possible to ensure it meets end-user needs and then convey this fully to your team.

The way you plan and organise your department's work will also determine the speed of progress and improved performance in your team.

Synergy

Once you have talented individuals working selflessly and cooperatively with one another on a task, perceiving themselves to be doing something of real value and purpose, then a new dynamic will begin. This is synergy in action. The gearing ratio between the resources used and the quality of output and outcomes begins to widen and productivity steadily increases. This is all down to having a happy and fulfilled team.

However, be warned, this doesn't happen overnight. You will have to pay a price, and that price is the effort and application needed to prepare and develop yourself properly; design and execute your work goals with careful thought; and unite a group of people into an effective team. This takes years of effort.

This book has attempted to distinguish and explain some of the factors that go into achieving excellence based on my personal experience at the 'sharp end' of operations management. I sincerely hope that the knowledge and insight you have found here will give you cause to pause and reflect on how you can become a truly outstanding operations manager. There is no other better cause in life than to actually make things happen and work successfully, whatever field of operation you are in.

References

Books

James, B (2011), 'Do It or Ditch It', Virgin Books

Jeffers, S (2007), 'Feel the Fear and Do It Anyway', Vermilion

Pink, D H (2006), 'A Whole New Mind', Riverhead Books

Clarke, R V & Eck J (2004), 'Become a Problem Solving Crime Analyst', Jill Dando Institute of Crime Science, University College London

Johnson, G & Scholes K (1989), 'Exploring Corporate Strategy', Prentice Hall

The Coaching Academy (2008) 'Diploma in Personal Performance Coaching', The Coaching Academy UK Ltd

University of West London (1995) 'MSc in Operations Management' University of West London

Easterby-Smith, M R Thorpe & A Lowe (1991) 'Management Research - An Introduction', London Sage Publications

Turner R J (1993), 'The Handbook of Project Based Management', McGraw-Hill International (UK) Ltd

Priestley D (2010), 'Become a Key Person of Influence', Ecademy Press

The Brian Tracy Personal Development Seminar DVD, (2008), The Coaching Academy UK Ltd

Covey S R, (1989) 'The Seven Habits of Highly Effective People', Free Press

References

Websites

DISC Personality Profiling, www.bevjames.com

Myers Briggs Profiling, http://www.myersbriggs.org/

Belbin's Team Role Profiling www.belbin.com

Kolb's Learning Preference Profile www.haygroup.com/
leadershipandtalentondemand/ourproducts

Business Leadership Programme Personality Profiling, Andrew
Priestley http://www.andrewpriestley.com/profiling.php

Professional Competency Framework, http://www.cipd.co.uk/hr-
resources/factsheets/competence-competency-frameworks.aspx

John Adair's Action-Centred Leadership,
http://www.johnadair.co.uk/index.html

The author as house captain of Rowan leading his Metropolitan Police Cadet Corps on parade at Hendon, London 1978.

Brixton Rioting 1981. My first introduction to extreme mass urban violence. Notice the hastily supplied army riot helmets to the ill equipped police.

Regents Park bandstand IRA bombing 1982 – seven Royal Green Jackets
Regiment bandsmen killed whilst playing pieces from the musical 'Oliver'-
The memory of this lives with me forever.

The author (back row with moustache) outside Bow Street Police Station, Covent
Garden, London, before it was closed in 1993, with fellow Bow Street Runners.
This unique historical building opened in 1829. It is still empty in 2012.

Miners Dispute 1984. Picket line duty was like entering the gladiators' arena.

The author as a young sergeant (25) at Bow Street Police Station in 1985 before losing his hair in the service of Queen and country.

A Metropolitan Police Marine Unit launch boat similar to that used to rescue my colleague from a suicide bid in the River Thames in 1984.

A Metropolitan Police Helicopter, 'India 99', frequently used by me for proactive problem solving and survey work to reduce crime.

1990-91 Pit Bull Terriers became the weapon of choice for drug dealers in the Notting Hill area. Several of my colleagues were severely injured with torn calf muscles. Their jaw clamp strength is incredible. I used the RSPCA Dangerous Dogs Unit to great effect in countering them on raids.

Scotland Yard's internal newspaper 'The Job' carries an article on the Capital Link Partnership launch in 1997.

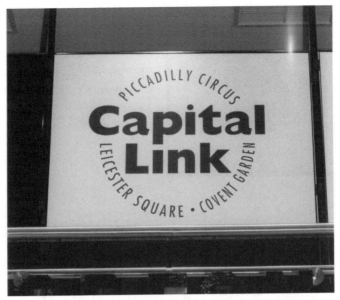

The Capital Link Logo 1999-2002.

The author greeting the Mayor of Westminster Jan Prendergast and The Rt
Hon. Sir John Wheeler, Chairman of the Joint Services Committee NCIS and
National Crime Squad at the Capital Link Exhibition,
The Odeon, Leicester Square, 1999.

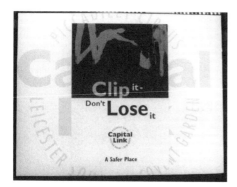

The table-top tent cards for pubs and bars drawing customers' attention to the risk of bag theft in a novel way. Designed by graphics students at Central St Martins, 1999.

Newspaper coverage of the launch of the security design changes at the Hogshead pub, Lisle Street, China Town, London 1999.

The chair back design for hanging handbags and holdalls in high-crime pubs and bars in London's West End. Developed by the Capital Link Partnership and Central St Martins School of Fashion and Design, 1999.

The author and his children together with Chubb staff at the launch of the new West End CCTV Control room beneath the Trocadero Centre, Piccadilly Circus 2002.

This is one of the seized replica firearms taken under operation 'Hand Over' 2008. It is indistinguishable from the real thing, a rapid fire Belgium Herstel P90 machine gun, firing 900 RPM. It is estimated that about 10,000 replicas enter the UK port of Felixstowe from the Far East each month without import licences posing as toys.

A replica sniper rifle, again indistinguishable from the real thing and capable of conversion to a live firing gun. This was ordered on the internet and imported without any controls whatsoever. It was seized during Operation Hand-Over in 2008.

The author on his final day at Scotland Yard with his daughter Sophie and son Tom. 2009.

The author, now a Chief Inspector, with police service medals. 2009.

The author (5th from left back row) with bushcraft expert, Ray Mears, in the Taiga Forest, Sweden on a self-development Arctic survival course, 2010.

The author open-Canadian canoeing on the River Wye, Herefordshire, 2008.

The author on a self-development and fitness course in the Scottish Highlands 2012.

The author with the Qatar Team Bronze Medal winner for the
2012 London Olympics High Jump.

The author outside Qatar House
on close protection duties
London 2012 Olympics.

The author on the specially installed roof garden of Qatar House, London Olympics 2012 overlooking the Thames.

The author inside Qatar House which was specially fitted out as a palace. London Olympics 2012.

About the Author

James Cooke spent most of his early years in rural Herefordshire where he was educated at Ross-On-Wye Grammar School.

In 1976, at the age of 16 he entered the Metropolitan Police Cadet Corps where he continued his studies and became House Captain. At the early age of 18 he started his policing career at Paddington Green where he was involved in responding to the IRA Regents Park Bombing and Brixton riots.

In 1983 he was promoted to Sergeant and started his junior management role at Bow Street Police Station covering Leicester Square and Covent Garden. During this time he was responsible for Divisional Intelligence and leading the Special Events Office which planned and implemented security for numerous VIP visits to the area including HM Queen Elizabeth's 60th Birthday celebrations.

In 1990 he moved to Notting Hill and was team leader for the All Saints Road policing unit combating drug supply and disorder with various covert and uniformed operations. This was followed by an

Acting Inspector role for the entire residential western sector of the Division. During this time he also studied for his Diploma and MSc in Operations Management at the University of West London.

In 1994 he was seconded to the Duke of Edinburgh's International Award for Young People and project managed a major canoeing expedition across the northern reaches of the Algonquin National Park in Ontario, Canada. This was sponsored by various corporate organizations such as British Airways, BP and Glaxo SmithKline.

Between 1996 and 2000 he established and developed what was to become the UK's first Business Improvement District between Piccadilly Circus and Covent Garden which involved numerous programmes of public space design, new policing tactics for high risk places and a pioneering community justice initiative. This was closely followed by a project officers role for the West End CCTV initiative during which he developed a new city centre management approach involving the proactive use of the camera system.

Between 2003 and 2009 he was repeatedly selected to lead on various initiatives to combat the growing threat of gun and gang crime developing several programmes of pioneering work to address this issue through comprehensive risk management systems and multi agency intervention. For this he was commended several times and then asked to lead Commissioner Ian Blair's review of all Public Protection departments in 2005. During the course of this intense period he was promoted on two further occasions to Chief Inspector.

After retiring in 2009 James established his new Company Standing Start Solutions. This has two trading arms World Ready which trains and coaches executives and World Safe which provides VIP Close Protection security services.

James is an active outdoor expedition enthusiast and in 2010 he travelled with Ray Mears to the Swedish Taiga region and was trained in Arctic survival techniques.

He lives in Soho, London.